THE COVID-19 IMPACT
ON PHILIPPINE BUSINESS

KEY FINDINGS FROM THE ENTERPRISE SURVEY

JULY 2020

ASIAN DEVELOPMENT BANK

ADB

© 2020 Asian Development Bank
6 ADB Avenue, Mandaluyong City, 1550 Metro Manila, Philippines
Tel +63 2 8632 4444; Fax +63 2 8636 2444
www.adb.org

Some rights reserved. Published in 2020.

ISBN 978-92-9262-307-4 (print); 978-92-9262-308-1 (electronic); 978-92-9262-309-8 (ebook)
Publication Stock No. SPR200214-2
DOI: http://dx.doi.org/10.22617/SPR200214-2

Note:
In this publication, "$" refers to United States dollars.

Cover design by Claudette Rodrigo.

Printed on recycled paper

CONTENTS

TABLE AND FIGURES

FOREWORD

The coronavirus disease (COVID-19) has shocked global, regional, and national economies. People's lives and economic activities have been strictly limited to safeguard health and control the spread of the virus. Travel bans, temporary closures of schools and businesses, and social distancing have accompanied quarantines. Meanwhile, private sector businesses have cut back production as well as service delivery, and have been forced to temporarily lay off employees. They face a lack of working capital, making it difficult to continue operating. Prolonged containment of COVID-19 increases the risk of business failure and bankruptcy. In particular, micro, small, and medium-sized firms are at great risk due to abrupt supply chain disruptions and tightened financial conditions.

The Philippines acted quickly to combat the virus and ease its impact. It imposed an Enhanced Community Quarantine (ECQ) in the National Capital Region and other high-risk regions to stop the spread of COVID-19. It provided a comprehensive set of support measures for households and businesses to help navigate the ECQ, such as an emergency subsidy program for Filipino families and wage supplements to employees of small businesses.

The Asian Development Bank (ADB) supports the Philippine COVID-19 response. It approved a $1.5 billion loan including funding for social protection, small business relief assistance, and a $200 million loan to support the Philippine government's effort to provide emergency cash transfers, among others. ADB also offered a $5 million grant to deliver nutritious food baskets to up to 140,000 vulnerable households across Metro Manila, and a $3 million grant to help the government buy emergency medical supplies and set up a new laboratory for COVID-19 testing.

To better assess the impact on business establishments, ADB's Economic Research and Regional Cooperation Department conducted an enterprise survey from 28 April to 15 May 2020 in collaboration with the Philippine Department of Finance. The 2,481 enterprises responding to the survey offered a real picture of the severe COVID-19 impact on Philippine business, the effects of the quarantine and lockdown measures, and what is needed to help the government develop economic bounce-back strategies as the crisis recedes.

The report provides a rich set of initial facts and ideas for the government to develop evidence-based policymaking to support the revival of Philippine enterprises hurt by the pandemic. It also provides survey-based information for current and future analytical use. We hope this report contributes to the ongoing policy discussions on firm-level support measures needed to reignite the Philippine economy.

Yasuyuki Sawada
Chief Economist and Director General
Economic Research and Regional Cooperation Department
Asian Development Bank

ACKNOWLEDGMENTS

The report was prepared by Shigehiro Shinozaki, senior economist, and Paul Vandenberg, senior economist, Economic Research and Regional Cooperation Department (ERCD) of the Asian Development Bank (ADB). The work was supervised by Yasuyuki Sawada, chief economist and ERCD director general; Joseph Ernest Zveglich Jr., deputy chief economist; and Edimon Ginting, deputy director general. The survey coordination with the Philippine Department of Finance (DOF) was provided by Kelly Bird, country director of ADB's Philippines Country Office (PhCO), and Cristina Lozano.

The survey questionnaire was redesigned based on the rapid survey of micro, small, and medium-sized enterprises conducted in March–April 2020, covering all Philippine enterprises requested by the DOF. It benefited from the advice and inputs from Rana Hasan, director of the Economic Analysis and Operational Support Division; David Anthony Raitzer; Matthias Helble; Liming Chen; and Eugenia Co Go.

The online survey was distributed through ADB's Facebook page assisted by Andrew Perrin and Reah Valerie Sy of ADB's Department of Communications and the networks of the Philippine Chamber of Commerce and Industry, led by Apolinar Aure, chairman of the SME Development Committee; and the Bankers Association of the Philippines, led by Benjamin Castillo, managing director. The survey team included Shigehiro Shinozaki, team leader; Josephine Penaflor Ferre, ADB consultant; and Chona Plete Guatlo, ADB consultant. Administrative support was provided by Richard Supangan and Maria Frederika Bautista.

EXECUTIVE SUMMARY

The Asian Development Bank conducted a Philippine enterprise survey from 28 April to 15 May 2020 to gauge the impact of the novel coronavirus disease (COVID-19) on the business community. Questions focused on production, finance, workforce, supply chains, and other issues. The survey also asked about the support measures needed from government, and the measures enterprises would take at reopening (e.g., social distancing in the workplace).

Section 1 describes the methodology adopted in this study. Responses were received from 2,481 enterprises, which included micro, small, and medium-sized enterprises as well as large firms. Due to the emergency situation—where businesses were unexpectedly disrupted but nimble data collection was needed—non-standard sampling procedures had to be adopted: the responses, while highly informative, are not based on a random or representative sample. In unweighted survey data, there appears to be overrepresentation from the National Capital Region and underrepresentation from the wholesale and retail trade sector.

Section 2 summarizes the key findings from the survey. Survey responses show that quarantine restrictions, which began on 16 March to contain the spread of the virus, had a significant impact on business activity. Two-thirds of businesses closed temporarily, with most others (29%) reducing operations. Of those remaining open, most (78%) operated at half capacity or less. Only 4% of the enterprises maintained full operations.

Liquidity was a serious concern for most enterprises as working capital became scarce. One-third of respondents had run out of cash and savings by the time of the survey, while another one-third expected to run out over the next 1–3 months. Constraints on additional credit were also binding: just over half (53%) could not arrange to borrow ₱50,000 within a week, if needed.

The situation and needs assessment questions in our survey revealed that the most pressing payment concern was wages and related social security contributions (37%). In line with this, a wage subsidy was the most frequently requested government support measure (57%). Micro and small enterprises were about 10 percentage points more likely to request a wage subsidy than large enterprises. Some 33% of those surveyed availed of the Department of Labor and Employment's grant program for workers unable to receive wages (Clarificatory Guidelines on the COVID-19 Adjustment Measures Program). Use of the program was higher among small and medium-sized enterprises (38%) than for microenterprises (28%) or large firms (35%).

Deferment of tax payments was the second most common policy support desired, cited by 52% of respondents. The third most common request was for low-interest or subsidized loans (36%) followed by tax reductions or credits (35%). Those surveyed were allowed multiple responses.

As just a few (14%) of the enterprises in our survey sell products or services via the internet, it was generally difficult for businesses to service customers and generate revenue during quarantine. Better connection to internet-based business platforms would not only help continue businesses operations currently, but also help prevent adverse impacts from a second wave of infections in the near future.

While enterprises are prepared to take required health and safety measures for reopening in general, our survey also identified different challenges to reopening businesses. The most frequently cited challenge after reopening is providing face masks to workers (63%). However, only 17% of enterprises would practice social distancing and create smaller working groups. Regular body temperature checks were planned by 13% of enterprises. Measures least likely to be used were contact tracing (6%) and canteen rationing (less than 1%).

Section 3 discusses the policy implications derived from the survey findings. Several current government initiatives, such as increasing the flow of credit and subsidizing wages, appear to respond to the expressed needs of business.

1. METHODOLOGY

In collaboration with the Philippine Department of Finance, the Asian Development Bank (ADB) conducted an enterprise survey during 28 April–15 May 2020. The questionnaire was designed to investigate the impact of coronavirus disease (COVID-19) on Philippine enterprises, along with the effect of the 16 March 2020 quarantine and lockdown measures—such as the enhanced community quarantine (ECQ) imposed by the government around the National Capital Region (NCR). It also aimed to help the government in developing their economic bounce-back strategies in response to the crisis.

The survey was designed to grasp each respondent's basic characteristics, the COVID-19 impact, potential needs for policy measures, and preparation for reopening. Accordingly, the survey questionnaire had four components: (i) the company's profile at the end of 2019; (ii) the COVID-19 impact on business operations, sales, employment, wage payments, and actions taken to retain business; (iii) the most needed policy interventions that could help enterprises both during and after the COVID-19 crisis; and (iv) the firm's social distancing practices.

The emergency unexpectedly disrupted businesses; yet nimble data collection was needed. Thus, non-standard sampling procedures were inevitably chosen. The survey was carried out online via social media (Facebook) and other internet portals through the networks of the Philippine Chamber of Commerce and Industry and the Bankers Association of the Philippines. As the sampling frame was not used, the data structure was compared with an existing Philippine enterprise survey to review potential data bias and guide the reader on how to interpret the survey results. A list of establishments surveyed by the Philippine Statistics Authority (PSA) in 2018 was used for comparison.

Follow-up surveys will be conducted every 2 months to continuously monitor the Philippine business environment and assess the effects government policy measures have in supporting Philippine enterprises. ADB plans follow-up surveys in July and September 2020.

2. KEY FINDINGS FROM THE ADB PHILIPPINE ENTERPRISE SURVEY

A. Data Structure

As of 15 May 2020, ADB had received 2,481 complete responses from private sector businesses including micro, small, medium-sized, and large enterprises. In general, the aggregate data had the same qualitative size, sectoral, and regional distribution structure as the list of establishments surveyed by the PSA in 2018 (Table): the smaller the firm size, the larger the numbers in the survey; the wholesale and retail trade sector held the largest share; and the largest numbers of responding firms were from the NCR. Quantitatively, the wholesale and retail trade sector appeared underrepresented and the NCR appeared overrepresented compared with the PSA survey.

By industry, the difference of each sector's share to total respondents between the ADB and PSA surveys was less than 5 percentage points, except for wholesale and retail trade (24.6 percentage points below the PSA survey), construction (8.2 percentage points above the PSA survey), and other services (7.7 percentage points above the PSA survey). By region, the difference of each region's share to total respondents between ADB and PSA surveys was below 5 percentage points, except for the NCR (29.2 percentage points above the PSA survey).

In the Philippines, there are two different official criteria to classify firm size: (i) employment levels as set by the PSA for statistical purposes and (ii) total assets (excluding land) as defined by the Small and Medium Enterprise Development Council Resolution No.01 Series of 2003.

In comparing ADB and PSA survey data, the definition of enterprise size based on the employment criterion set by the PSA—a microenterprise has 1–9 employees, a small enterprise has 10–99 employees, a medium-sized enterprise has 100–199 employees, and a large enterprise has more than 200 employees—was adopted.

For the rest of this report, ADB uses total assets to define firm size as it provides a more realistic picture for analysis. Under this criterion, a microenterprise has assets (excluding land) of ₱3 million or less, a small enterprise up to ₱15 million, a medium-sized enterprise has total assets up to ₱100 million, and a large enterprise has total assets exceeding ₱100 million.

B. Company Profile

Corporations or partnerships accounted for 71% of survey respondents, followed by sole proprietors (26.9%) (Figure 1). By firm size (using the total asset criterion), microenterprises comprised 51.9% of respondents, followed by small enterprises (27.2%), medium-sized enterprises (13.3%), and large enterprises (7.5%) (Figure 2).

The majority of enterprises surveyed belonged to the services sector. More concretely, enterprises engaged in wholesale and retail trade (including repair of motor vehicles and motorcycles) had the largest share of respondents (21.5%), followed by accommodation and food services which includes tourism (14.3%); other services such as

Table: Survey Comparison between Asian Development Bank and Philippine Statistics Authority

Item	ADB Philippine Enterprise Survey — Employment Grouping						PSA List of Establishments, 2018 — Employment Grouping						Difference between ADB and PSA Surveys (%)
	Micro	Small	Medium-Sized	Large	Total	Share (%)	Micro	Small	Medium-Sized	Large	Total	Share (%)	
By industrial sector, total	1,425	959	47	50	2,481	100.0	887,272	106,175	4,895	4,769	1,003,111	100.0	
Agriculture, Forestry, and Fishing	9	9	–	–	18	0.7	5,837	2,512	157	173	8,679	0.9	(0.1)
Mining and Quarrying	–	–	–	–	–	–	492	302	21	35	850	0.1	(0.1)
Manufacturing	86	154	15	6	261	10.5	103,590	11,678	1,067	1,133	117,468	11.7	(1.2)
Electricity, Gas, Steam, and Air Conditioning Supply	15	14	–	–	29	1.2	478	633	98	89	1,298	0.1	1.0
Water Supply; Sewerage, Waste Management, and Remediation Activities	1	4	–	–	5	0.2	677	711	49	29	1,466	0.1	0.1
Construction	116	91	5	2	214	8.6	2,304	1,715	226	262	4,507	0.4	8.2
Wholesale and Retail Trade; Repair of Motor Vehicles and Motorcycles	326	196	7	5	534	21.5	427,101	33,577	1,087	584	462,349	46.1	(24.6)
Transport and Storage	40	40	1	1	82	3.3	7,264	3,511	231	194	11,200	1.1	2.2
Accommodation and Food Service Activities	235	118	2	–	356	14.3	125,396	18,802	337	105	144,640	14.4	(0.1)
Information and Communication	84	93	4	8	189	7.6	27,421	1,973	153	140	29,687	3.0	4.7
Financial and Insurance Activities	61	42	2	4	109	4.4	37,813	8,053	167	183	46,216	4.6	(0.2)
Real Estate Activities	56	19	–	–	75	3.0	9,478	1,975	79	63	11,595	1.2	1.9
Professional, Scientific, and Technical Activities	64	32	1	–	97	3.9	13,617	2,164	104	89	15,974	1.6	2.3
Administrative and Support Service Activities	25	21	2	5	53	2.1	14,073	3,022	474	1,144	18,713	1.9	0.3
Public Administration and Defense; Compulsary Social Security	–	–	–	1	1	0.0	–	–	–	–	–	–	0.0
Education	21	10	–	–	31	1.2	9,105	8,312	391	271	18,079	1.8	(0.6)
Human Health and Social Work Activities	11	4	–	–	15	0.6	26,076	2,325	200	223	28,824	2.9	(2.3)
Arts, Entertainment, and Recreation	38	17	1	1	57	2.3	13,755	1,563	34	41	15,393	1.5	0.8
Other Service Activities	237	95	7	16	355	14.3	62,795	3,347	20	11	66,173	6.6	7.7
By region, total	1,425	959	47	50	2,481	100.0	887,272	106,175	4,895	4,769	1,003,111	100.0	
National Capital Region	684	504	20	23	1,231	49.6	166,921	34,523	1,868	1,938	205,250	20.5	29.2
Cordillera Administrative Region	15	7	–	1	23	0.9	18,783	1,587	47	49	20,466	2.0	(1.1)
Region 1 (Ilocos Region)	15	9	1	1	26	1.0	46,708	3,977	122	70	50,877	5.1	(4.0)
Region 2 (Cagayan Valley)	14	9	–	–	23	0.9	28,547	2,119	52	35	30,753	3.1	(2.1)
Region 3 (Central Luzon)	147	74	4	5	230	9.3	104,875	10,754	444	385	116,458	11.6	(2.3)
Region 4A (Calabarzon)	202	129	12	4	347	14.0	133,640	13,778	778	811	149,007	14.9	(0.9)
MIMAROPA Region	24	21	1	–	46	1.9	21,948	1,914	57	33	23,952	2.4	(0.5)
Region 5 (Bicol Region)	33	16	1	1	51	2.1	37,111	3,215	118	70	40,514	4.0	(2.0)
Region 6 (Western Visayas)	68	31	1	–	100	4.0	55,482	5,894	214	193	61,783	6.2	(2.1)
Region 7 (Central Visayas)	91	83	3	8	185	7.5	61,176	8,775	444	537	70,932	7.1	0.4
Region 8 (Eastern Visayas)	16	7	–	2	25	1.0	28,324	2,355	70	40	30,789	3.1	(2.1)
Region 9 (Zamboanga Peninsula)	11	8	–	1	20	0.8	30,888	2,216	73	67	33,244	3.3	(2.5)
Region 10 (Northern Mindanao)	33	12	–	3	48	1.9	33,040	4,079	155	138	37,412	3.7	(1.8)
Region 11 (Davao Region)	51	31	3	–	85	3.4	52,449	5,758	252	226	58,685	5.9	(2.4)
Region 12 (SOCCSKSARGEN)	9	9	1	1	20	0.8	41,581	3,121	120	118	44,940	4.5	(3.7)
Region 13 (Caraga)	11	9	–	–	20	0.8	18,069	1,687	67	50	19,873	2.0	(1.2)
BARMM (formerly ARMM)	1	–	–	–	1	0.0	7,730	423	14	9	8,176	0.8	(0.8)

– = no number; ADB = Asian Development Bank; BARMM = Bangsamoro Autonomous Region in Muslim Mindanao; MIMAROPA = Mindoro, Marinduque, Romblon, and Palawan (Southwestern Tagalog Region); PSA = Philippine Statistics Authority; SOCCSKSARGEN = South Cotabato, Cotabato, Sultan Kudarat, Sarangani, and General Santos.

Note: Firm size classification of ADB survey data is based on the number of employees for comparison with PSA data.

Source: Asian Development Bank, Philippine Enterprise Survey.

Figure 1: Type of Respondent

Others, 32 , 1.3%

Sole Proprietorship, 667, 26.9%

Corporation or Partnership, 1,762, 71.0%

Cooperative or Foundation, 20, 0.8%

Source: Asian Development Bank, Philippine Enterprise Survey.

Figure 2: Enterprises Surveyed by Firm Size
(by total assets)

Large, 186, 7.5%

Medium, 331, 13.3%

Micro, 1,288, 51.9%

Small, 676, 27.2%

Source: Asian Development Bank, Philippine Enterprise Survey.

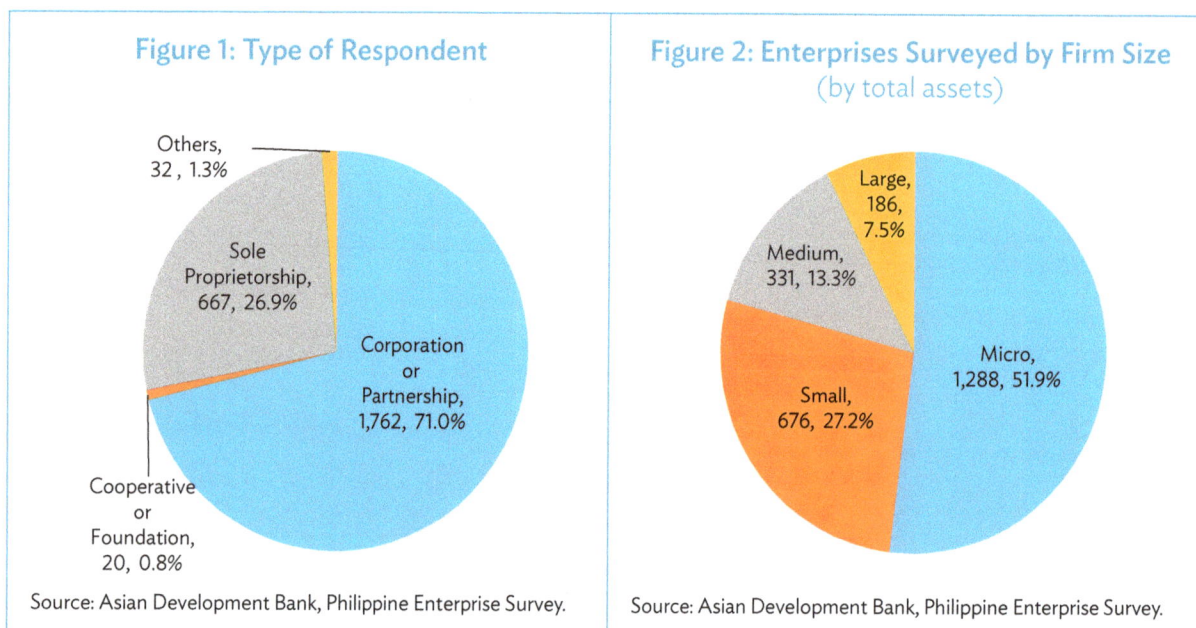

worker dispatching, beauty salons, laundry, personal repairs, and publishing (14.3%); manufacturing (10.5%); construction (8.6%); and information and communication (7.6%) (Figure 3).

By firm size (total asset criterion) and sector, microenterprises in wholesale and retail trade held the largest share (22.0% of total microenterprises), followed by other services (17.9%), accommodation and food services (14.8%), and construction (8.3%). Small enterprises engaged in wholesale and retail trade were highest (22.9% of total small enterprises), followed by accommodation and food services (13.5%), manufacturing (11.7%), and other services (10.5%). Medium-sized enterprises in wholesale and retail trade had a 19.0% share of total medium-sized enterprises, followed by manufacturing (18.4%), accommodation and food services (16.9%), and construction (9.1%). Large enterprises engaged in wholesale and retail trade held a 17.7% share of total large enterprises, followed by other services (15.6%), manufacturing (15.1%), and accommodation and food services (10.2%).

By region, 79.7% of those surveyed operated on Luzon Island (49.6% in the NCR, 14.0% in Calabarzon, 9.3% in Central Luzon, and 6.8% in other areas—Cordillera Administrative Region, Ilocos, Cagayan Valley, MIMAROPA, and Bicol), followed by the Central Visayas (7.5%), Western Visayas (4.0%), and Davao (3.4%) (Figure 4).

By firm size in each region, microenterprises operating in the NCR held a 48.2% share of total microenterprises, followed by Calabarzon (14.2%) and Central Luzon (9.9%). Small enterprises operating in the NCR had a 51.0% share of total small enterprises, followed by Calabarzon (12.4%) and Central Luzon (9.2%). Medium-sized enterprises operating in the NCR were 50.8% of total medium-sized enterprises, followed by Calabarzon (14.5%) and Central Visayas (8.2%). Large enterprises operating in the NCR stood at 52.2% of total large enterprises, followed by Calabarzon (17.2%) and Central Luzon (11.3%).

The majority of enterprises surveyed were relatively young firms, operating for 5 years or less (accounting for 56.7% of total respondents), followed by firms operating for 6–10 years (18.2%), firms operating for 16–30 years (18.2%), firms operating for 11–15 years (9.4%), and firms operating for 31 years and above (3.5%) (Figure 5).

Figure 3: Enterprises Surveyed by Sector

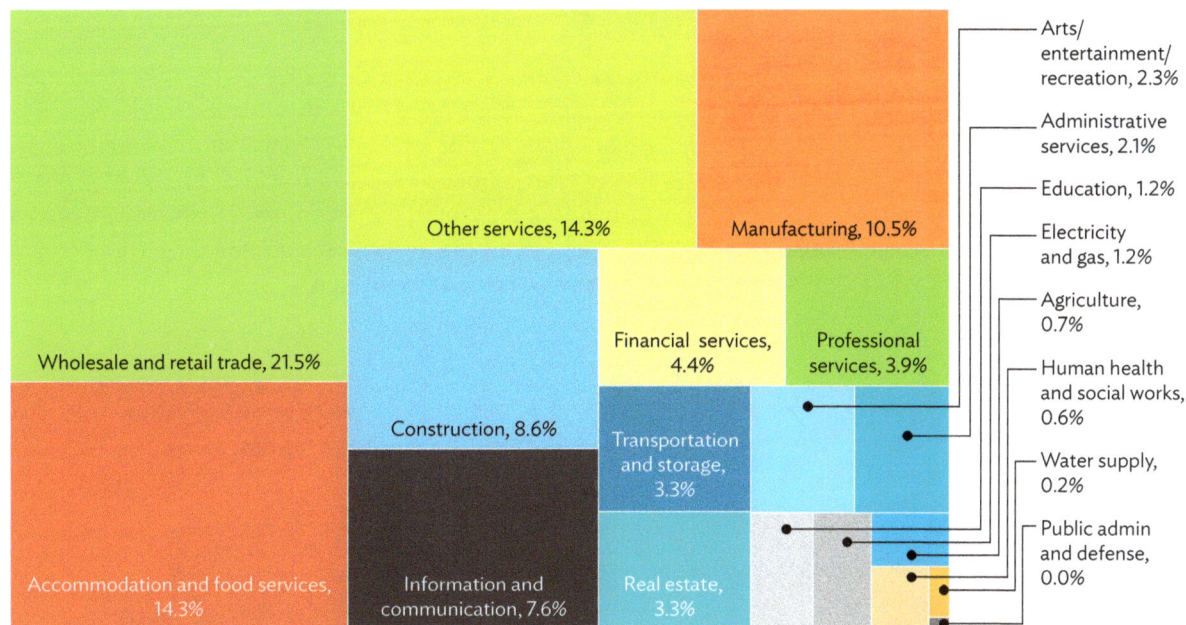

Other services, 14.3%

Manufacturing, 10.5%

Wholesale and retail trade, 21.5%

Financial services, 4.4%

Professional services, 3.9%

Construction, 8.6%

Transportation and storage, 3.3%

Accommodation and food services, 14.3%

Information and communication, 7.6%

Real estate, 3.3%

Arts/entertainment/recreation, 2.3%

Administrative services, 2.1%

Education, 1.2%

Electricity and gas, 1.2%

Agriculture, 0.7%

Human health and social works, 0.6%

Water supply, 0.2%

Public admin and defense, 0.0%

Source: Asian Development Bank, Philippine Enterprise Survey.

Figure 4: Enterprises Surveyed by Region

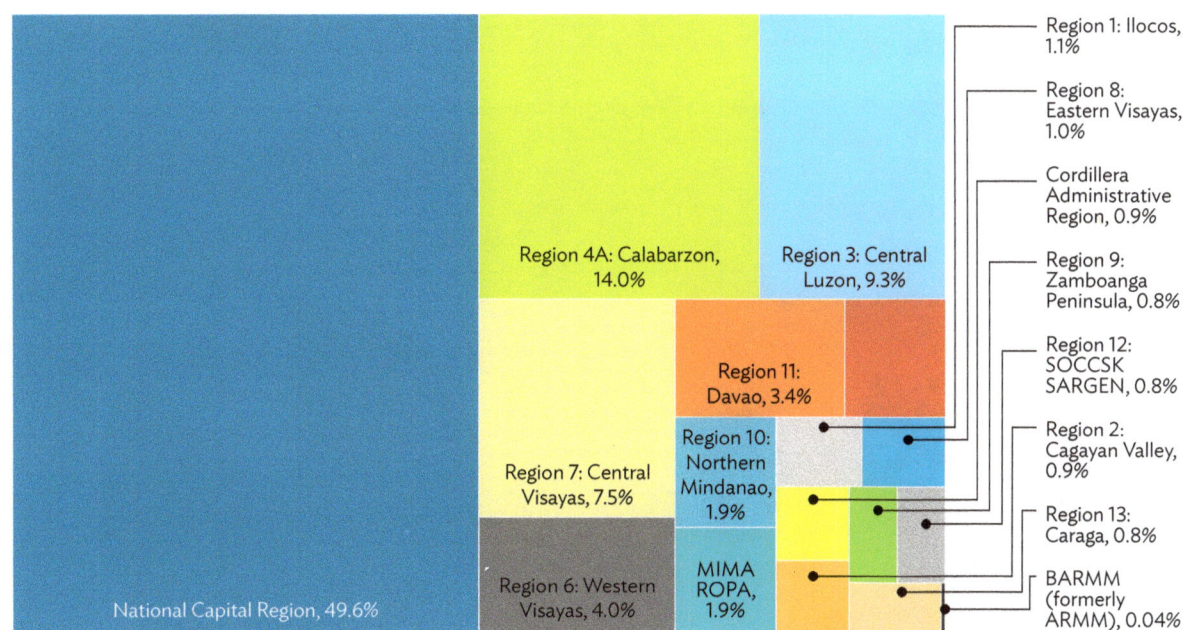

National Capital Region, 49.6%

Region 4A: Calabarzon, 14.0%

Region 3: Central Luzon, 9.3%

Region 7: Central Visayas, 7.5%

Region 11: Davao, 3.4%

Region 10: Northern Mindanao, 1.9%

Region 6: Western Visayas, 4.0%

MIMAROPA, 1.9%

Region 1: Ilocos, 1.1%

Region 8: Eastern Visayas, 1.0%

Cordillera Administrative Region, 0.9%

Region 9: Zamboanga Peninsula, 0.8%

Region 12: SOCCSKSARGEN, 0.8%

Region 2: Cagayan Valley, 0.9%

Region 13: Caraga, 0.8%

BARMM (formerly ARMM), 0.04%

BARMM = Bangsamoro Autonomous Region in Muslim Mindanao; MIMAROPA = Mindoro, Marinduque, Romblon, and Palawan (Southwestern Tagalog Region); SOCCSKSARGEN = South Cotabato, Cotabato, Sultan Kudarat, Sarangani, and General Santos.
Source: Asian Development Bank, Philippine Enterprise Survey.

In terms of the gender composition of workers, more than one-third (34.9%) of the enterprises surveyed reported that only 10% or less of a firm's total employees were women (Figure 6). However, another one-third (15.8% plus 15.4%) of those surveyed said women comprised 50% or more of the firm's total workforce.

As for international trade orientation, most enterprises concentrated on domestic markets. Only 7.8% of enterprises surveyed were engaged in exports while 15.9% were importers (Figures 7 and 8). Of those exporting, 40.1% said that exports were their primary business (accounting for more than 90% of total sales), while for 41.7% exporting was a supplementary business (accounting for 50% or less of sales). Production relied highly on imported goods and services for 17.9% of importers (accounting for more than 90% of their total production inputs), while 49.3% reported imports accounted for not more than 50% of inputs. Just 14.2% of those surveyed used online selling or e-commerce, suggesting traditional channels for marketing products and services remain dominant.

Figure 5: Operating Period

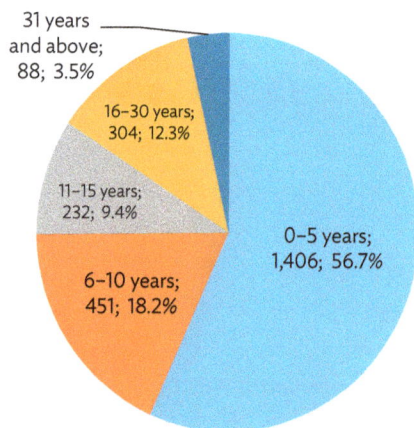

- 31 years and above; 88; 3.5%
- 16–30 years; 304; 12.3%
- 11–15 years; 232; 9.4%
- 6–10 years; 451; 18.2%
- 0–5 years; 1,406; 56.7%

Source: Asian Development Bank, Philippine Enterprise Survey.

Figure 6: Share of Female Employees to Total Employment

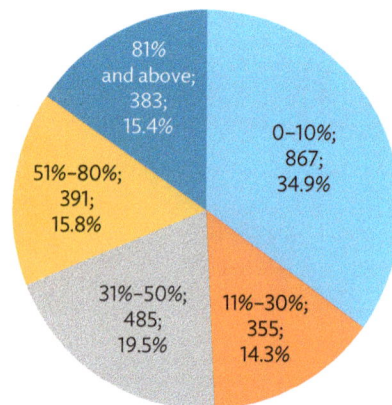

- 81% and above; 383; 15.4%
- 51%–80%; 391; 15.8%
- 31%–50%; 485; 19.5%
- 11%–30%; 355; 14.3%
- 0–10%; 867; 34.9%

Source: Asian Development Bank, Philippine Enterprise Survey.

Figure 7: Engagement in Export Business

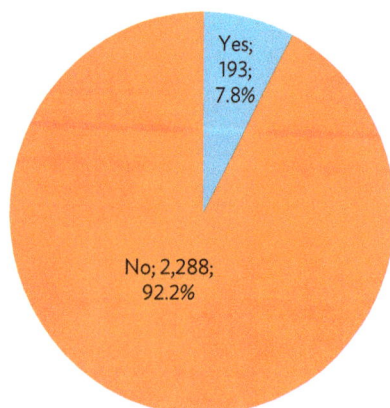

- Yes; 193; 7.8%
- No; 2,288; 92.2%

Source: Asian Development Bank, Philippine Enterprise Survey.

Figure 8: Engagement in Import Business

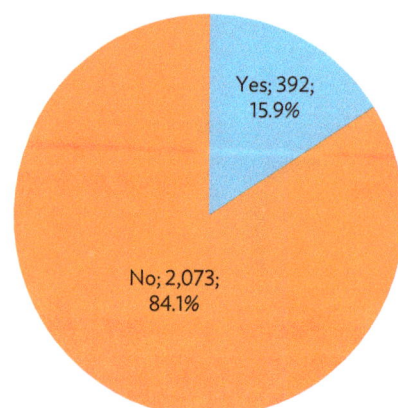

- Yes; 392; 15.9%
- No; 2,073; 84.1%

Source: Asian Development Bank, Philippine Enterprise Survey.

C.   COVID-19 Impact on Business

Business Conditions after Quarantine Implemented

- Two-thirds of firms surveyed immediately suspended business activity, while those still operating cut operations by half.
- The smaller the firm size, the lower the share of businesses remaining open.
- Wholesale and retail trade was the sector most adversely affected by the ECQ.
- Half of firms temporarily closed were based in the NCR.

While critical in safeguarding public health against the spread of COVID-19, the enhanced community quarantine and other quarantine/lockdown measures (henceforth referred to as ECQ) dramatically limited business activities throughout much of the Philippines. After the 16 March[1] lockdown of the NCR, Calabarzon, and other regions, most Philippine enterprises faced the immediate closure of business or limitation of business operations. According to the survey, 65.9% of enterprises surveyed temporarily closed their business after the ECQ came into effect (Figure 9). Limited operations continued in 29.1% of the enterprises surveyed. Among those with limited operations, one-fifth reported more than 50% of their business continued, while 78.4% reported less than 50% of their business operational (Figure 10). Only 4% of those surveyed remained fully open. Meanwhile, 1.1% closed permanently.

There was a clear correlation between business closures and firm size. Temporary closures were most widespread among microenterprises (71.2% of total microenterprises), followed by small enterprises (63.2%), medium-sized enterprises (57.4%), and large enterprises (53.8%). Among large enterprises, 7% remained fully operational while 38.2% stayed partially open. The smaller the firm size, the lower the share of businesses remaining open: medium-sized (5.1%), small (3.7%), and microenterprises (3.3%). The same was true for those partially open: medium-sized (36.3%), small (32.5%), and microenterprises (24.1%). Only a small fraction of enterprises surveyed permanently closed: 1.3% of microenterprises, 0.6% of small, 1.2% of medium-sized, and 1.1% of large enterprises.

By sector, wholesale and retail trade was the most affected by the ECQ, with 21.8% temporarily closed, followed by accommodation and food services (16.9%) and other services (14.7%). Wholesale and retail trade accounted for 21.5% of enterprises maintaining limited operations, followed by "other sectors" (14.7%) and information and communication (11.5%).

When looking at enterprises with limited operations in detail, 80.0% of enterprises engaged in wholesale and retail trade reported their business not more than 50% operational. Meanwhile, 20.0% of enterprises in wholesale and retail trade reported more than 50% operational. For accommodation and food services including the tourism industry, 89.8% of firms in this category reported not more than 50% operational while 10.2% reported more than 50% operational. For other services, 68.9% of firms in this category reported not more than 50% operational while 31.1% reported more than 50% operational. For information and communication, 63.9% of firms in this category reported not more than 50% operational while 36.1% reported more than 50% operational.

The wholesale and retail trade and information and communication sectors accounted for the same share of fully operating enterprises (16.3%), followed by construction (15.3%). Meanwhile, 25.9% of those permanently closed were in wholesale and retail trade, followed by accommodation and food services (22.2%) and information and communication (11.1%), although a small number of enterprises identified in this category.

---

[1]   Throughout the report, references to specific months (for example, February, March, and April) refer to 2020 unless otherwise indicated.

By region, NCR-based firms accounted for 49.9% of temporarily closed enterprises, followed by firms in Calabarzon (14.3%) and Central Visayas (7.2%). Meanwhile, 61.2% of those operating fully were in the NCR, followed by firms in Calabarzon (15.3%) and Central Visayas (7.1%). Enterprises with limited operations were concentrated in the NCR (47.5%), followed by Calabarzon (13.4%) and Central Visayas (8.0%). For NCR-based firms, 66.3% temporarily closed their business, 4.9% remained fully open, 27.9% opened but with limited operations, and 1.0% closed permanently.

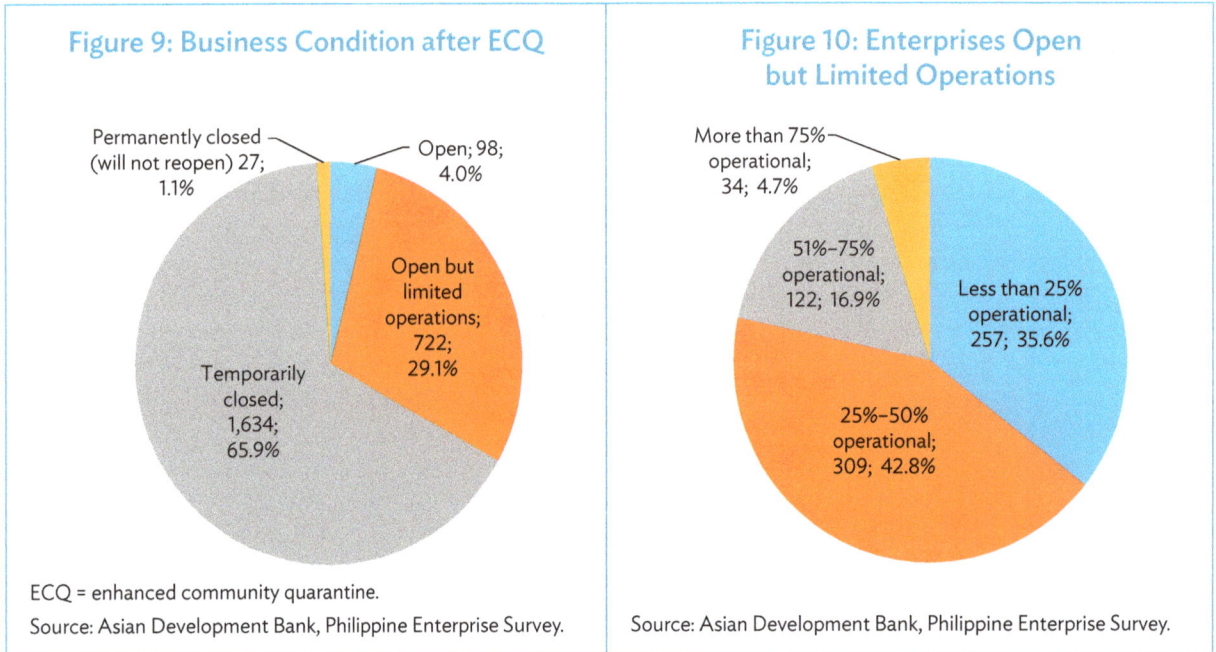

Figure 9: Business Condition after ECQ

Permanently closed (will not reopen) 27; 1.1%
Open; 98; 4.0%
Open but limited operations; 722; 29.1%
Temporarily closed; 1,634; 65.9%

ECQ = enhanced community quarantine.
Source: Asian Development Bank, Philippine Enterprise Survey.

Figure 10: Enterprises Open but Limited Operations

More than 75% operational; 34; 4.7%
51%–75% operational; 122; 16.9%
Less than 25% operational; 257; 35.6%
25%–50% operational; 309; 42.8%

Source: Asian Development Bank, Philippine Enterprise Survey.

Expected Time Frame for Business Recovery

The majority of respondents could not assess the expected time frame for business recovery following the lifting of the ECQ, due to the uncertain business environment. Meanwhile, 29.9% of enterprises responded that it might take more than 3 months for business to recover after the ECQ ends, and 14.6% anticipated the recovery would take 1 to 3 months. Only 4% of enterprises surveyed expected a recovery within a month (Figure 11).

Status of Sales after the ECQ

- COVID-19 and associated containment measures triggered a sharp decline in April sales for most enterprises.
- Sales in wholesale and retail trade were most affected, both by decreased value (those closed) and increased value (those servicing special demand).
- NCR-based firms accounted for around half of those with decreasing sales values.

The COVID-19 outbreak and lockdown measures led to a sharp decline in April sales (80.4% on average by value) compared with March for 76.8% of enterprises surveyed (Figure 12). Sales remained the same for 22.1% of enterprises. Only 1.2% reported an increase in April sales (23.8% on average) as they supplied households with essential needs after the lockdown began.

This sales trend was common across all enterprise size categories: sales decreased for 76.7% of microenterprise respondents, 76.9% of small firms, 76.7% of medium-sized, and 76.3% of large firms; they remained the same for 22.1% of micro, 22.3% small, 21.5% medium-sized, and 22.0% of large firms; and sales rose for 1.2% of micro, 0.7% small, 1.8% medium-sized, and 1.6% of large firms reporting. Among those with declining sales, small enterprises had the largest decrease (by 82.0% on average) in April from March, followed by micro (81.5%), medium-sized (76.4%), and large (74.9%) firms. Meanwhile, among enterprises whose sales grew, medium-sized enterprises had the largest increase (by 37.5% on average in April), followed by small (29.0%), micro (20.2%), and large (15.0%) firms.

By sector, sales were the most affected in wholesale and retail trade, by both decrease and increase in value. The wholesale and retail trade sector accounted for 22.4% of enterprises experiencing a decline in March/April sales, followed by accommodation and food services (15.8%), other services (14.1%), manufacturing (10.9%), and information and communication (7.3%). Sales fell for accommodation and food services by 88.0% on average in April from March, other services by 81.2%, wholesale and retail trade by 80.8%, manufacturing by 80.7%, and information and communication by 69.9%. Wholesale and retail trade also led enterprises maintaining sales during March and April (17.7%), followed by other services (15.2%), construction (15.8%), accommodation and food services (10.1%), and manufacturing (9.3%). The wholesale and retail trade sector accounted for 37.9% of enterprises that increased sales during March and April, followed by information and communication (17.2%) and manufacturing (10.3%). This suggests that business performance in wholesale and retail trade largely split into two groups: (i) the most devastated group—forced to close or limit business and (ii) the group enjoying special demand from households due to the need for essential goods after the lockdown began.

By region, of all the enterprises with decreasing sales values from March to April, 48.5% were based in the NCR, followed by firms in Calabarzon (12.7%), Central Luzon (9.7%), and Central Visayas (8.0%). In terms of magnitude, NCR-based firms decreased sales by 81.9% on average in April, Calabarzon by 82.2%, Central Luzon by 82.0%, and Central Visayas by 73.7%. Meanwhile, 53.6% of enterprises with no change of sales during March and April were NCR-based, followed by firms in Calabarzon (18.1%) and Central Visayas (5.3%). Although a small fraction of enterprises reported an increase in sales between March and April, 44.8% were NCR-based, followed by firms

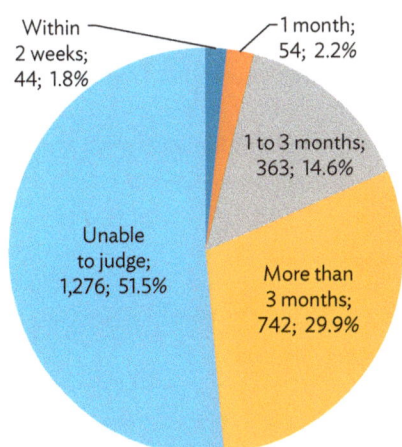

Figure 11: Expected Time Frame for Business Recovery after ECQ

Within 2 weeks; 44; 1.8%
1 month; 54; 2.2%
1 to 3 months; 363; 14.6%
More than 3 months; 742; 29.9%
Unable to judge; 1,276; 51.5%

ECQ = enhanced community quarantine.
Source: Asian Development Bank, Philippine Enterprise Survey.

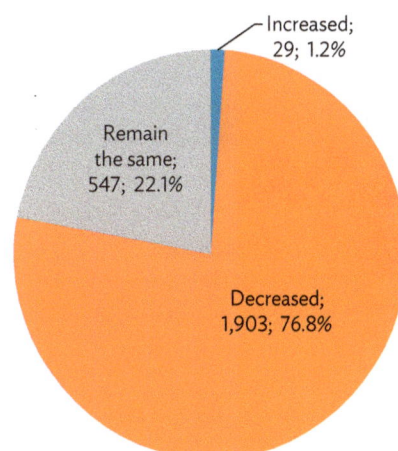

Figure 12: Status of Sales in April versus March 2020

Increased; 29; 1.2%
Remain the same; 547; 22.1%
Decreased; 1,903; 76.8%

Source: Asian Development Bank, Philippine Enterprise Survey.

in Calabarzon (20.7%) and Central Visayas (13.8%). Among NCR-based firms, 75.1% had a decline in sales, 23.8% maintained the same level, and 1.1% saw sales increase between March and April.

Employment

- During April, regular workers would more likely be granted leave or have hours and salaries reduced than be laid off.
- While most enterprises did not change employment arrangements for part-time workers, many had their working hours reduced.
- Regular and part-time workers in microenterprises were worse off in April.
- Regular and part-time workers in traditional trade and services were hurt most by the ECQ. Construction reported relatively large layoffs.
- By region, NCR-based firms most actively adopted new arrangements for regular and part-time workers.

a. Full-time regular workers

Most firms faced immediate temporary closures or limited business operations during the ECQ, forcing them to make employment adjustments. In April, 41.9% of enterprises surveyed granted leave to full-time regular employees, had their working hours cut (41.4%), or salary and benefits reduced (32.0%); just 14.7% resorted to layoffs (Figure 13). Meanwhile, 20.7% of enterprises hired new regular employees to meet special household demand.

From March to April, the surveyed enterprises, on average, granted leave to 8.1 employees; reduced working hours for 10.1 employees; reduced salaries, wages, or benefits for 6.4 employees; and laid off 2 employees. Meanwhile, on average, they hired 2.7 new employees to full-time regular positions. The average number of regular employees in the enterprises surveyed was 33.2 persons.

By firm size, microenterprises most actively altered arrangements for regular employees in April, with 37.2% of microenterprises surveyed granting leave to regular employees, followed by reduced working hours (36.6%), reduced salary and benefits (30.9%), and layoffs (14.6%). Meanwhile, 22.1% of microenterprises hired new regular employees. On average, 3.7 regular employees per microenterprise were granted leave; 3.7 employees had their working hours reduced; and 3.8 employees had their salary, wages, or benefits reduced. An average 1.3 employees were laid off, but 1.5 new regular employees were hired.

In April, regular employees in micro, small, medium-sized, and large enterprises were also directly impacted by the ECQ, with 47.8% of small firms and 45.3% of large firms reducing working hours of regular employees, followed by leaves granted (45.9% for small and 43.6% for large firms), salary and benefits reduced (34.9% and 30.4%), and layoffs (14.2% and 17.7%). Meanwhile, 20.0% of small firms and 24.9% of large firms hired new regular employees. On average, 9.3 regular employees in small firms and 50.6 in large firms had their working hours reduced; 6.8 in small firms and 29.4 in large firms were granted leave; 7.5 employees in small firms and 15.2 in large firms had salaries, wages, or benefits reduced; and 2.5 employees in small firms and 3.1 in large firms were laid off. Yet, on average, small firms hired 3.2 new regular employees and large firms 7.5 new regular employees in April.

Of the medium-sized enterprises surveyed, 50.9% granted leave to regular employees, 45.0% reduced working hours, 30.9% reduced salaries and benefits, while 14.4% resorted to layoffs. Still, 14.7% hired new regular employees. By number of regular employees, 16.4 per medium-sized firm were granted leave; 14.6 were forced to reduce working hours; 9.8 faced a reduction in salary, wages, or benefits; and 3.4 employees were laid off (more than the 3.1 employees in large firms). But, on average, 3.7 regular employees in medium-sized firms were hired in April.

As to the impact of employment disruption to overall employment size, survey data also indicate that microenterprises were most seriously affected, based on the number of employees in each category—micro (with employment of 1–9), small (10–99), medium-sized (100–199), and large firms (employing 200 or over).

Regular employees across all industrial sectors were hurt by ECQ measures. But they were more pronounced in wholesale and retail trade, accommodation and food services, and other services (in terms of the number of survey responses). For firms in wholesale and retail trade, 42.8% granted leave to regular employees, 41.9% reduced working hours, 30.9% reduced salaries and benefits, and 9.5% resorted to layoffs. In April, 19.5% hired new regular employees. In terms of average number of regular employees, wholesale and retail trade firms reduced working hours for 8.1 regular employees; granted leave to 5.3 employees; reduced salaries, wages, or benefits for 4.1 employees; and laid off 0.7 employees. But 1.8 regular employees were hired on average in April.

In accommodation and food services, 43.6% of firms granted leave to regular employees, 40.8% reduced working hours, 33.4% reduced salaries and benefits, and 22.7% resorted to layoffs. In the sector, 22.7% hired new regular employees. By number of employees affected, on average, 5.1 had salaries or benefits reduced, another 5.1 employees were granted leave, 5.0 reduced working hours, and 2.4 were laid off. An average 2.4 new employees were hired during April in the accommodation and food services sector.

For firms in "other services," 40.9% granted leaves, 38.8% reduced working hours, 33.3% reduced salaries and benefits, while 15.7% laid off employees. However, 21.4% of firms in other services hired new regular employees in April. By number of employees affected, average 9.9 regular employees had salaries, wages, or benefits reduced; 12.0 employees were granted leave; 10.5 reduced working hours; with 2.8 employees laid off. An average 2.8 regular employees were hired per firm during April.

By type of employment arrangement and sector, on average, firms in construction resorted to layoffs most (4.5 regular employees per firm), followed by manufacturing and other services (2.8 persons each). Firms in water supply granted leave to an average 17.0 regular employees in April, followed by transportation and storage (13.9 persons) and manufacturing (12.4 persons). Firms in financial services reduced working hours for an average 46.6 regular employees, followed by administrative services (24.7 persons) and water supply (16.8 persons). Firms in administrative services reduced salaries, wages, or benefits for 12.5 regular employees on average in April, followed by information and communication (10.5 persons) and manufacturing (10.3 persons). By contrast, firms in financial services hired an average 5.5 regular employees in April, followed by transportation and storage (4.9 persons), and manufacturing (4.2 persons).

By region, NCR-based firms were most affected by the ECQ in changing employment arrangements in terms of the number of responses, followed by Central Luzon, Calabarzon, and Central Visayas. For NCR-based firms, 42.4% granted leave to regular employees, followed by reduced working hours (41.7%), reduced salaries and benefits (33.7%), and layoffs (11.7%). In April, 20.6% of NCR-based firms hired new regular employees. On average, 11.9 regular employees per NCR-based firm were forced to reduce working hours; 10.0 employees were granted leave; 5.8 employees faced reduced salaries, wages, or benefits; and 1.8 employees were laid off. But 2.8 new regular employees were hired.

For Central Luzon, Calabarzon, and Central Visayas-based firms, 33.2%, 39.2%, and 48.6%, respectively, granted leave to regular employees, followed by reduced working hours (32.8%, 36.2%, and 44.3%), reduced salaries and benefits (28.8%, 29.4%, and 31.7%), and layoffs (20.5%, 13.9%, and 20.2%). In the three regions, 17.9%, 20.8%, and 21.3%, respectively, hired new regular employees in April. On average, within Central Luzon, Calabarzon, and Central Visayas-based firms, 6.9, 8.7, and 9.9 regular employees, respectively, reduced working hours; salaries, wages, or benefits were reduced for 4.1, 8.9, and 7.5 employees, respectively; leave was granted for 3.7, 6.3, and 7.5 employees, respectively; and 2.0, 2.5, and 3.8 employees, respectively, were laid off. On average, firms in Central Luzon, Calabarzon, and Central Visayas hired 1.8, 3.3, and 2.5 regular employees, respectively, in April.

b. Part-time or contractual workers

For part-time or contractual workers (henceforth "part-time workers"), changes in employment arrangements were similar to those for full-time regular workers, but differed slightly by frequency of use. In April, 21.4% of enterprises surveyed reduced working hours of part-time workers, followed by leaves granted to workers (17.7%), reduced salaries and benefits (17.3%), and layoffs (11.9%) (Figure 14). Meanwhile, 8.9% of enterprises reported new part-time workers hired to supplement the workforce in response to special demand. Some 80% of enterprises surveyed reported no change in employment status for part-time workers from March to April.

The surveyed enterprises on average reduced working hours for 4.1 part-time workers between from March to April; granted leave to 4.3 workers; reduced salaries, wages, or benefits for 3.7 workers; and laid off 1.4 workers. Meanwhile, on average they hired 1 new part-time worker to supplement workforces. The average number of part-time workers in the enterprises surveyed was 12.7 persons.

By firm size, similar to full-time workers, part-time workers in microenterprises were worse off in April, with 19.8% of microenterprises surveyed reducing working hours of part-time workers, followed by reduced salaries and benefits (17.1%), leaves granted (16.5%), and layoffs (11.6%). Yet, 9.8% of the microenterprises surveyed hired new part-time workers. On average, each microenterprise reduced working hours for 2.7 part-time workers; 4.2 workers were granted leave; 3.1 workers faced a reduction of salary, wages, or benefits; and 1.2 workers were laid off. But 0.5 part-time workers were hired in April.

Part-time workers in micro, small, medium-sized, and large enterprises were also adversely affected by the ECQ. For small enterprises, 23.1% reduced working hours of part-time workers, followed by reduced salaries and benefits (19.2%), leaves granted (17.9%), and layoffs (12.5%). On average, 8.3% of them hired new part-time workers in April. By number of employees per small firm, 4.6 part-time workers had to reduce working hours; 2.5 workers were granted leave; 3.7 workers had salaries, wages, or benefits reduced; and 1.7 workers were laid off. On average, 1.2 part-time workers were hired in April.

For medium-sized and large firms, 24.4% and 21.0%, respectively, reduced working hours of part-time workers. This was followed by leaves granted (22.2% for medium-sized and 17.7% for large firms), reduced salaries and benefits (15.9% and 14.9%), and layoffs (10.6% and 13.8%). Still, 5.9% of medium-sized firms and 9.4% of large firms hired new part-time workers in April. On average, working hours were reduced for 7.1 part-time workers and 6.5 part-time workers per medium-sized and large firm, respectively; 5.4 and 9.6 workers were granted leave; 4.0 and 7.0 workers had salaries, wages, or benefits reduced; and 1.1 and 1.5 workers were laid off. On average, medium-sized firms hired 1.3 new part-time workers in April and large firms 3.1 part-time workers.

By sector, similar to regular workers, part-time workers across all sectors felt the impact of the ECQ. It was more pronounced in wholesale and retail trade, accommodation and food services, and other services. In wholesale and retail trade, 20.1% of firms reduced working hours of part-time workers, followed by granted leave (17.8%), reduced salaries and benefits (15.2%), and layoffs (6.8%). In April, 8.0% hired new part-time workers.

By type of employment arrangements and sector, construction firms once again laid off more part-time workers (5.3 per firm) on average in April, followed by other services (1.9 persons) and transportation and storage (1.7 persons). Firms in administrative services reduced working hours for 20.3 part-time workers on average in April, followed by other services (6.7 persons) and construction (6.4 persons). Firms in transportation and storage granted leave to 33.8 part-time workers on average in April, followed by other services (8.1 persons) and information and communication (6.0 persons). Firms in administrative services reduced the salary, wages, or benefits of 20.2 part-time workers on average in April, followed by information and communication (8.0 persons) and other services (6.6 persons). By contrast, firms in human health and social work services hired 5.3 part-tome workers on average in April, followed by administrative services (3.3 persons), and construction (3.0 persons).

By region, NCR-based firms most actively adopted new employment arrangements for part-time workers in April in terms of the number of responses. Among NCR-based firms, 20.9% reduced working hours of part-time workers, followed by reduced salaries and benefits (17.9%), leaves granted (16.7%), and layoffs (10.1%). In April, 7.7% hired new part-time workers. On average, 3.5 part-time workers per NCR-based firm were forced to reduce working hours; 6.5 workers were granted leave; 2.4 workers had salaries, wages, or benefits reduced; and 1.5 workers were laid off. On average, 0.9 part-time workers were hired in April.

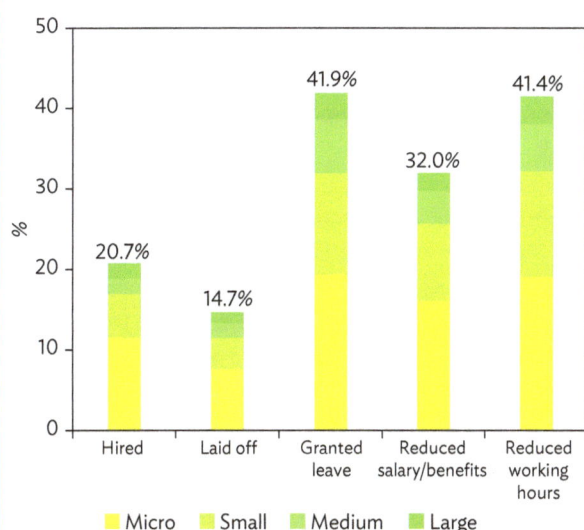

Figure 13: Full-Time Regular Workers (% share of total responses)

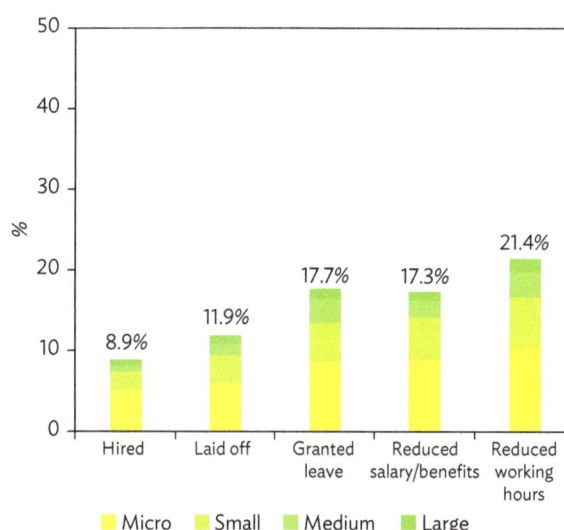

Figure 14: Part-Time or Contractual Workers (% share of total responses)

Source: Asian Development Bank, Philippine Enterprise Survey.

Wage Payments

- Half of the firms surveyed suspended wage payments after the COVID-19 outbreak, with the suspension more pronounced in microenterprises.
- The wholesale and retail trade sector and the NCR region were most affected by suspended or reduced wage payments.

As the majority of enterprises surveyed temporarily closed their business after the ECQ began on 16 March, many enterprises reported either no wage payments to employees or a decrease in total wage payments. More concretely, 49.3% of enterprises did not pay wages to employees temporarily after 15 March (Figure 15), 28.9% reduced the total amount of wage payments, and 19.9% reported no change in payment conditions to employees. Just 2% of enterprises reported an increase in total wage payments to employees after the pandemic began, suggesting special needs identified by specific industries.

By firm size, this pattern was apparent especially among microenterprises, which were most likely to either stop paying wages or sharply decrease wage payments to employees after the beginning of the ECQ (compared with small, medium-sized, and large firms). Yet, the survey also found microenterprises more likely to increase total wage payments to employees relative to small, medium-sized, and large firms. Microenterprises accounted for 58.7% of enterprises with no wage payment change after the ECQ began, followed by small enterprises (24.3%), medium-sized enterprises (10.1%), and large enterprises (6.9%). Microenterprises reduced wage payments by more than 50% most (44.2%), followed by small (31.8%), medium-sized (16.4%), and large (7.6%) enterprises. Meanwhile, 49.9% of enterprises with no change in wage payment conditions were microenterprises, followed by small (28.6%), medium-sized (12.0%), and large (9.5%) enterprises. Microenterprises also accounted for 35.3% of enterprises increasing wage payments by 10%–30%, 44.4% of those increasing wage payments by 31%–50%, and 50.0% of those increasing wage payments more than 50%.

By sector, wholesale and retail trade was the most affected in terms of either no wage payment or a decrease of wage payments after the ECQ began. Firms in wholesale and retail trade accounted for 20.4% of total enterprises with no wage payment after the ECQ, followed by those in accommodation and food services (17.3%) and other services (15.1%). Enterprises that decreased wage payments by more than 50% were in wholesale and retail trade (20.0%), followed by those in accommodation and food services (14.2%) and other services (11.5%). Meanwhile, 27.0% of enterprises with no change in wage payment conditions were firms in wholesale and retail trade, followed by those in other services (15.0%) and manufacturing (10.3%).

By region, the NCR was the most affected for either no wage payment or a decrease of wage payments. NCR-based firms accounted for 48.0% of total enterprises with no wage payment after ECQ began, followed by firms in Calabarzon (15.8%) and Central Luzon (11.0%). Enterprises that reduced wage payments by more than 50% were primarily NCR-based firms (53.3%), followed by firms in Calabarzon (11.2%) and Central Luzon (7.3%). Meanwhile, 53.8% of enterprises with no change in wage payment conditions were NCR-based, followed by firms in Calabarzon (12.0%) and Central Luzon (8.5%).

Status of "Work from Home"

- Work from home was not a feasible option for any workers in most enterprises; it was more pronounced in microenterprises.
- Wholesale and retail trade had the greatest difficulty conducting work from home.
- Half of NCR-based firms reported that work from home was not possible for any workers.

After the ECQ began, many enterprises were forced to close their businesses, and "work from home" (WFH) became an oft-used alternative approach to maintain business activity. However, the survey findings revealed that WFH was not necessarily feasible or ideal. More than half (57.0%) of enterprises reported that it was not possible to adopt WFH for any workers (Figure 16). Less than 50% of workers could WFH without major operational disruptions in 32.2% of the enterprises surveyed. Only 10.8% reported that more than 50% of workers could WFH without major disruptions.

By firm size, 63.0% of microenterprises reported WFH was not possible for any workers, 12.7% reported 1%–5% of employees could WFH, 6.4% reported 6%–25% of employees could WFH, and 6.7% reported 26%–50% of employees could WFH, while 11.3% reported more than 50% of employees could WFH. For small enterprises, 52.4% reported WFH was not possible for any workers, 22.8% reported 1%–5% of employees could WFH, 10.2% reported 6%–25% of employees could WFH, and 5.2% reported 26%–50% of employees could WFH, while 9.5% of small enterprises reported more than 50% of employees could WFH. For medium-sized enterprises, 47.4% reported WFH was not possible for any workers, 26.0% reported 1%–5% of employees could WFH, 10.6% reported 6%–25% of employees could WFH, and 6.3% reported 26%–50% of employees could WFH, while 9.7% of small enterprises reported more than 50% of employees could WFH. For large enterprises, 50.0% reported WFH was not possible for any workers, 18.3% reported 1%–5% of employees could WFH, 10.2% reported 6%–25% of employees could WFH, and 7.5% reported 26%–50% of employees could WFH, while 14.0% of large enterprises reported more than 50% of employees could WFH.

By sector, wholesale and retail trade had the greatest difficulty practicing WFH. Firms in wholesale and retail trade accounted for 22.4% of total enterprises that reported WFH was not possible for any workers, followed by those in accommodation and food services (18.9%) and other services (15.1%). Firms in wholesale and retail trade also accounted for 22.1% of those where WFH was possible for 1%–5% of employees, 25.4% for 6%–25%, and 18.6% for 26%–50% of WFH employees. Other services followed at 14.4%, 12.7%, and 16.7%, respectively. Meanwhile, firms in information and communication accounted for 29.1% of enterprises that reported WFH was possible for more than 50% of employees, followed by those in wholesale and retail trade (16.4%) and professional services (11.6%).

By region, NCR-based firms accounted for 43.0% of total enterprises that reported WFH was not possible for any workers, followed by firms in Calabarzon (14.8%) and Central Luzon (10.5%). NCR-based firms also accounted for 49.4% of enterprises that reported WFH was possible for 1%–5% of employees, followed by firms in Calabarzon (14.4%) and Central Luzon (11.2%). Meanwhile, NCR-based firms accounted for 69.4% of total enterprises that reported WFH was possible for more than 50% of employees, followed by Calabarzon (9.0%) and Central Visayas (6.7%).

Figure 15: Changes in Wage Payments after the COVID-19 Outbreak

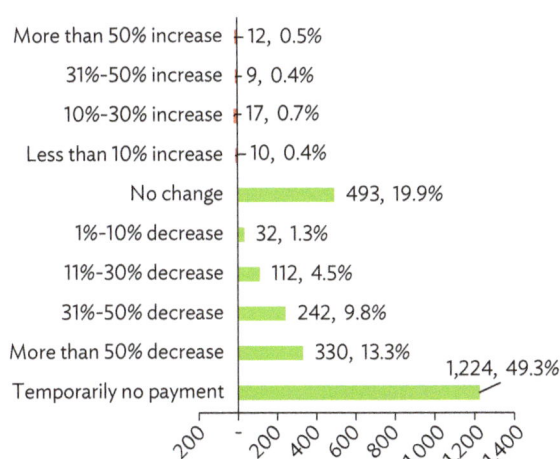

Source: Asian Development Bank, Philippine Enterprise Survey.

Figure 16: Workers Able to Work From Home

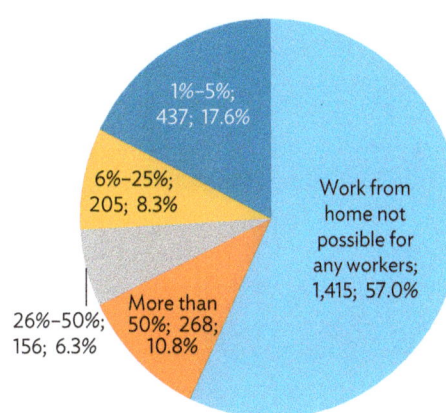

Source: Asian Development Bank, Philippine Enterprise Survey.

Enterprise Assistance to Employees during the ECQ

Enterprises provided several types of assistance to their employees during the ECQ. In the multiple answer section of the questionnaire, 884 firms (35.6% of total respondents) reported providing vitamins and hygiene products such as alcohol-based disinfectant to employees; 816 firms (32.9%) reported delivering personal protective equipment such as face masks; 377 firms (15.2%) provided accommodation near the workplace; 340 firms (13.7%) provided a shuttle service to and from home or designated pickup points; 339 firms (13.7%) offered additional leave credits; and 330 firms (13.3%) provided an internet/data allowance to employees.

Product Supply Chain Bottlenecks

- More than one-third of enterprises faced severe bottlenecks in the product supply chain, negatively affecting more than half their production capacity.
- Supply chain bottlenecks were mainly caused by slow customs clearance on imported goods, limited operations with local suppliers, and shortage of trucks/drivers.
- More than half of enterprises reported no change in the cost of supplies after the ECQ began, regardless of firm size.
- Traditional trade, accommodation and food services, and manufacturing accounted for more than half of enterprises reporting an increase in the cost of supplies.
- Half of enterprises facing an increase in the cost of supplies were based in the NCR.

The lockdown measures immediately affected the logistics of supplying goods and services. Accordingly, 39.1% of those surveyed faced severe bottlenecks in the product supply chain, negatively affecting more than half their production capacity (Figure 17). However, 26.7% reported only minor bottlenecks, affecting less than half their production capacity, while 34.2% did not experience any bottlenecks. In the multiple answer section of the questionnaire where respondents can select up to three reasons, 1,109 firms (44.7% of total respondents) reported that slow customs clearance on goods and/or raw material imports caused the supply chain bottleneck, followed by contract termination or reduced operations with local suppliers or distributors (773 responses or 31.2% of total respondents) and the limited availability of trucks/drivers that delayed logistics (558 responses or 22.5%).

There was no change in the cost of supplies and raw materials after the ECQ began for 52.6% of enterprises; 26.1% reported an increase in cost; while 21.3% reported a decrease (Figure 18).

By firm size, 53.0% of microenterprises reported no change in cost of supplies and raw materials, 24.6% reported an increase, while 22.4% reported a supply cost decrease. For small enterprises, 52.9% reported no change in the cost of supplies and raw materials, 26.8% reported a cost increase, while 20.3% reported a cost decrease. For medium-sized enterprises, 51.5% reported no change in the cost of supplies and raw materials, 31.8% reported a cost increase, while 16.7% reported a cost decrease. For large enterprises, 51.1% reported no change in the cost of supplies and raw materials, 23.1% reported a cost increase, while 25.8% reported a cost decrease.

By sector, firms in wholesale and retail trade accounted for 26.2% of enterprises reporting an increase in the cost of supplies and raw materials after the ECQ began, followed by those in accommodation and food services (15.5%) and manufacturing (13.6%). Meanwhile, firms in wholesale and retail trade also accounted for 20.8% of total enterprises reporting a cost decrease, followed by those in accommodation and food services (16.1%) and other services (12.9%). These mixed results of cost increases and decreases depended on the extent of bottlenecks within the supply chain.

By region, NCR-based firms accounted for 49.2% of enterprises reporting an increase in the cost of supplies and raw materials after the ECQ began, followed by firms in Calabarzon (14.2%) and Central Luzon (9.8%). Meanwhile, NCR-based firms also accounted for 37.3% of total enterprises that reported a cost decrease, followed by firms in Calabarzon (15.3%) and Central Luzon (12.1%).

Figure 17: Bottlenecks in Supply Chain?

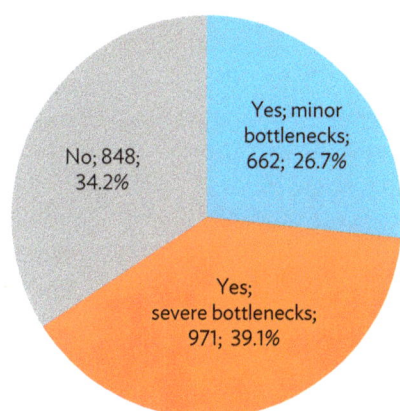

No; 848; 34.2%
Yes; minor bottlenecks; 662; 26.7%
Yes; severe bottlenecks; 971; 39.1%

Source: Asian Development Bank, Philippine Enterprise Survey.

Figure 18: Any Change in Cost of Supplies/Raw Materials during ECQ?

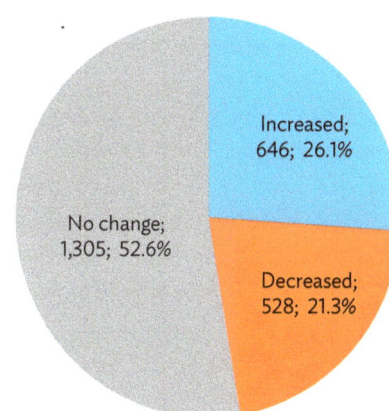

Increased; 646; 26.1%
No change; 1,305; 52.6%
Decreased; 528; 21.3%

ECQ = enhanced community quarantine.
Source: Asian Development Bank, Philippine Enterprise Survey.

Financial Condition of Enterprises after the COVID-19 Outbreak

- One-third of enterprises already had no cash and savings to cover operations; another one-third reported running out of cash and funds within 1–3 months.
- The most significant financial problem for enterprises was paying staff wages and social security charges.
- Microenterprises faced the most serious shortage of working capital, while large firms had sufficient liquidity to survive for over 6 months.
- Services sector and NCR-based firms had a serious liquidity problem due to a lack of working capital.

Enterprises faced sharp deterioration of financial conditions after the COVID-19 outbreak—33.6% of survey respondents already had no cash or savings to cover operation costs at the time of the survey (Figure 19). Another 36.5% reported that cash and funds covering operation costs would run out in 1–3 months, and 17.4% reported cash would run out in 3–6 months. Only 9.3% of enterprises indicated they had enough savings, liquid assets, and other contingency budget to maintain their business for more than 6 months. The most significant financial problem for enterprises during the COVID-19 pandemic is paying staff wages and social security charges. This was cited by 37.4% of respondents, followed by repayment of loans (17.0%), office rent (16.8%), and invoice payments (15.0%) (Figure 20).

By firm size, microenterprises faced the most serious shortage of working capital, while large enterprises tended to have sufficient liquidity to survive for more than 6 months. More concretely, 41.1% of microenterprises reported having no cash and savings for business operations at the time of the survey; 36.3% reported they expected to run out of cash and funds within 1–3 months; 14.1% would run out cash and funds within 3–6 months; while 5.3% reported having enough funds to cover more than 6 months of operations. For small enterprises, 26.7% reported no cash and savings for business operations, 37.5% reported they would run out of cash and funds within 1–3 months, 20.9% would run out cash and funds within 3–6 months, while 11.6% reported sufficient funds to cover more than 6 months of operations. For medium-sized enterprises, 21.8% reported no cash and savings for business operations, 37.9% reported they would run out of cash and funds within 1–3 months, 21.8% would run out cash and funds within 3–6 months, while 15.8% reported having enough money to cover more than 6 months of operations. For large enterprises, 27.6% reported no cash and savings for business operations, 31.4% reported they would run out of cash and funds within 1–3 months, 19.5% would run out cash and funds within 3–6 months, while 16.8% reported having enough money to cover more than 6 months of operations.

By sector, firms in other services such as worker dispatching, beauty salons, laundry, personal repairs, and publishing accounted for 19.8% of enterprises with no cash and savings for business operations at the time of the survey, followed by those in accommodation and food services (17.7%) and wholesale and retail trade (15.8%). Firms in wholesale and retail trade accounted for 24.1% of those reporting they would run out of cash and funds within 1–3 months, followed by those in accommodation and food services (15.0%) and other services (12.4%). Meanwhile, firms in wholesale and retail trade accounted for 25.3% of those reporting having sufficient funds to cover more than 6 months of operations, followed by those in manufacturing (13.5%) and financial services (10.9%).

By region, NCR-based firms accounted for 48.1% of enterprises without cash and savings for business operations at the time of the survey, followed by firms in Calabarzon (13.8%) and Central Visayas (6.9%). NCR-based firms accounted for 49.7% of those reporting they would run out of cash and funds within 1–3 months, followed by firms in Calabarzon (14.4%) and Central Visayas (7.3%). Meanwhile, NCR-based firms accounted for 53.7% of enterprises reporting they had enough money to cover more than 6 months of operations, followed by firms in Calabarzon (9.6%), Central Visayas (8.7%), and Central Luzon (8.7%).

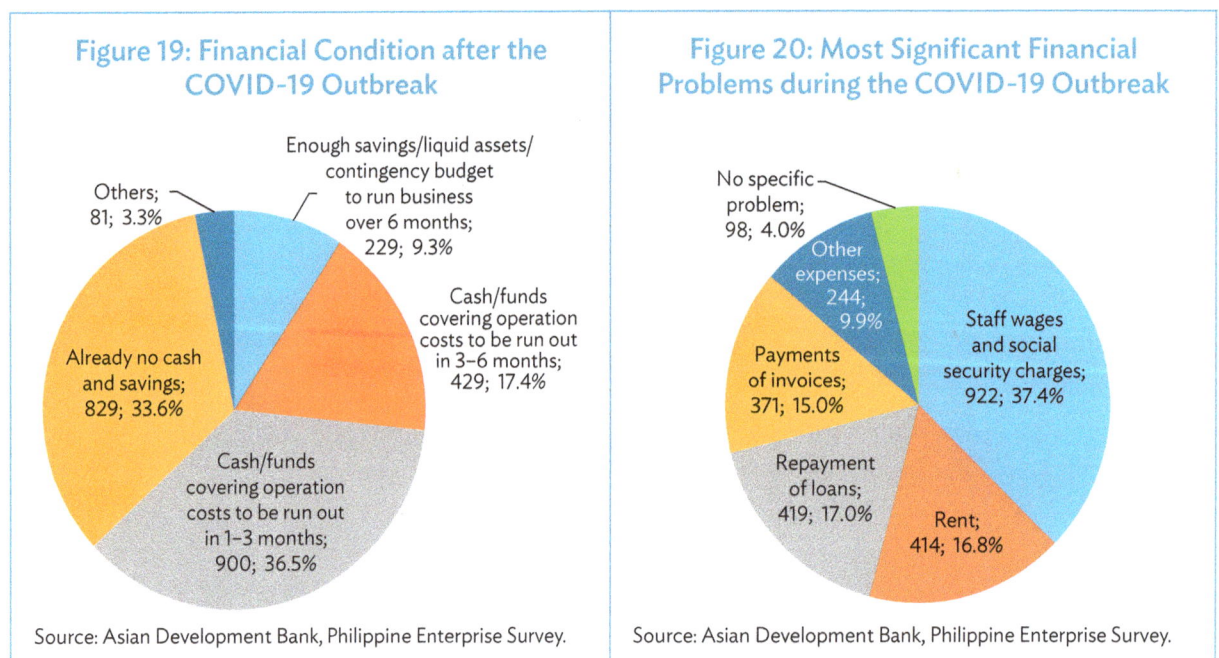

Figure 19: Financial Condition after the COVID-19 Outbreak

- Enough savings/liquid assets/contingency budget to run business over 6 months; 229; 9.3%
- Others; 81; 3.3%
- Cash/funds covering operation costs to be run out in 3–6 months; 429; 17.4%
- Already no cash and savings; 829; 33.6%
- Cash/funds covering operation costs to be run out in 1–3 months; 900; 36.5%

Source: Asian Development Bank, Philippine Enterprise Survey.

Figure 20: Most Significant Financial Problems during the COVID-19 Outbreak

- No specific problem; 98; 4.0%
- Other expenses; 244; 9.9%
- Payments of invoices; 371; 15.0%
- Repayment of loans; 419; 17.0%
- Staff wages and social security charges; 922; 37.4%
- Rent; 414; 16.8%

Source: Asian Development Bank, Philippine Enterprise Survey.

Funding during the ECQ and Desired Source of Funds for Business

- Most enterprises relied on their own funds and/or retained profit to maintain their business during the ECQ.
- Microenterprises, mostly in wholesale and retail trade, borrowed from close relatives and informal moneylenders to survive the ECQ.
- Enterprises surveyed cited bank credit as the top financing method desired.
- Overall credit constraints are tightening even for relatively small amounts of liquidity.

During the ECQ, most enterprises surveyed relied heavily on their own funds and/or retained profit to maintain their business, while exploring external funding to fill gaps in working capital. In the multiple answer section of the questionnaire, 1,334 firms (53.8% of total respondents) reported they used their own funds and/or retained profit to continue business activities (Figure 21); 553 firms (22.3%) borrowed from family, relatives, and friends; 379 firms (15.3%) applied for loans/overdrafts/lines of credit from banks for working capital; 255 firms (10.3%) received funding support from business partners; 245 firms (9.9%) could obtain loans/overdrafts/lines of credit from banks for working capital; 221 firms (8.9%) received government funding support; 217 firms (8.7%) borrowed from informal moneylenders; 151 firms (6.1%) tapped nonbank finance institutions (such as microfinance institutions and pawnshops) for working capital; only 41 firms (1.7%) used digital finance platforms such as peer-to-peer lending or crowdfunding for working capital financing.

Regardless of firm size, using one's own funds and/or retained profit was a key funding source during the ECQ. Microenterprises, mostly in wholesale and retail trade, had the largest share (66.2%) of firms borrowing from close relatives and the largest share (61.3%) borrowing from informal moneylenders. Half of those applying for bank loans were also microenterprises, which may have been supported by government programs increasing access to finance.

For sources of future funds, those surveyed cited bank credit as the top financing method desired, with 1,050 responses (42.3%) (Figure 22). Meanwhile, 892 firms (36.0%) would continue to rely on their own funds, 572 firms (23.1%) would tap informal funds from close relatives to survive the ECQ, 492 firms (19.8%) would seek financial support from business partners, and 353 firms (14.2%) would look to nonbank finance institutions to fill their working capital needs. Only 95 firms said they would seek loans from digital finance platforms.

Given the serious shortage of working capital, the survey examined the availability of short-term access to small amounts of funding by asking a hypothetical question whether each respondent could borrow ₱50,000 within a week. Over half (53%) of those surveyed said they could not (Figure 23); 57.3% reported it was more difficult now to borrow ₱50,000 in a short period than in 2019 (Figure 24). These figures suggest that overall credit constraints are becoming more binding even for a relatively small amount of liquidity.

Policy Measures Required during and after the COVID-19 Crisis

- A payroll subsidy for workers was the policy measure most needed for firms to survive during the pandemic, followed by deferred tax payments and concessional loans.
- Enterprises are exploring a new post-COVID-19 business model that avoids physical contact, requesting the government to review current regulations to facilitate digital transactions; associated skill training for workers is also required.
- The most cited measure that enterprises would take upon reopening is to provide face masks to workers; social distancing and creating smaller work groups were not major actions considered by firms after the business reopens.

Figure 21: Funding during the ECQ

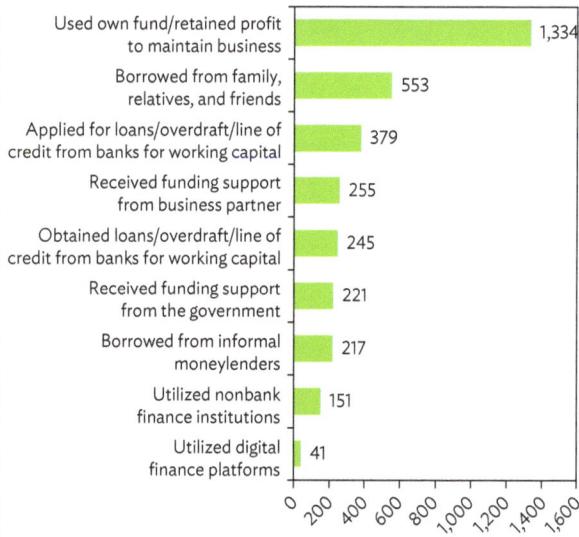

Category	Value
Used own fund/retained profit to maintain business	1,334
Borrowed from family, relatives, and friends	553
Applied for loans/overdraft/line of credit from banks for working capital	379
Received funding support from business partner	255
Obtained loans/overdraft/line of credit from banks for working capital	245
Received funding support from the government	221
Borrowed from informal moneylenders	217
Utilized nonbank finance institutions	151
Utilized digital finance platforms	41

ECQ = enhanced community quarantine.
Source: Asian Development Bank, Philippine Enterprise Survey.

Figure 22: Desired Source of Funds for Business

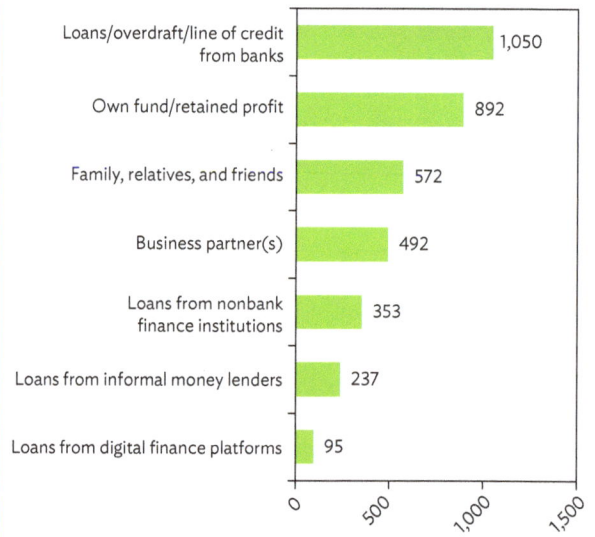

Category	Value
Loans/overdraft/line of credit from banks	1,050
Own fund/retained profit	892
Family, relatives, and friends	572
Business partner(s)	492
Loans from nonbank finance institutions	353
Loans from informal money lenders	237
Loans from digital finance platforms	95

Source: Asian Development Bank, Philippine Enterprise Survey.

Figure 23: Can You Borrow ₱50,000 within a Week?

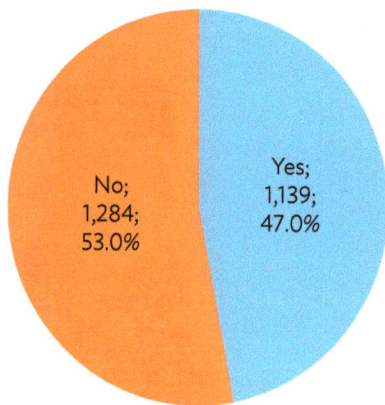

No; 1,284; 53.0%
Yes; 1,139; 47.0%

Source: Asian Development Bank, Philippine Enterprise Survey.

Figure 24: Is It More Difficult to Borrow ₱50,000 Now than 2019?

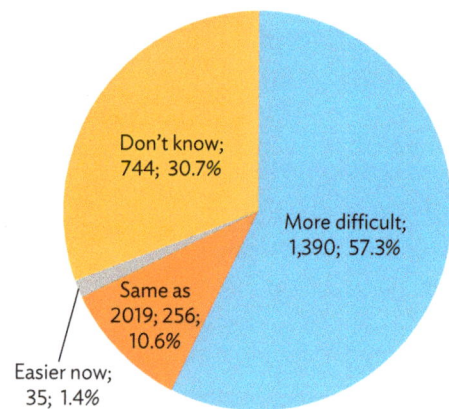

Don't know; 744; 30.7%
More difficult; 1,390; 57.3%
Same as 2019; 256; 10.6%
Easier now; 35; 1.4%

Source: Asian Development Bank, Philippine Enterprise Survey.

The survey also included questions to identify appropriate policy needs. In multiple choice questions (up to three answers can be selected), respondents said the most needed policy measures to help their businesses survive during the COVID-19 crisis was a payroll subsidy for workers (1,421 responses or 57.3% of total respondents), followed by deferment of payments to government (such as tax payments, withholding tax, and value-added tax [VAT]) (1,283 responses or 51.7%), and low-interest and subsidized loans (894 responses or 36.0%) (Figure 25).

Following the COVID-19 crisis, the most popular request from respondents was a review of existing regulations by the Bureau of Internal Revenue, the Securities and Exchange Commission, and the Commission on Audit on compatibility with digital payments and transactions (1,054 responses or 42.5%). This suggests that enterprises are exploring a new business model shifting to digital transactions as the crisis recedes. Enterprises also want policy support to upgrade worker skills to maintain competitiveness under the new normal (893 responses or 36.0%). Firms also want tax incentives for adopting digital technologies such as digital payments and e-commerce (767 responses or 32.1%) (Figure 26).

Businesses and their employees will need to be protected against the spread of the virus even if lockdown measures are lifted and businesses reopened. Enterprises surveyed cited several possible ways to deal with social contact issues: providing face masks to all employees (63.4%), separating staff into smaller groups and restricting group interaction (16.9%), routinely checking the staff temperature (12.9%), maintaining records for contact tracing (6.1%), and canteen rationing to ensure social distancing during lunch (0.7%).

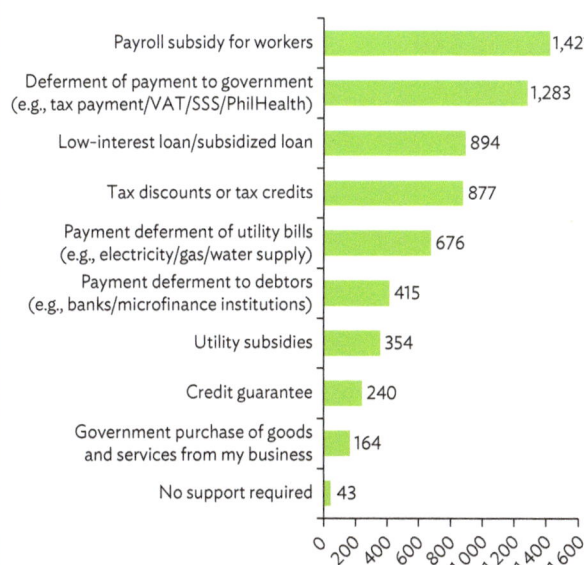

Figure 25: Policy Measures Needed during the COVID-19 Crisis

PhilHealth = Philippine Health Insurance Corporation, SSS = Social Security System, VAT = value-added tax.
Source: Asian Development Bank, Philippine Enterprise Survey.

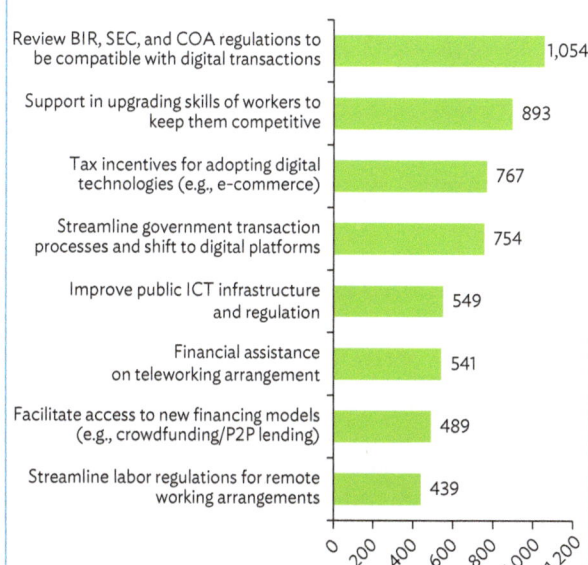

Figure 26: Policy Measures Needed after the COVID-19 Crisis

BIR = Bureau of Internal Revenue, COA = Commission on Audit, ICT = information and communication technology, P2P = peer-to-peer, SEC = Securities and Exchange Commission.
Source: Asian Development Bank, Philippine Enterprise Survey.

3. POLICY IMPLICATIONS

The survey findings indicate that enterprises faced severe difficulties due to the ECQ measures that restricted the movement of workers and consumers and business operations. These restrictions forced many businesses to temporarily close or reduce their operations. As a result, revenue has dried up while fixed costs must still be paid. From a business standpoint, the economy needs to reopen, but this must be balanced against the threat to public health and the need to control the spread of the virus. Like other countries around the world, the Philippines continues to face very difficult decisions in balancing these health and economic imperatives.

By mid-June, the government (and central bank) had put in place a variety of policies and programs. These include (i) quarantine and social distancing measures to reduce person-to-person contact and contain the spread of the virus; (ii) health measures to test and trace, and to provide medical care to those infected; and (iii) economic relief and support measures for households, workers, and businesses. The government has been active in all three areas and continues to modify, reduce, and enhance measures. Some of the key measures supporting business are the

- MSME Credit Guarantee Program,
- Small Business Corporation loans to micro and small businesses,
- Small Business Wage Subsidy Program,
- Corporate Recovery and Tax Incentives for Enterprises Act, and
- Bangko Sentral ng Pilipinas (BSP) regulations of commercial banks' MSME lending.

The Philippines is transitioning through the initial phase of the pandemic and will move to subsequent phases in the months ahead. Economic and business support policies, linked to the evolving health situation, might be considered along three main phases:

Phase 1—Relief and Support
Phase 2—Reopening and Bounce Back
Phase 3—Recovery and Continued Transformation

The phases may overlap and a policy in one phase may continue unmodified, continue as modified, or be discontinued in the following phase. Wholly new policies may arise in subsequent phases. The specific periodization (dates) of the phases is difficult to determine and depends on the evolving health situation, notably the control of the virus. The Philippines recorded its first case of COVID-19 on 30 January, but it was several weeks before the first local transmission was recorded on 7 March. Quarantine measures were instituted in mid-March which precipitated a steep decline in economic activity. The number of daily new, reported cases peaked at over 1,000 in late May and varies considerably day-to-day. It was just over 600 on 13 June. Quarantine measures have eased in June. A chief concern is whether the spread is being adequately contained and whether, despite a lull, a second wave may begin in the months ahead.

Phase 1: Economic Relief and Support

Continue to support access to finance. Enterprises are facing serious working capital constraints. One-third of enterprises surveyed were out of cash and savings by the time the survey was conducted in early May, with another one-third (37%) expected to run out in the next 1–3 months. Further, more than half (53%) could not arrange to borrow even ₱50,000 within one week, and 57% said it was more difficult to borrow that amount now than in 2019. Thus, additional finance in the form of loans and overdraft facilities should be a high priority for government assistance.

The government (and central bank) understands the financing constraint. Additional financing for MSMEs has been provided in three ways: (i) use of credit guarantees; (ii) lending by the Small Business Corporation, and (iii) changes in central bank regulations.

The government has provided ₱60 billion to the MSME Credit Guarantee Program, administered by the Philippine Guarantee Corporation. A 50% guarantee on working capital loans will support ₱120 billion in lending by commercial banks. In addition, the Agriculture Guarantee Fund Pool reduced its guarantee fee from 1.0% to 0.5% for borrowers hit by the crisis and increased its coverage ratio (share of the loan that is guaranteed) from 85% to 90%.

Small Business Corporation, under the Department of Trade and Industry, is providing loans totaling ₱1 billion to micro and small businesses affected by the crisis. Microenterprises can borrow up to ₱200,000 and small businesses up to ₱500,000. The interest rate will be set at 0.5% per month with a 6-month grace period on principal repayments. The loans were available in areas where the ECQ was lifted, starting in mid-May.

The BSP announced that it will count loans granted to MSMEs as part of bank reserve requirements. Also, there is a temporary reduction to 50% of the credit weight rate of MSME loans (from 75% to 100% normally). In addition, the weight risk has been reduced to zero for MSME loans covered by guarantee (Philippine Guarantee Corporation and the agriculture guarantee). Overall, these BSP measures are designed to free up commercial bank funds and encourage more lending to MSMEs.

Wage subsidy program can be extended. Paying wages and social security contributions is the single most important payment concern for most enterprises (37%). Also, a wage subsidy was the most frequently requested government support measure (57%).

The Small Business Wage Subsidy Program has been a very timely instrument to meet the needs for business while supporting the livelihoods of workers and their families.[2] Subsidies have targeted 3.4 million workers, with payouts expected to total ₱51 billion. The subsidy covers 2 months (from mid-March to May) and provides support for enterprises forced to close operations under the ECQ. The use of online payment systems greatly increased the efficiency of getting payments to workers, with about 97% of payments made by early June. It would be useful to extend the program, particularly for sectors hardest hit by the downturn, notably in retail, transport, and tourism.

Assist enterprises to sell online. A small share of enterprises surveyed (14%) sell their products or services on the internet. This makes it difficult to service customers and generate revenue during quarantine or other mobility restrictions. Efforts can be made to encourage firms to get connected to advertise, offer, and sell over the internet. Enterprises often need help even with the e-commerce basics, such as creating a website and uploading photographs of their products. In addition, an enterprise needs to link with an e-payments service provider to

---

[2]   Department of Labor and Employment operated an initial wage subsidy program called the COVID-19 Adjustment Measures Program (CAMP) from 23 March to 15 April. It was folded subsequently into the Small Business Wage Subsidy Program.

receive revenue. Platforms, e-commerce service companies, and e-payment providers are available, but enterprises need to know how to link up. Getting connected in this way will not only assist businesses to keep operating in the current situation but will also help during a possible second wave later, and more generally to expand their customer base under normal and "new normal" business conditions.

Tax deferrals are helpful. Deferrals on tax filings were the second most frequently requested policy measure by respondents (52%). Deferrals ease cash flow and enhance liquidity by reducing outflows. The government was proactive in this regard during the first few months of the crisis. Deadlines were extended by 1–2 months depending on the type of tax. Extensions were from their original dates in April to May to various dates in June. In all, 13 deadlines were extended including income tax for 2019 and the first quarter of 2020. Tax filings due for the first 4 months of 2020 for VAT, expanded withholding tax, compensation withholding tax, and percentage tax were also extended.

These deferrals have delayed the receipt of government revenues, which are needed not only to fund the government's regular operations but also to finance measures to counteract the economic effects of the pandemic. As such, the government decided not to extend further the filing deadlines for 2019 income tax which was set at a revised date of 15 June.

Phase 2: Reopening and Bounce-Back Initiatives

Support enterprises as quarantines ease. The government imposed the Community Quarantine (CQ) and ECQ in various parts of the country beginning mid-March. These measures, necessary to contain the spread of the virus, had a dramatic impact on businesses. As mentioned, two-thirds of enterprises surveyed were temporarily closed by the time of the survey and most others (29%) remained open but with limited operations. Of those remaining open, most (78%) operated at 50% or less capacity. Only 4% of enterprises remained open with full operations. Some firms felt it would take up to 3 months to recover from the quarantine (19%), but a larger portion (30%) expected it to take longer. These results suggest that it is imperative that the government continues to provide assistance to firms as quarantines are lifted. The difficulties for business will not end immediately after the virus is brought under control.

Quarantines are being revised in a phased manner. Several areas moved from an ECQ to a modified ECQ or general community quarantine (GCQ) in early June. This has allowed more businesses to operate and consumers to spend. The move also led to a resumption of work on infrastructure (transport) projects, notably those under the Build, Build, Build program. Increased construction activity will mean more workers with wages that are spent on goods and services in other parts of the economy. A further review of quarantines was held on 15 June, with Cebu City returning to an ECQ because of increased infections. The NCR remains under GCQ at least until 15 July. As restrictions ease, more businesses can open and resume operations to generate revenue.

Continue providing access to formal sources of business finance. Despite the need for working capital, only 10% of those surveyed had accessed a loan, overdraft, or line of credit from a financial institution to meet their working capital needs during the first months of the pandemic. Nearly the same percentage (9%) had borrowed from informal moneylenders to maintain operations. The same share (9%) received funding support from government. The largest single source of finance was savings and retained business earnings, used by 54% of enterprises to sustain operations. The latter is a finite source and will run out as long as restrictions remain. Enterprises also relied on funds from family and friends (22%).

Keep financing costs low. A total of 36% of enterprises surveyed cited the need for low interest or subsidized loans. It was the third most cited policy measure desired by enterprises.

Tax reform will help businesses recover. Enterprises surveyed favored tax credits and reductions. These measures were requested by 35% of enterprises and were the fourth most frequently requested measure of the nine government support options provided. Prior to the crisis, the government developed a tax reform program, which has been expanded to address the needs of business due to the crisis.

The Corporate Recovery and Tax Incentives for Enterprises Act (CREATE) has three key components. First, it reduces the corporate tax rate from 30% to 25% beginning in July. The rate will be reduced by a further one percentage point each year from 2023 to 2027. Second, the net operating loss carryover will be expanded from the current 3 years to 5 years for losses incurred by small business in 2020. And third, the 5% tax on gross income earned incentive has been extended 2 years, from the original 2 to 7 years to a revised 4 to 9 years. These measures will reduce the tax burden for companies and will provide extra breathing space for enterprises as they emerge from the first two quarters of the crisis.

Ensure enterprises implement social distancing measures. Businesses are resuming operations even as the virus continues to spread. The survey found that businesses were starting to think about the health and social distancing measures they could implement to allow workers a safe return to work. Providing face masks to workers was the most common initiative enterprises expected to take after reopening (63%). However, only 17% would conduct social distancing and create smaller working groups. Thus, it may be important to issue directives to enterprises to practice adequate social distancing, especially at the initial stages of reopening. Regular temperature checks were planned by 13% of enterprises. Measures least likely to be used were contact tracing (6%) and canteen rationing (less than 1%).

Restart businesses that source workers locally. There is less chance of workers spreading the virus if their employer is in the same locality. The survey found considerable variation in the share of workers sourced locally. Some 28% of enterprises employ three-quarters or more of their workers from the local municipality. A further 19% source half to three-quarters of workers locally. This means that a full 53% of enterprises source less than half their workers locally. Thus, ensuring the selective reopening of businesses that employ a large share of local workers may reduce the chance of inter-municipal transmission.

Ease mobility restrictions where work-from-home (WFH) practices are least feasible. The survey found considerable variation in WFH possibilities. Enterprises in information and communication and professional services were most likely to WFH. These are sectors whether mobility restrictions are least in need of easing. At the same time, WFH opportunities are limited or negligible for health and social work, accommodation and food services (including tourism), utilities, and manufacturing. There is a greater urgency, subject to health conditions, to ease restrictions for these sectors.

Phase 3: Recovery Programs and Policies

Facilitate debt restructuring. Borrowing that occurred during the crisis will need to be repaid. Even as businesses regain precrisis revenue levels, this will be difficult. Commercial banks and the central bank should closely monitor debt levels and repayment capabilities. In many cases, debt will need to be further restructured to give firms time to repay.

Deepen market networks and value chains. Reopening will provide an opportunity for firms to return to precrisis levels of activity. This may be a slow process as it may take time for demand to revive because consumers and clients (other businesses) will spend cautiously. Enterprises will need to reestablish and develop markets and renew value chain participation. Continuing with precrisis strategies for enterprise development—digitization, online transacting, technology advancements (Fourth Industrial Revolution), and skilling the workforce—can then be resumed in earnest.

Other Issues Arising from the Survey Results

Nonbank finance (microcredit, pawnshops) could play a larger role. Nonbank finance played a minor role in providing access to finance during the ECQ. Few enterprises surveyed (6%) used this form of finance to address low revenue caused by the pandemic. This source is best suited to micro and the "smaller" small enterprises, which in normal times would have difficulty accessing bank finance.

Limited need to monitor supply prices. More than half of enterprises (53%) saw no change in the price of supplies—indeed, 21% experienced a decrease. This appears similar for imported supplies. Only a modest share of enterprises surveyed accessed supplies from abroad (16%). Of those that do import, more than half (54%) have either seen no change or indeed a decrease in import supply prices since 15 March. A further 12% saw a modest increase of 5% or less. This suggests that a problem of price increases may not be a serious issue for businesses and may not require government intervention.

Long-Term Strategic Direction

In May 2020, the Philippine Department of Finance (DOF) announced a large-scale, four-pillar socioeconomic strategy against COVID-19, costing ₱1.74 trillion or 9.1% of country's gross domestic product (GDP). The pillars include (i) emergency support for vulnerable groups and individuals (₱595.6 billion or 3.1% of GDP) including wage subsidies, soft loans and credit guarantees to MSMEs, and cash assistance; (ii) expanded medical resources to fight COVID-19 (₱58.6 billion or 0.3% of GDP) including assistance for purchasing medical equipment and supplies, along with special compensation to health-care workers; (iii) fiscal and monetary actions to finance emergency initiatives including the BSP's purchase of government bonds to fund COVID-19 response measures; and (iv) an economic recovery program focused on creating and sustaining jobs (₱1.1 trillion or 5.7% of GDP, for (iii) and (iv)).

It is critical that massive, timely government spending support those households, workers, and enterprises devastated by COVID-19 during the early stage of the pandemic. Given the uncertainty on when COVID-19 can be contained, a flexible but focused policy approach is needed to account for different time scenarios. The Philippine government, led by the National Economic and Development Authority (NEDA) and the DOF, has explored a phased approach addressing emergency, recovery, and resiliency stages to allow the Philippine economy to bounce back from a longer perspective. To build resiliency, the government has proposed a series of structural reform options: (i) health (for example, medical supply production and health infrastructure development); (ii) agriculture (value chain intervention); (iii) logistics (warehousing and cold-chain systems); (iv) digitization (online transactions with government and the private sector); (v) investments (economic liberalization to attract foreign investors); (vi) business (credit easing and regulatory reforms); (vii) labor (employment retention and wage reduction); (viii) social protection (digital delivery and unemployment insurance); (ix) education (e-learning); (x) public transport (promote non-motorized transport); and (xi) disaster and emergency management.

These flexible yet focused policy interventions can effectively reach out and benefit targeted groups. But it is crucial to continuously monitor the impact on households, workers, and enterprises, by industrial sector and region. ADB stands ready to support the government through follow-up business surveys in the Philippines.

ANNEX 1: SURVEY DATA TABLES

Part 1: Company Profile
Type of Business

		Part 1														
		q1.1: What best describes your company?														
		Corporation or Partnership			Cooperative or Foundation			Sole Proprietorship			Others			Total		
Item		No.	%*	%***	No.	%*	%***	No.	%*	%***	No.	%*	%***	No.	%*	%***
Firm size	Micro	769	43.6	59.7	6	30.0	0.5	499	74.8	38.7	14	43.8	1.1	1,288	51.9	100.0
	Small	575	32.6	85.1	5	25.0	0.7	89	13.3	13.2	7	21.9	1.0	676	27.3	100.0
	Medium-sized	275	15.6	83.1	8	40.0	2.4	40	6.0	12.1	8	25.0	2.4	331	13.3	100.0
	Large	143	8.1	76.9	1	5.0	0.5	39	5.9	21.0	3	9.4	1.6	186	7.5	100.0
	Total	1,762	100.0	71.0	20	100.0	0.8	667	100.0	26.9	32	100.0	1.3	2,481	100.0	100.0
Sector	Agriculture, Forestry, and Fishing	11	0.6	61.1	–	–	–	7	1.1	38.9	–	–	–	18	0.7	100.0
	Manufacturing	204	11.6	78.2	2	10.0	0.8	51	7.7	19.5	4	12.5	1.5	261	10.5	100.0
	Electricity, Gas, Steam, and Air Conditioning Supply	20	1.1	69.0	–	–	–	9	1.4	31.0	–	–	–	29	1.2	100.0
	Water Supply, Sewerage, Waste Management, and Remediation Activities	4	0.2	80.0	1	5.0	20.0	–	–	–	–	–	–	5	0.2	100.0
	Construction	158	9.0	73.8	1	5.0	0.5	52	7.8	24.3	3	9.4	1.4	214	8.6	100.0
	Wholesale and Retail Trade; Repair of Motor Vehicles and Motorcycles	380	21.6	71.2	1	5.0	0.2	150	22.5	28.1	3	9.4	0.6	534	21.5	100.0
	Transportation and storage	61	3.5	74.4	1	5.0	1.2	19	2.9	23.2	1	3.1	1.2	82	3.3	100.0
	Accommodation and Food Service Activities	198	11.2	55.6	1	5.0	0.3	154	23.1	43.3	3	9.4	0.8	356	14.4	100.0
	Information and Communication	160	9.1	84.7	–	–	–	26	3.9	13.8	3	9.4	1.6	189	7.6	100.0
	Financial and Insurance Activities	93	5.3	85.3	7	35.0	6.4	6	0.9	5.5	3	9.4	2.8	109	4.4	100.0
	Real Estate Activities	68	3.9	90.7	–	–	–	7	1.1	9.3	–	–	–	75	3.0	100.0
	Professional, Scientific, and Technical Activities	78	4.4	80.4	–	–	–	18	2.7	18.6	1	3.1	1.0	97	3.9	100.0
	Administrative and Support Service Activities	45	2.6	84.9	2	10.0	3.8	6	0.9	11.3	–	–	–	53	2.1	100.0
	Public Administration and Defense; Compulsory Social Security	–	–	–	–	–	–	–	–	–	1	3.1	100.0	1	0.0	100.0

continued on next page

Type of Business continued

Item		Corporation or Partnership			Cooperative or Foundation			Sole Proprietorship			Others			Total		
		No.	%*	%**	No.	%*	%**	No.	%*	%**	No.	%*	%**	No.	%*	%**
	Education	21	1.2	67.7	2	10.0	6.5	6	0.9	19.4	2	6.3	6.5	31	1.3	100.0
	Human Health and Social Work Activities	8	0.5	53.3	–	–	–	7	1.1	46.7	–	–	–	15	0.6	100.0
	Arts, Entertainment, and Recreation	41	2.3	71.9	–	–	–	16	2.4	28.1	–	–	–	57	2.3	100.0
	Other Service Activities	212	12.0	59.7	2	10.0	0.6	133	19.9	37.5	8	25.0	2.3	355	14.3	100.0
	Total	1,762	100.0	71.0	20	100.0	0.8	667	100.0	26.9	32	100.0	1.3	2,481	100.0	100.0
Location	National Capital Region	984	55.9	79.9	6	30.0	0.5	230	34.5	18.7	11	34.4	0.9	1,231	49.6	100.0
	Cordillera Administrative Region	14	0.8	60.9	–	–	–	8	1.2	34.8	1	3.1	4.3	23	0.9	100.0
	Region 1: Ilocos	13	0.7	50.0	–	–	–	13	2.0	50.0	–	–	–	26	1.1	100.0
	Region 2: Cagayan Valley	11	0.6	47.8	–	–	–	12	1.8	52.2	–	–	–	23	0.9	100.0
	Region 3: Central Luzon	126	7.2	54.8	2	10.0	0.9	99	14.8	43.0	3	9.4	1.3	230	9.3	100.0
	Region 4A: Calabarzon	243	13.8	70.0	4	20.0	1.2	97	14.5	28.0	3	9.4	0.9	347	14.0	100.0
	MIMAROPA	23	1.3	50.0	–	–	–	22	3.3	47.8	1	3.1	2.2	46	1.9	100.0
	Region 5: Bicol	26	1.5	51.0	1	5.0	2.0	24	3.6	47.1	–	–	–	51	2.1	100.0
	Region 6: Western Visayas	60	3.4	60.0	3	15.0	3.0	35	5.3	35.0	2	6.3	2.0	100	4.0	100.0
	Region 7: Central Visayas	140	8.0	75.7	–	–	–	42	6.3	22.7	3	9.4	1.6	185	7.5	100.0
	Region 8: Eastern Visayas	11	0.6	44.0	2	10.0	8.0	11	1.7	44.0	1	3.1	4.0	25	1.0	100.0
	Region 9: Zamboanga Peninsula	11	0.6	55.0	–	–	–	8	1.2	40.0	1	3.1	5.0	20	0.8	100.0
	Region 10: Northern Mindanao	28	1.6	58.3	–	–	–	17	2.6	35.4	3	9.4	6.3	48	1.9	100.0
	Region 11: Davao	54	3.1	63.5	–	–	–	31	4.7	36.5	–	–	–	85	3.4	100.0
	Region 12: SOCCSKSARGEN	8	0.5	40.0	2	10.0	10.0	9	1.4	45.0	1	3.1	5.0	20	0.8	100.0
	Region 13: Caraga	9	0.5	45.0	–	–	–	9	1.4	45.0	2	6.3	10.0	20	0.8	100.0
	BARMM (formerly ARMM)	1	0.1	100.0	–	–	–	–	–	–	–	–	–	1	0.0	100.0
	Total	1,762	100.0	71.0	20	100.0	0.8	667	100.0	26.9	32	100.0	1.3	2,481	100.0	100.0

Part 1 — q1.1: What best describes your company?

– = no number; BARMM = Bangsamoro Autonomous Region in Muslim Mindanao; MIMAROPA = Mindoro, Marinduque, Romblon, and Palawan (Southwestern Tagalog Region); SOCCSKSARGEN = South Cotabato, Cotabato, Sultan Kudarat, Sarangani, and General Santos.

* Share of vertical column. ** Share of horizontal line.

Source: Asian Development Bank, Philippine Enterprise Survey.

Status of Business Registration

		Part 1														
		q.1.2: Is the company registered with the following government agency?														
		DTI		SEC		PSE		SSS		BIR		CDA		LGU		None of the above	
Item		No.	%	No.	%	No.	%	No.	%	No.	%	No.	%	No.	%	No.	%
Firm size	Micro	606	64.5	784	43.7	10	40.0	1,096	51.1	1,133	51.6	8	34.8	757	52.8	2	40.0
	Small	184	19.6	582	32.4	4	16.0	585	27.3	594	27.1	5	21.7	395	27.6	–	–
	Medium-sized	90	9.6	281	15.7	7	28.0	296	13.8	299	13.6	9	39.1	191	13.3	2	40.0
	Large	59	6.3	149	8.3	4	16.0	169	7.9	169	7.7	1	4.4	90	6.3	1	20.0
	Total	939	100.0	1,796	100.0	25	100.0	2,146	100.0	2,195	100.0	23	100.0	1,433	100.0	5	100.0
Sector	Agriculture, Forestry, and Fishing	9	1.0	11	0.6	–	–	13	0.6	14	0.6	–	–	9	0.6	–	–
	Manufacturing	18	1.9	19	1.1	1	4.0	25	1.2	28	1.3	–	–	17	1.2	–	–
	Electricity, Gas, Steam, and Air Conditioning Supply	3	0.3	12	0.7	1	4.0	11	0.5	12	0.6	–	–	6	0.4	–	–
	Water Supply, Sewerage, Waste Management, and Remediation Activities	13	1.4	14	0.8	–	–	22	1.0	22	1.0	–	–	11	0.8	–	–
	Construction	60	6.4	152	8.5	2	8.0	162	7.6	167	7.6	3	13.0	97	6.8	1	20.0
	Wholesale and Retail Trade; Repair of Motor Vehicles and Motorcycles	14	1.5	20	1.1	–	–	27	1.3	27	1.2	–	–	17	1.2	–	–
	Transportation and storage	80	8.5	159	8.9	2	8.0	182	8.5	186	8.5	–	–	114	8.0	–	–
	Accommodation and Food Service Activities	177	18.9	323	18.0	3	12.0	393	18.3	397	18.1	3	13.0	258	18.0	–	–
	Information and Communication	12	1.3	13	0.7	–	–	16	0.8	15	0.7	–	–	9	0.6	–	–
	Financial and Insurance Activities	22	2.3	41	2.3	–	–	47	2.2	48	2.2	–	–	34	2.4	–	–
	Real Estate Activities	59	6.3	103	5.7	1	4.0	124	5.8	128	5.8	1	4.4	94	6.6	–	–
	Professional, Scientific, and Technical Activities	118	12.6	90	5.0	2	8.0	167	7.8	170	7.7	2	8.7	119	8.3	–	–
	Administrative and Support Service Activities	16	1.7	76	4.2	–	–	69	3.2	71	3.2	–	–	51	3.6	–	–
	Public Administration and Defense; Compulsory Social Security	24	2.6	58	3.2	1	4.0	58	2.7	59	2.7	–	–	38	2.7	–	–
	Education	9	1.0	67	3.7	4	16.0	56	2.6	60	2.7	2	8.7	45	3.1	–	–
	Human Health and Social Work Activities	15	1.6	66	3.7	1	4.0	66	3.1	68	3.1	1	4.4	45	3.1	–	–

continued on next page

Status of Business Registration continued

		Part 1 q.1.2: Is the company registered with the following government agency?														
		DTI		SEC		PSE		SSS		BIR		CDA		LGU		None of the above	
Item		No.	%	No.	%	No.	%	No.	%	No.	%	No.	%	No.	%	No.	%
	Arts, Entertainment, and Recreation	17	1.8	37	2.1	1	4.0	44	2.1	42	1.9	1	4.4	32	2.2	–	–
	Other Service Activities	273	29.1	535	29.8	6	24.0	664	30.9	681	31.0	10	43.5	437	30.5	4	80.0
	Total	939	100.0	1,796	100.0	25	100.0	2,146	100.0	2,195	100.0	23	100.0	1,433	100.0	5	100.0
Location	National Capital Region	365	38.9	999	55.6	15	60.0	1,057	49.3	1,077	49.1	7	30.4	697	48.6	2	40.0
	Cordillera Administrative Region	11	1.2	15	0.8	–	–	19	0.9	20	0.9	–	–	14	1.0	–	–
	Region 1: Ilocos	15	1.6	14	0.8	–	–	22	1.0	23	1.1	–	–	21	1.5	–	–
	Region 2: Cagayan Valley	13	1.4	11	0.6	–	–	22	1.0	22	1.0	1	4.4	15	1.1	–	–
	Region 3: Central Luzon	119	12.7	129	7.2	4	16.0	198	9.2	201	9.2	2	8.7	124	8.7	2	40.0
	Region 4A: Calabarzon	132	14.1	245	13.6	4	16.0	294	13.7	304	13.9	6	26.1	200	14.0	1	20.0
	MIMAROPA	29	3.1	23	1.3	–	–	42	2.0	42	1.9	–	–	35	2.4	–	–
	Region 5: Bicol	26	2.8	27	1.5	–	–	43	2.0	43	2.0	2	8.7	37	2.6	–	–
	Region 6: Western Visayas	45	4.8	60	3.3	1	4.0	87	4.1	91	4.2	2	8.7	58	4.1	–	–
	Region 7: Central Visayas	63	6.7	141	7.9	1	4.0	162	7.6	166	7.6	–	–	93	6.5	–	–
	Region 8: Eastern Visayas	14	1.5	11	0.6	–	–	21	1.0	23	1.1	1	4.4	18	1.3	–	–
	Region 9: Zamboanga Peninsula	10	1.1	12	0.7	–	–	20	0.9	20	0.9	–	–	15	1.1	–	–
	Region 10: Northern Mindanao	27	2.9	33	1.8	–	–	44	2.1	46	2.1	–	–	32	2.2	–	–
	Region 11: Davao	47	5.0	55	3.1	–	–	79	3.7	81	3.7	–	–	48	3.4	–	–
	Region 12: SOCCSKSARGEN	11	1.2	10	0.6	–	–	15	0.7	15	0.7	2	8.7	10	0.7	–	–
	Region 13: Caraga	12	1.3	10	0.6	–	–	20	0.9	20	0.9	–	–	15	1.1	–	–
	BARMM (formerly ARMM)	–	–	1	0.1	–	–	1	0.1	1	0.1	–	–	1	0.1	–	–
	Total	939	100.0	1,796	100.0	25	100.0	2,146	100.0	2,195	100.0	23	100.0	1,433	100.0	5	100.0

– = no number; BARMM = Bangsamoro Autonomous Region in Muslim Mindanao; BIR = Bureau of Internal Revenue; CDA = Cooperative Development Agency; DTI = Department of Trade and Industry; LGU = local government unit; MIMAROPA = Mindoro, Marinduque, Romblon, and Palawan (Southwestern Tagalog Region); PSE = Philippine Stock Exchange; SEC = Securities and Exchange Commission; SOCCSKSARGEN = South Cotabato, Cotabato, Sultan Kudarat, Sarangani, and General Santos; SSS = Social Security System.

Source: Asian Development Bank, Philippine Enterprise Survey.

Primary Business Sector

Part 1

q1.3: What is your primary business sector?

Item		Agriculture, Forestry, and Fishing			Manufacturing			Electricity, Gas, Steam, and Air Conditioning Supply			Water Supply; Sewerage, Waste Management, and Remediation Activities			Construction			Wholesale and Retail Trade; Repair of Motor Vehicles and Motorcycles			Transportation and storage		
		No.	%*	%**	No.	%*	%**	No.	%*	%**	No.	%*	%**	No.	%*	%**	No.	%*	%**	No.	%*	%**
Firm size	Micro	7	38.9	0.5	93	35.6	7.2	16	55.2	1.2	1	20.0	0.1	107	50.0	8.3	283	53.0	22.0	31	37.8	2.4
	Small	5	27.8	0.7	79	30.3	11.7	6	20.7	0.9	2	40.0	0.3	64	29.9	9.5	155	29.0	22.9	30	36.6	4.4
	Medium-sized	5	27.8	1.5	61	23.4	18.4	7	24.1	2.1	2	40.0	0.6	30	14.0	9.1	63	11.8	19.0	11	13.4	3.3
	Large	1	5.6	0.5	28	10.7	15.1	–	–	–	–	–	–	13	6.1	7.0	33	6.2	17.7	10	12.2	5.4
	Total	18	100.0	0.7	261	100.0	10.5	29	100.0	1.2	5	100.0	0.2	214	100.0	8.6	534	100.0	21.5	82	100.0	3.3
Location	National Capital Region	2	11.1	0.2	98	37.6	8.0	7	24.1	0.6	3	60.0	0.2	98	45.8	8.0	292	54.7	23.7	44	53.7	3.6
	Cordillera Administrative Region	–	–	–	3	1.2	13.0	–	–	–	–	–	–	2	0.9	8.7	6	1.1	26.1	–	–	–
	Region 1: Ilocos	–	–	–	1	0.4	3.8	–	–	–	–	–	–	3	1.4	11.5	6	1.1	23.1	–	–	–
	Region 2: Cagayan Valley	1	5.6	4.3	2	0.8	8.7	1	3.5	4.3	–	–	–	–	–	–	8	1.5	34.8	–	–	–
	Region 3: Central Luzon	6	33.3	2.6	40	15.3	17.4	4	13.8	1.7	–	–	–	18	8.4	7.8	40	7.5	17.4	10	12.2	4.3
	Region 4A: Calabarzon	2	11.1	0.6	66	25.3	19.0	4	13.8	1.2	2	40.0	0.6	34	15.9	9.8	61	11.4	17.6	12	14.6	3.5
	MIMAROPA	–	–	–	1	0.4	2.2	–	–	–	–	–	–	4	1.9	8.7	8	1.5	17.4	1	1.2	2.2
	Region 5: Bicol	2	11.1	3.9	2	0.8	3.9	1	3.5	2.0	–	–	–	6	2.8	11.8	9	1.7	17.6	2	2.4	3.9
	Region 6: Western Visayas	–	–	–	6	2.3	6.0	3	10.3	3.0	–	–	–	10	4.7	10.0	13	2.4	13.0	4	4.9	4.0
	Region 7: Central Visayas	–	–	–	27	10.3	14.6	4	13.8	2.2	–	–	–	14	6.5	7.6	31	5.8	16.8	1	1.2	0.5
	Region 8: Eastern Visayas	–	–	–	2	0.8	8.0	1	3.5	4.0	–	–	–	4	1.9	16.0	5	0.9	20.0	3	3.7	12.0
	Region 9: Zamboanga Peninsula	1	5.6	5.0	1	0.4	5.0	–	–	–	–	–	–	1	0.5	5.0	8	1.5	40.0	1	1.2	5.0
	Region 10: Northern Mindanao	1	5.6	2.1	4	1.5	8.3	1	3.5	2.1	–	–	–	7	3.3	14.6	9	1.7	18.8	–	–	–
	Region 11: Davao	3	16.7	3.5	6	2.3	7.1	3	10.3	3.5	–	–	–	9	4.2	10.6	24	4.5	28.2	3	3.7	3.5
	Region 12: SOCCSKSARGEN	–	–	–	–	–	–	–	–	–	–	–	–	3	1.4	15.0	4	0.8	20.0	1	1.2	5.0
	Region 13: Caraga	–	–	–	2	0.8	10.0	–	–	–	–	–	–	1	0.5	5.0	9	1.7	45.0	–	–	–
	BARMM (formerly ARMM)	–	–	–	–	–	–	–	–	–	–	–	–	–	–	–	1	0.2	100.0	–	–	–
	Total	18	100.0	0.7	261	100.0	10.5	29	100.0	1.2	5	100.0	0.2	214	100.0	8.6	534	100.0	21.5	82	100.0	3.3

continued on next page

Primary Business Sector continued

Part 1

q1.3: What is your primary business sector?

Item		Accommodation and Food Service Activities			Information and Communication			Financial and Insurance Activities			Real Estate Activities			Professional, Scientific, and Technical Activities			Administrative and Support Service Activities			Public Administration and Defense; Compulsory Social Security		
		No.	%*	%**	No.	%*	%**	No.	%*	%**	No.	%*	%**	No.	%*	%**	No.	%*	%**	No.	%*	%**
Firm size	Micro	190	53.4	14.8	104	55.0	8.1	54	49.5	4.2	32	42.7	2.5	59	60.8	4.6	23	43.4	1.8	–	–	–
	Small	91	25.6	13.5	49	25.9	7.2	30	27.5	4.4	24	32.0	3.6	21	21.7	3.1	22	41.5	3.3	–	–	–
	Medium-sized	56	15.7	16.9	23	12.2	6.9	15	13.8	4.5	12	16.0	3.6	11	11.3	3.3	5	9.4	1.5	–	–	–
	Large	19	5.3	10.2	13	6.9	7.0	10	9.2	5.4	7	9.3	3.8	6	6.2	3.2	3	5.7	1.6	1	100.0	0.5
	Total	356	100.0	14.3	189	100.0	7.6	109	100.0	4.4	75	100.0	3.0	97	100.0	3.9	53	100.0	2.1	1	100.0	0.0
Location	National Capital Region	138	38.8	11.2	120	63.5	9.7	39	35.8	3.2	43	57.3	3.5	72	74.2	5.8	40	75.5	3.2	1	100.0	0.1
	Cordillera Administrative Region	4	1.1	17.4	3	1.6	13.0	1	0.9	4.3	–	–	–	–	–	–	1	1.9	4.3	–	–	–
	Region 1: Ilocos	7	2.0	26.9	1	0.5	3.8	2	1.8	7.7	1	1.3	3.8	1	1.0	3.8	–	–	–	–	–	–
	Region 2: Cagayan Valley	2	0.6	8.7	1	0.5	4.3	2	1.8	8.7	–	–	–	–	–	–	–	–	–	–	–	–
	Region 3: Central Luzon	41	11.5	17.8	9	4.8	3.9	13	11.9	5.7	4	5.3	1.7	7	7.2	3.0	2	3.8	0.9	–	–	–
	Region 4A: Calabarzon	39	11.0	11.2	8	4.2	2.3	15	13.8	4.3	14	18.7	4.0	11	11.3	3.2	5	9.4	1.4	–	–	–
	MIMAROPA	26	7.3	56.5	–	–	–	–	–	–	–	–	–	–	–	–	–	–	–	–	–	–
	Region 5: Bicol	9	2.5	17.6	1	0.5	2.0	7	6.4	13.7	–	–	–	1	1.0	2.0	1	1.9	2.0	–	–	–
	Region 6: Western Visayas	21	5.9	21.0	7	3.7	7.0	8	7.3	8.0	1	1.3	1.0	–	–	–	1	1.9	1.0	–	–	–
	Region 7: Central Visayas	35	9.8	18.9	22	11.6	11.9	13	11.9	7.0	11	14.7	5.9	4	4.1	2.2	1	1.9	0.5	–	–	–
	Region 8: Eastern Visayas	2	0.6	8.0	3	1.6	12.0	1	0.9	4.0	1	1.3	4.0	–	–	–	–	–	–	–	–	–
	Region 9: Zamboanga Peninsula	2	0.6	10.0	3	1.6	15.0	1	0.9	5.0	–	–	–	1	1.0	5.0	–	–	–	–	–	–
	Region 10: Northern Mindanao	7	2.0	14.6	6	3.2	12.5	2	1.8	4.2	–	–	–	–	–	–	–	–	–	–	–	–
	Region 11: Davao	16	4.5	18.8	4	2.1	4.7	3	2.8	3.5	–	–	–	–	–	–	2	3.8	2.4	–	–	–
	Region 12: SOCCSKSARGEN	3	0.8	15.0	–	–	–	1	0.9	5.0	–	–	–	–	–	–	–	–	–	–	–	–
	Region 13: Caraga	4	1.1	20.0	1	0.5	5.0	1	0.9	5.0	–	–	–	–	–	–	–	–	–	–	–	–
	BARMM (formerly ARMM)	–	–	–	–	–	–	–	–	–	–	–	–	–	–	–	–	–	–	–	–	–
	Total	356	100.0	14.3	189	100.0	7.6	109	100.0	4.4	75	100.0	3.0	97	100.0	3.9	53	100.0	2.1	1	100.0	0.0

continued on next page

Primary Business Sector continued

Part 1

q1.3: What is your primary business sector?

Item		Education			Human Health and Social Work Activities			Arts, Entertainment, and Recreation			Other Service Activities			Total		
		No.	%*	%***	No.	%*	%***	No.	%*	%***	No.	%*	%***	No.	%*	%**
Firm size	Micro	19	61.3	1.5	9	60.0	0.7	30	52.6	2.3	230	64.8	17.9	1,288	51.9	100.0
	Small	6	19.4	0.9	2	13.3	0.3	19	33.3	2.8	71	20.0	10.5	676	27.3	100.0
	Medium-sized	1	3.2	0.3	3	20.0	0.9	1	1.8	0.3	25	7.0	7.6	331	13.3	100.0
	Large	5	16.1	2.7	1	6.7	0.5	7	12.3	3.8	29	8.2	15.6	186	7.5	100.0
	Total	31	100.0	1.2	15	100.0	0.6	57	100.0	2.3	355	100.0	14.3	2,481	100.0	100.0
Location	National Capital Region	8	25.8	0.6	6	40.0	0.5	39	68.4	3.2	181	51.0	14.7	1,231	49.6	100.0
	Cordillera Administrative Region	–	–	–	–	–	–	–	–	–	3	0.9	13.0	23	0.9	100.0
	Region 1: Ilocos	–	–	–	1	6.7	3.8	–	–	–	3	0.9	11.5	26	1.1	100.0
	Region 2: Cagayan Valley	2	6.5	8.7	–	–	–	–	–	–	4	1.1	17.4	23	0.9	100.0
	Region 3: Central Luzon	4	12.9	1.7	2	13.3	0.9	1	1.8	0.4	29	8.2	12.6	230	9.3	100.0
	Region 4A: Calabarzon	7	22.6	2.0	4	26.7	1.2	5	8.8	1.4	58	16.3	16.7	347	14.0	100.0
	MIMAROPA	1	3.2	2.2	–	–	–	1	1.8	2.2	4	1.1	8.7	46	1.9	100.0
	Region 5: Bicol	2	6.5	3.9	–	–	–	1	1.8	2.0	7	2.0	13.7	51	2.1	100.0
	Region 6: Western Visayas	2	6.5	2.0	1	6.7	1.0	4	7.0	4.0	19	5.4	19.0	100	4.0	100.0
	Region 7: Central Visayas	1	3.2	0.5	1	6.7	0.5	3	5.3	1.6	17	4.8	9.2	185	7.5	100.0
	Region 8: Eastern Visayas	1	3.2	4.0	–	–	–	–	–	–	2	0.6	8.0	25	1.0	100.0
	Region 9: Zamboanga Peninsula	–	–	–	–	–	–	–	–	–	1	0.3	5.0	20	0.8	100.0
	Region 10: Northern Mindanao	1	3.2	2.1	–	–	–	2	3.5	4.2	8	2.3	16.7	48	1.9	100.0
	Region 11: Davao	1	3.2	1.2	–	–	–	–	–	–	11	3.1	12.9	85	3.4	100.0
	Region 12: SOCCSKSARGEN	–	–	–	–	–	–	1	1.8	5.0	7	2.0	35.0	20	0.8	100.0
	Region 13: Caraga	1	3.2	5.0	–	–	–	–	–	–	1	0.3	5.0	20	0.8	100.0
	BARMM (formerly ARMM)	–	–	–	–	–	–	–	–	–	–	–	–	1	0.0	100.0
	Total	31	100.0	1.2	15	100.0	0.6	57	100.0	2.3	355	100.0	14.3	2,481	100.0	100.0

– = no number; BARMM = Bangsamoro Autonomous Region in Muslim Mindanao; MIMAROPA = Mindoro, Marinduque, Romblon, and Palawan (Southwestern Tagalog Region); SOCCSKSARGEN = South Cotabato, Cotabato, Sultan Kudarat, Sarangani, and General Santos.

Note: Survey data was reclassified based on the Philippine Standard Industrial Classification (PSIC).

* Share of vertical column. ** Share of horizontal line.

Source: Asian Development Bank, Philippine Enterprise Survey.

Company Location

Part 1

q1.5: Your company location:

Item	National Capital Region			Cordillera Administrative Region			Region 1: Ilocos			Region 2: Cagayan Valley			Region 3: Central Luzon			Region 4A: Calabarzon		
	No.	%*	%**	No.	%*	%***	No.	%*	%***	No.	%*	%***	No.	%*	%***	No.	%	%***
Firm size																		
Micro	621	50.5	48.2	18	78.3	1.4	18	69.2	1.4	13	56.5	1.0	127	55.2	9.9	183	52.7	14.2
Small	345	28.0	51.0	2	8.7	0.3	5	19.2	0.7	6	26.1	0.9	62	27.0	9.2	84	24.2	12.4
Medium-sized	168	13.7	50.8	3	13.0	0.9	3	11.5	0.9	2	8.7	0.6	20	8.7	6.0	48	13.8	14.5
Large	97	7.9	52.2	–	–	–	–	–	–	2	8.7	1.1	21	9.1	11.3	32	9.2	17.2
Total	1,231	100.0	49.6	23	100.0	0.9	26	100.0	1.0	23	100.0	0.9	230	100.0	9.3	347	100.0	14.0
Sector																		
Agriculture, Forestry, and Fishing	2	0.2	11.8	–	–	–	–	–	–	1	4.4	5.9	6	2.6	35.3	2	0.6	11.8
Manufacturing	98	8.0	37.4	3	13.0	1.1	1	3.9	0.4	2	8.7	0.8	40	17.4	15.3	66	19.0	25.2
Electricity, Gas, Steam, and Air Conditioning Supply	7	0.6	23.3	–			–			1	4.4	3.3	4	1.7	13.3	4	1.2	13.3
Water Supply, Sewerage, Waste Management, and Remediation Activities	3	0.2	60.0	–			–			–			–			2	0.6	40.0
Construction	98	8.0	45.2	2	8.7	0.9	3	11.5	1.4	–			18	7.8	8.3	34	9.8	15.7
Wholesale and Retail Trade; Repair of Motor Vehicles and Motorcycles	292	23.7	55.1	6	26.1	1.1	6	23.1	1.1	8	34.8	1.5	40	17.4	7.5	61	17.6	11.5
Transportation and storage	44	3.6	52.4	–			–			–			10	4.4	11.9	12	3.5	14.3
Accommodation and Food Service Activities	138	11.2	38.8	4	17.4	1.1	7	26.9	2.0	2	8.7	0.6	41	17.8	11.5	39	11.2	11.0
Information and Communication	120	9.8	63.5	3	13.0	1.6	1	3.9	0.5	1	4.4	0.5	9	3.9	4.8	8	2.3	4.2
Financial and Insurance Activities	39	3.2	35.8	1	4.4	0.9	2	7.7	1.8	2	8.7	1.8	13	5.7	11.9	15	4.3	13.8
Real Estate Activities	43	3.5	56.6	–			1	3.9	1.3	–			4	1.7	5.3	14	4.0	18.4
Professional, Scientific, and Technical Activities	72	5.9	75.0	–	–		1	3.9	1.0	–	–		7	3.0	7.3	11	3.2	11.5
Administrative and Support Service Activities	40	3.3	75.5	1	4.4	1.9	–			–			2	0.9	3.8	5	1.4	9.4
Public Administration and Defense; Compulsory Social Security	1	0.1	100.0	–			–			–			–			–		–
Education	8	0.7	25.0	–			–			2	8.7	6.3	4	1.7	12.5	7	2.0	21.9
Human Health and Social Work Activities	6	0.5	40.0	–			1	3.9	6.7	–			2	0.9	13.3	4	1.2	26.7
Arts, Entertainment, and Recreation	39	3.2	68.4	–			–			–			1	0.4	1.8	5	1.4	8.8
Other Service Activities	181	14.7	50.8	3	13.0	0.8	3	11.5	0.8	4	17.4	1.1	29	12.6	8.1	58	16.7	16.3
Total	1,231	100.0	49.5	23	100.0	0.9	26	100.0	1.0	23	100.0	0.9	230	100.0	9.3	347	100.0	14.0

continued on next page

Company Location continued

								Part 1													
								q1.5: Your company location:													
		MIMAROPA			Region 5: Bicol			Region 6: Western Visayas			Region 7: Central Visayas			Region 8: Eastern Visayas			Region 9: Zamboanga Peninsula		
Item		No.	%*	%**	No.	%*	%**	No.	%*	%**	No.	%*	%**	No.	%*	%**	No.	%*	%**
Firm size	Micro	21	45.7	1.6	29	56.9	2.3	53	53.0	4.1	87	47.0	6.8	10	40.0	0.8	10	50.0	0.8
	Small	11	23.9	1.6	13	25.5	1.9	22	22.0	3.3	60	32.4	8.9	12	48.0	1.8	7	35.0	1.0
	Medium-sized	10	21.7	3.0	7	13.7	2.1	16	16.0	4.8	27	14.6	8.2	3	12.0	0.9	2	10.0	0.6
	Large	4	8.7	2.2	2	3.9	1.1	9	9.0	4.8	11	6.0	5.9	–	–	–	1	5.0	0.5
	Total	46	100.0	1.9	51	100.0	2.1	100	100.0	4.0	185	100.0	7.5	25	100.0	1.0	20	100.0	0.8
Sector	Agriculture, Forestry, and Fishing	–	–	–	2	3.9	11.8	–	–	–	–	–	–	–	–	–	–	–	–
	Manufacturing	1	2.2	0.4	2	3.9	0.8	6	6.0	2.3	27	14.6	10.3	2	8.0	0.8	2	8.0	0.8
	Electricity, Gas, Steam, and Air Conditioning Supply	–	–	–	1	2.0	3.3	3	3.0	10.0	4	2.2	13.3	1	4.0	3.3	1	4.0	3.3
	Water Supply, Sewerage, Waste Management, and Remediation Activities	–	–	–	–	–	–	–	–	–	–	–	–	–	–	–	–	–	–
	Construction	4	8.7	1.8	6	11.8	2.8	10	10.0	4.6	14	7.6	6.5	4	16.0	1.8	4	16.0	1.8
	Wholesale and Retail Trade; Repair of Motor Vehicles and Motorcycles	8	17.4	1.5	9	17.7	1.7	13	13.0	2.5	31	16.8	5.8	5	20.0	0.9	5	20.0	0.9
	Transportation and storage	1	2.2	1.2	2	3.9	2.4	4	4.0	4.8	1	0.5	1.2	3	12.0	3.6	3	12.0	3.6
	Accommodation and Food Service Activities	26	56.5	7.3	9	17.7	2.5	21	21.0	5.9	35	18.9	9.8	2	8.0	0.6	2	8.0	0.6
	Information and Communication	–	–	–	1	2.0	0.5	7	7.0	3.7	22	11.9	11.6	3	12.0	1.6	3	12.0	1.6
	Financial and Insurance Activities	–	–	–	7	13.7	6.4	8	8.0	7.3	13	7.0	11.9	1	4.0	0.9	1	4.0	0.9
	Real Estate Activities	–	–	–	–	–	–	1	1.0	1.3	11	6.0	14.5	1	4.0	1.3	1	4.0	1.3
	Professional, Scientific, and Technical Activities	–	–	–	1	2.0	1.0	–	–	–	4	2.2	4.2	–	–	–	–	–	–
	Administrative and Support Service Activities	–	–	–	1	2.0	1.9	1	1.0	1.9	1	0.5	1.9	–	–	–	–	–	–
	Public Administration and Defense; Compulsory Social Security	–	–	–	–	–	–	–	–	–	–	–	–	–	–	–	–	–	–
	Education	1	2.2	3.1	2	3.9	6.3	2	2.0	6.3	1	0.5	3.1	1	4.0	3.1	1	4.0	3.1
	Human Health and Social Work Activities	–	–	–	–	–	–	1	1.0	6.7	1	0.5	6.7	–	–	–	–	–	–
	Arts, Entertainment, and Recreation	1	2.2	1.8	1	2.0	1.8	4	4.0	7.0	3	1.6	5.3	–	–	–	–	–	–
	Other Service Activities	4	8.7	1.1	7	13.7	2.0	19	19.0	5.3	17	9.2	4.8	2	8.0	0.6	2	8.0	0.6
	Total	46	100.0	1.9	51	100.0	2.1	100	100.0	4.0	185	100.0	7.4	25	100.0	1.0	25	100.0	1.0

continued on next page

Part 1

q1.5: Your company location:

Item		Region 10: Northern Mindanao			Region 11: Davao			Region 12: SOCCSKSARGEN			Region 13: Caraga			BARMM (formerly ARMM)			Total		
		No.	%*	%**	No.	%*	%**	No.	%*	%**	No.	%*	%**	No.	%*	%**	No.	%*	%**
Firm size	Micro	24	50.0	1.9	50	58.8	3.9	9	45.0	0.7	15	75.0	1.2	–	–	–	1,288	51.9	100.0
	Small	15	31.3	2.2	23	27.1	3.4	7	35.0	1.0	1	5.0	0.1	1	100.0	0.1	676	27.3	100.0
	Medium-sized	6	12.5	1.8	9	10.6	2.7	4	20.0	1.2	3	15.0	0.9	–	–	–	331	13.3	100.0
	Large	3	6.3	1.6	3	3.5	1.6	–	–	–	1	5.0	0.5	–	–	–	186	7.5	100.0
	Total	48	100.0	1.9	85	100.0	3.4	20	100.0	0.8	20	100.0	0.8	1	100.0	0.0	2,481	100.0	100.0
Sector	Agriculture, Forestry, and Fishing	1	2.1	5.9	3	3.5	17.6	–	–	–	–	–	–	–	–	–	17	0.7	100.0
	Manufacturing	4	8.3	1.5	6	7.1	2.3	–	–	–	2	10.0	0.8	–	–	–	262	10.5	100.0
	Electricity, Gas, Steam, and Air Conditioning Supply	1	2.1	3.3	3	3.5	10.0	–	–	–	–	–	–	–	–	–	30	1.2	100.0
	Water Supply, Sewerage, Waste Management, and Remediation Activities	–	–	–	–	–	–	–	–	–	–	–	–	–	–	–	5	0.2	100.0
	Construction	7	14.6	3.2	9	10.6	4.1	3	15.0	1.4	1	5.0	0.5	–	–	–	217	8.6	100.0
	Wholesale and Retail Trade; Repair of Motor Vehicles and Motorcycles	9	18.8	1.7	24	28.2	4.5	4	20.0	0.8	9	45.0	1.7	1	100.0	0.2	530	21.5	100.0
	Transportation and storage	–	–	–	3	3.5	3.6	1	5.0	1.2	–	–	–	–	–	–	84	3.3	100.0
	Accommodation and Food Service Activities	7	14.6	2.0	16	18.8	4.5	3	15.0	0.8	4	20.0	1.1	–	–	–	356	14.4	100.0
	Information and Communication	6	12.5	3.2	4	4.7	2.1	–	–	–	1	5.0	0.5	–	–	–	189	7.6	100.0
	Financial and Insurance Activities	2	4.2	1.8	3	3.5	2.8	1	5.0	0.9	1	5.0	0.9	–	–	–	109	4.4	100.0
	Real Estate Activities	–	–	–	–	–	–	–	–	–	–	–	–	–	–	–	76	3.0	100.0
	Professional, Scientific, and Technical Activities	–	–	–	–	–	–	–	–	–	–	–	–	–	–	–	96	3.9	100.0
	Administrative and Support Service Activities	–	–	–	2	2.4	3.8	–	–	–	–	–	–	–	–	–	53	2.1	100.0
	Public Administration and Defense; Compulsory Social Security	–	–	–	–	–	–	–	–	–	–	–	–	–	–	–	1	0.0	100.0
	Education	1	2.1	3.1	1	1.2	3.1	–	–	–	1	5.0	3.1	–	–	–	32	1.3	100.0
	Human Health and Social Work Activities	–	–	–	–	–	–	–	–	–	–	–	–	–	–	–	15	0.6	100.0
	Arts, Entertainment, and Recreation	2	4.2	3.5	–	–	–	1	5.0	1.8	–	–	–	–	–	–	57	2.3	100.0
	Other Service Activities	8	16.7	2.2	11	12.9	3.1	7	35.0	2.0	1	5.0	0.3	–	–	–	356	14.3	100.0
	Total	48	100.0	1.9	85	100.0	3.4	20	100.0	0.8	20	100.0	0.8	1	100.0	0.0	2,485	100.0	100.0

– = no number; BARMM = Bangsamoro Autonomous Region in Muslim Mindanao; MIMAROPA = Mindoro, Marinduque, Romblon, and Palawan (Southwestern Tagalog Region); SOCCSKSARGEN = South Cotabato, Cotabato, Sultan Kudarat, Sarangani, and General Santos.

* Share of vertical column. ** Share of horizontal line.

Source: Asian Development Bank, Philippine Enterprise Survey.

Business Operating Period

Part 1

q1.6: Period of your operations since establishment (as of the end of 2019):

Item		0–5 years			6–10 years			11–15 years			16–30 years			31 years and above			Total		
		No.	%*	%**	No.	%*	%**	No.	%*	%**	No.	%*	%**	No.	%*	%**	No.	%*	%**
Firm size	Micro	894	63.6	69.4	204	45.2	15.8	95	41.0	7.4	82	27.0	6.4	13	14.8	1.0	1,288	51.9	100.0
	Small	314	22.3	46.4	145	32.2	21.4	76	32.8	11.2	113	37.2	16.7	28	31.8	4.1	676	27.3	100.0
	Medium-sized	128	9.1	38.7	65	14.4	19.6	41	17.7	12.4	69	22.7	20.8	28	31.8	8.5	331	13.3	100.0
	Large	70	5.0	37.6	37	8.2	19.9	20	8.6	10.8	40	13.2	21.5	19	21.6	10.2	186	7.5	100.0
	Total	1,406	100.0	56.7	451	100.0	18.2	232	100.0	9.4	304	100.0	12.3	88	100.0	3.5	2,481	100.0	100.0
Sector	Agriculture, Forestry, and Fishing	7	0.5	38.9	4	0.9	22.2	1	0.4	5.6	5	1.6	27.8	1	1.1	5.6	18	0.7	100.0
	Manufacturing	114	8.1	43.7	44	9.8	16.9	23	9.9	8.8	53	17.4	20.3	27	30.7	10.3	261	10.5	100.0
	Electricity, Gas, Steam, and Air Conditioning Supply	15	1.1	51.7	8	1.8	27.6	5	2.2	17.2	1	0.3	3.4	–	–	–	29	1.2	100.0
	Water Supply, Sewerage, Waste Management, and Remediation Activities	1	0.1	20.0	1	0.2	20.0	–	–	–	3	1.0	60.0	–	–	–	5	0.2	100.0
	Construction	143	10.2	66.8	35	7.8	16.4	13	5.6	6.1	20	6.6	9.3	3	3.4	1.4	214	8.6	100.0
	Wholesale and Retail Trade; Repair of Motor Vehicles and Motorcycles	284	20.2	53.2	99	22.0	18.5	59	25.4	11.0	73	24.0	13.7	19	21.6	3.6	534	21.5	100.0
	Transportation and storage	43	3.1	52.4	21	4.7	25.6	6	2.6	7.3	11	3.6	13.4	1	1.1	1.2	82	3.3	100.0
	Accommodation and Food Service Activities	250	17.8	70.2	51	11.3	14.3	21	9.1	5.9	28	9.2	7.9	6	6.8	1.7	356	14.4	100.0
	Information and Communication	110	7.8	58.2	37	8.2	19.6	21	9.1	11.1	19	6.3	10.1	2	2.3	1.1	189	7.6	100.0
	Financial and Insurance Activities	62	4.4	56.9	14	3.1	12.8	12	5.2	11.0	14	4.6	12.8	7	8.0	6.4	109	4.4	100.0
	Real Estate Activities	28	2.0	37.3	14	3.1	18.7	12	5.2	16.0	15	4.9	20.0	6	6.8	8.0	75	3.0	100.0
	Professional, Scientific, and Technical Activities	54	3.8	55.7	25	5.5	25.8	8	3.5	8.2	9	3.0	9.3	1	1.1	1.0	97	3.9	100.0
	Administrative and Support Service Activities	25	1.8	47.2	8	1.8	15.1	6	2.6	11.3	12	4.0	22.6	2	2.3	3.8	53	2.1	100.0
	Public Administration and Defense; Compulsory Social Security	–	–	–	–	–	–	–	–	–	–	–	–	1	1.1	100.0	1	0.0	100.0
	Education	14	1.0	45.2	7	1.6	22.6	3	1.3	9.7	5	1.6	16.1	2	2.3	6.5	31	1.3	100.0
	Human Health and Social Work Activities	9	0.6	60.0	3	0.7	20.0	1	0.4	6.7	2	0.7	13.3	–	–	–	15	0.6	100.0
	Arts, Entertainment, and Recreation	32	2.3	56.1	12	2.7	21.1	8	3.5	14.0	5	1.6	8.8	–	–	–	57	2.3	100.0
	Other Service Activities	215	15.3	60.6	68	15.1	19.2	33	14.2	9.3	29	9.5	8.2	10	11.4	2.8	355	14.3	100.0
	Total	1,406	100.0	56.7	451	100.0	18.2	232	100.0	9.4	304	100.0	12.3	88	100.0	3.5	2,481	100.0	100.0

continued on next page

Business Operating Period continued

Part 1

q1.6: Period of your operations since establishment (as of the end of 2019):

Item	Location	0–5 years			6–10 years			11–15 years			16–30 years			31 years and above			Total		
		No.	%*	%**	No.	%*	%**	No.	%*	%**	No.	%*	%**	No.	%*	%**	No.	%*	%**
Location	National Capital Region	652	46.4	53.0	229	50.8	18.6	125	53.9	10.2	168	55.3	13.6	57	64.8	4.6	1,231	49.6	100.0
	Cordillera Administrative Region	17	1.2	73.9	3	0.7	13.0	2	0.9	8.7	1	0.3	4.3	–	–	–	23	0.9	100.0
	Region 1: Ilocos	17	1.2	65.4	4	0.9	15.4	3	1.3	11.5	2	0.7	7.7	–	–	–	26	1.1	100.0
	Region 2: Cagayan Valley	10	0.7	43.5	8	1.8	34.8	2	0.9	8.7	2	0.7	8.7	1	1.1	4.3	23	0.9	100.0
	Region 3: Central Luzon	146	10.4	63.5	40	8.9	17.4	15	6.5	6.5	22	7.2	9.6	7	8.0	3.0	230	9.3	100.0
	Region 4A: Calabarzon	211	15.0	60.8	50	11.1	14.4	27	11.6	7.8	52	17.1	15.0	7	8.0	2.0	347	14.0	100.0
	MIMAROPA	32	2.3	69.6	5	1.1	10.9	3	1.3	6.5	6	2.0	13.0	–	–	–	46	1.9	100.0
	Region 5: Bicol	33	2.4	64.7	13	2.9	25.5	2	0.9	3.9	1	0.3	2.0	2	2.3	3.9	51	2.1	100.0
	Region 6: Western Visayas	70	5.0	70.0	12	2.7	12.0	9	3.9	9.0	7	2.3	7.0	2	2.3	2.0	100	4.0	100.0
	Region 7: Central Visayas	90	6.4	48.6	45	10.0	24.3	24	10.3	13.0	19	6.3	10.3	7	8.0	3.8	185	7.5	100.0
	Region 8: Eastern Visayas	11	0.8	44.0	7	1.6	28.0	4	1.7	16.0	2	0.7	8.0	1	1.1	4.0	25	1.0	100.0
	Region 9: Zamboanga Peninsula	10	0.7	50.0	6	1.3	30.0	–	–	–	4	1.3	20.0	–	–	–	20	0.8	100.0
	Region 10: Northern Mindanao	26	1.9	54.2	12	2.7	25.0	3	1.3	6.3	4	1.3	8.3	3	3.4	6.3	48	1.9	100.0
	Region 11: Davao	51	3.6	60.0	12	2.7	14.1	11	4.7	12.9	10	3.3	11.8	1	1.1	1.2	85	3.4	100.0
	Region 12: SOCCSKSARGEN	12	0.9	60.0	3	0.7	15.0	1	0.4	5.0	4	1.3	20.0	–	–	–	20	0.8	100.0
	Region 13: Caraga	17	1.2	85.0	2	0.4	10.0	1	0.4	5.0	–	–	–	–	–	–	20	0.8	100.0
	BARMM (formerly ARMM)	1	0.1	100.0	–	–	–	–	–	–	–	–	–	–	–	–	1	0.0	100.0
	Total	1,406	100.0	56.7	451	100.0	18.2	232	100.0	9.4	304	100.0	12.3	88	100.0	3.5	2,481	100.0	100.0

– = no number; BARMM = Bangsamoro Autonomous Region in Muslim Mindanao; MIMAROPA = Mindoro, Marinduque, Romblon, and Palawan (Southwestern Tagalog Region); SOCCSKSARGEN = South Cotabato, Cotabato, Sultan Kudarat, Sarangani, and General Santos.

* Share of vertical column. ** Share of horizontal line.

Source: Asian Development Bank, Philippine Enterprise Survey.

Employment

Part 1

q1.7. How many full-time and part-time paid workers did your company have (as of the end of 2019)?

Item		Full-time workers					Part-time or contractual workers				
		Average	Range		# of responses		Average	Range		# of responses	
			Min	Max	No.	%		Min	Max	No.	%
Firm size	Micro	16.2	–	6,000	1,287	51.9	10.3	–	3,000	1,288	51.9
	Small	28.7	–	1,000	676	27.3	11.8	–	553	676	27.2
	Medium-sized	41.9	–	609	331	13.3	13.9	–	812	331	13.3
	Large	151.6	–	6,625	186	7.5	30.6	–	1,000	186	7.5
	Total	33.2	–	6,625	2,480	100.0	12.7	–	3,000	2,481	100.0
Sector	Agriculture, Forestry, and Fishing	18.4	1	73	18	0.7	3.3	–	18	18	0.7
	Manufacturing	40.9	–	1,400	261	10.5	13.2	–	600	261	10.5
	Electricity, Gas, Steam, and Air Conditioning Supply	13.3	1	55	29	1.2	1.6	–	15	29	1.2
	Water Supply, Sewerage, Waste Management, and Remediation Activities	22.8	5	62	5	0.2	6.0	–	20	5	0.2
	Construction	18.5	–	246	214	8.6	25.2	–	300	214	8.6
	Wholesale and Retail Trade; Repair of Motor Vehicles and Motorcycles	18.0	–	1,262	534	21.5	3.7	–	300	534	21.5
	Transportation and storage	28.5	–	800	82	3.3	11.9	–	281	82	3.3
	Accommodation and Food Service Activities	29.7	–	6,000	356	14.4	12.5	–	3,000	356	14.3
	Information and Communication	51.6	–	3,000	189	7.6	25.8	–	3,000	189	7.6
	Financial and Insurance Activities	147.2	–	6,625	109	4.4	15.1	–	1,000	109	4.4
	Real Estate Activities	7.1	–	43	75	3.0	2.3	–	50	75	3.0
	Professional, Scientific, and Technical Activities	11.2	1	117	97	3.9	5.5	–	102	97	3.9
	Administrative and Support Service Activities	64.8	1	1,000	53	2.1	30.2	–	754	53	2.1
	Public Administration and Defense; Compulsory Social Security	343.0	343	343	1	0.0	100.0	100	100	1	0.0
	Education	8.1	–	48	31	1.3	4.6	–	20	31	1.2
	Human Health and Social Work Activities	11.5	1	50	15	0.6	2.2	–	20	15	0.6
	Arts, Entertainment, and Recreation	10.7	1	100	56	2.3	4.5	–	81	57	2.3
	Other Service Activities	34.4	–	1,800	355	14.3	16.5	–	812	355	14.3
	Total	33.2	–	6,625	2,480	100.0	12.7	–	3,000	2,481	100.0
Location	National Capital Region	36.1	–	6,625	1,230	49.6	11.0	–	1,000	1,231	49.6
	Cordillera Administrative Region	36.1	1	600	23	0.9	3.3	–	39	23	0.9
	Region 1: Ilocos	32.4	1	350	26	1.0	8.0	–	100	26	1.0
	Region 2: Cagayan Valley	14.6	1	60	23	0.9	6.6	–	100	23	0.9
	Region 3: Central Luzon	24.0	–	764	230	9.3	6.1	–	300	230	9.3
	Region 4A: Calabarzon	21.3	1	377	347	14.0	14.1	–	754	347	14.0
	MIMAROPA	15.1	–	114	46	1.9	6.9	–	76	46	1.9
	Region 5: Bicol	18.9	–	256	51	2.1	8.8	–	116	51	2.1
	Region 6: Western Visayas	13.0	–	156	100	4.0	7.2	–	200	100	4.0
	Region 7: Central Visayas	62.0	–	6,000	185	7.5	20.2	–	3,000	185	7.5
	Region 8: Eastern Visayas	153.5	–	3,000	25	1.0	153.3	–	3,000	25	1.0
	Region 9: Zamboanga Peninsula	23.4	1	246	20	0.8	1.6	–	18	20	0.8
	Region 10: Northern Mindanao	40.4	–	1,000	48	1.9	20.3	–	494	48	1.9
	Region 11: Davao	15.7	–	119	85	3.4	11.2	–	270	85	3.4
	Region 12: SOCCSKSARGEN	39.1	1	400	20	0.8	12.4	–	150	20	0.8
	Region 13: Caraga	14.0	–	75	20	0.8	1.8	–	10	20	0.8
	BARMM (formerly ARMM)	9.0	9	9	1	0.0	–	–	–	1	0.0
	Total	33.2	–	6,625	2,480	100.0	12.7	–	3,000	2,481	100.0

– = no number; BARMM = Bangsamoro Autonomous Region in Muslim Mindanao; MIMAROPA = Mindoro, Marinduque, Romblon, and Palawan (Southwestern Tagalog Region); SOCCSKSARGEN = South Cotabato, Cotabato, Sultan Kudarat, Sarangani, and General Santos.

Source: Asian Development Bank, Philippine Enterprise Survey.

Female Employees

Part 1

q1.8: Percentage (%) of female employees to total employees (as of the end of 2019):

Item		0–10%			11%–30%			31%–50%			51%–80%			81% and above			Total		
		No.	%*	%**	No.	%*	%**	No.	%*	%**	No.	%*	%**	No.	%*	%**	No.	%*	%**
Firm size	Micro	495	57.1	38.4	145	40.9	11.3	211	43.5	16.4	178	45.5	13.8	259	67.6	20.1	1,288	51.9	100.0
	Small	217	25.0	32.1	124	34.9	18.3	148	30.5	21.9	119	30.4	17.6	68	17.8	10.1	676	27.3	100.0
	Medium-sized	99	11.4	29.9	52	14.7	15.7	85	17.5	25.7	60	15.4	18.1	35	9.1	10.6	331	13.3	100.0
	Large	56	6.5	30.1	34	9.6	18.3	41	8.5	22.0	34	8.7	18.3	21	5.5	11.3	186	7.5	100.0
	Total	867	100.0	34.9	355	100.0	14.3	485	100.0	19.5	391	100.0	15.8	383	100.0	15.4	2,481	100.0	100.0
Sector	Agriculture, Forestry, and Fishing	5	0.6	27.8	3	0.9	16.7	8	1.7	44.4	1	0.3	5.6	1	0.3	5.6	18	0.7	100.0
	Manufacturing	115	13.3	44.1	39	11.0	14.9	41	8.5	15.7	37	9.5	14.2	29	7.6	11.1	261	10.5	100.0
	Electricity, Gas, Steam, and Air Conditioning Supply	16	1.9	55.2	5	1.4	17.2	6	1.2	20.7	1	0.3	3.4	1	0.3	3.4	29	1.2	100.0
	Water Supply, Sewerage, Waste Management, and Remediation Activities	3	0.4	60.0	–	–	–	2	0.4	40.0	–	–	–	–	–	–	5	0.2	100.0
	Construction	148	17.1	69.2	38	10.7	17.8	16	3.3	7.5	5	1.3	2.3	7	1.8	3.3	214	8.6	100.0
	Wholesale and Retail Trade; Repair of Motor Vehicles and Motorcycles	168	19.4	31.5	88	24.8	16.5	123	25.4	23.0	90	23.0	16.9	65	17.0	12.2	534	21.5	100.0
	Transportation and storage	51	5.9	62.2	11	3.1	13.4	9	1.9	11.0	7	1.8	8.5	4	1.0	4.9	82	3.3	100.0
	Accommodation and Food Service Activities	77	8.9	21.6	44	12.4	12.4	90	18.6	25.3	72	18.4	20.2	73	19.1	20.5	356	14.4	100.0
	Information and Communication	50	5.8	26.5	31	8.7	16.4	48	9.9	25.4	36	9.2	19.0	24	6.3	12.7	189	7.6	100.0
	Financial and Insurance Activities	24	2.8	22.0	18	5.1	16.5	19	3.9	17.4	30	7.7	27.5	18	4.7	16.5	109	4.4	100.0
	Real Estate Activities	21	2.4	28.0	12	3.4	16.0	14	2.9	18.7	17	4.4	22.7	11	2.9	14.7	75	3.0	100.0
	Professional, Scientific, and Technical Activities	21	2.4	21.6	11	3.1	11.3	22	4.5	22.7	20	5.1	20.6	23	6.0	23.7	97	3.9	100.0
	Administrative and Support Service Activities	17	2.0	32.1	6	1.7	11.3	10	2.1	18.9	11	2.8	20.8	9	2.4	17.0	53	2.1	100.0
	Public Administration and Defense; Compulsory Social Security	–	–	–	–	–	–	–	–	–	1	0.3	100.0	–	–	–	1	0.0	100.0
	Education	2	0.2	6.5	–	–	–	4	0.8	12.9	10	2.6	32.3	15	3.9	48.4	31	1.3	100.0
	Human Health and Social Work Activities	4	0.5	26.7	2	0.6	13.3	1	0.2	6.7	2	0.5	13.3	6	1.6	40.0	15	0.6	100.0
	Arts, Entertainment, and Recreation	20	2.3	35.1	6	1.7	10.5	17	3.5	29.8	8	2.1	14.0	6	1.6	10.5	57	2.3	100.0
	Other Service Activities	125	14.4	35.2	41	11.6	11.5	55	11.3	15.5	43	11.0	12.1	91	23.8	25.6	355	14.3	100.0
	Total	867	100.0	34.9	355	100.0	14.3	485	100.0	19.5	391	100.0	15.8	383	100.0	15.4	2,481	100.0	100.0

continued on next page

Female Employment continued

Part 1

q1.8: Percentage (%) of female employees to total employees (as of the end of 2019):

Item / Location	0–10%			11%–30%			31%–50%			51%–80%			81% and above			Total		
	No.	%*	%**	No.	%*	%**	No.	%*	%**	No.	%*	%**	No.	%*	%**	No.	%*	%**
National Capital Region	382	44.1	31.0	181	51.0	14.7	253	52.2	20.6	216	55.2	17.5	199	52.0	16.2	1,231	49.6	100.0
Cordillera Administrative Region	6	0.7	26.1	3	0.9	13.0	4	0.8	17.4	5	1.3	21.7	5	1.3	21.7	23	0.9	100.0
Region 1: Ilocos	6	0.7	23.1	3	0.9	11.5	4	0.8	15.4	4	1.0	15.4	9	2.4	34.6	26	1.1	100.0
Region 2: Cagayan Valley	4	0.5	17.4	2	0.6	8.7	10	2.1	43.5	2	0.5	8.7	5	1.3	21.7	23	0.9	100.0
Region 3: Central Luzon	93	10.7	40.4	34	9.6	14.8	36	7.4	15.7	37	9.5	16.1	30	7.8	13.0	230	9.3	100.0
Region 4A: Calabarzon	146	16.8	42.1	45	12.7	13.0	59	12.2	17.0	46	11.8	13.3	51	13.3	14.7	347	14.0	100.0
MIMAROPA	13	1.5	28.3	5	1.4	10.9	12	2.5	26.1	9	2.3	19.6	7	1.8	15.2	46	1.9	100.0
Region 5: Bicol	23	2.7	45.1	9	2.5	17.6	4	0.8	7.8	9	2.3	17.6	6	1.6	11.8	51	2.1	100.0
Region 6: Western Visayas	40	4.6	40.0	16	4.5	16.0	18	3.7	18.0	10	2.6	10.0	16	4.2	16.0	100	4.0	100.0
Region 7: Central Visayas	53	6.1	28.6	27	7.6	14.6	42	8.7	22.7	35	9.0	18.9	28	7.3	15.1	185	7.5	100.0
Region 8: Eastern Visayas	12	1.4	48.0	3	0.9	12.0	5	1.0	20.0	1	0.3	4.0	4	1.0	16.0	25	1.0	100.0
Region 9: Zamboanga Peninsula	7	0.8	35.0	2	0.6	10.0	6	1.2	30.0	4	1.0	20.0	1	0.3	5.0	20	0.8	100.0
Region 10: Northern Mindanao	19	2.2	39.6	11	3.1	22.9	9	1.9	18.8	4	1.0	8.3	5	1.3	10.4	48	1.9	100.0
Region 11: Davao	44	5.1	51.8	11	3.1	12.9	14	2.9	16.5	6	1.5	7.1	10	2.6	11.8	85	3.4	100.0
Region 12: SOCCSKSARGEN	9	1.0	45.0	2	0.6	10.0	4	0.8	20.0	–	–	–	5	1.3	25.0	20	0.8	100.0
Region 13: Caraga	9	1.0	45.0	1	0.3	5.0	5	1.0	25.0	3	0.8	15.0	2	0.5	10.0	20	0.8	100.0
BARMM (formerly ARMM)	1	0.1	100.0	–	–	–	–	–	–	–	–	–	–	–	–	1	0.0	100.0
Total	867	100.0	34.9	355	100.0	14.3	485	100.0	19.5	391	100.0	15.8	383	100.0	15.4	2,481	100.0	100.0

– = no number; BARMM = Bangsamoro Autonomous Region in Muslim Mindanao; MIMAROPA = Mindoro, Marinduque, Romblon, and Palawan (Southwestern Tagalog Region); SOCCSKSARGEN = South Cotabato, Cotabato, Sultan Kudarat, Sarangani, and General Santos.

* Share of vertical column. ** Share of horizontal line.

Source: Asian Development Bank, Philippine Enterprise Survey.

Total Assets (excluding Land)

Part 1

q1.10: Total assets (including fixed assets such as buildings and equipment, and financial assets such as bank savings, but excluding land, as of the end of 2019):

Item		Not more than ₱3,000,000			₱3,000,001–₱15,000,000			₱15,000,001–₱100,000,000			Over ₱100,000,000			Total		
		No.	%*	%**	No.	%*	%**	No.	%*	%**	No.	%*	%**	No.	%*	%**
Firm size	Micro	1,288	100.0	100.0	–	–	–	–	–	–	–	–	–	1,288	51.9	100.0
	Small	–	–	–	676	100.0	100.0	–	–	–	–	–	–	676	27.3	100.0
	Medium-sized	–	–	–	–	–	–	331	100.0	100.0	–	–	–	331	13.3	100.0
	Large	–	–	–	–	–	–	–	–	–	186	100.0	100.0	186	7.5	100.0
	Total	1,288	100.0	51.9	676	100.0	27.2	331	100.0	13.3	186	100.0	7.5	2,481	100.0	100.0
Sector	Agriculture, Forestry, and Fishing	7	0.5	38.9	5	0.7	27.8	5	1.5	27.8	1	0.5	5.6	18	0.7	100.0
	Manufacturing	93	7.2	35.6	79	11.7	30.3	61	18.4	23.4	28	15.1	10.7	261	10.5	100.0
	Electricity, Gas, Steam, and Air Conditioning Supply	16	1.2	55.2	6	0.9	20.7	7	2.1	24.1	–	–	–	29	1.2	100.0
	Water Supply, Sewerage, Waste Management, and Remediation Activities	1	0.1	20.0	2	0.3	40.0	2	0.6	40.0	–	–	–	5	0.2	100.0
	Construction	107	8.3	50.0	64	9.5	29.9	30	9.1	14.0	13	7.0	6.1	214	8.6	100.0
	Wholesale and Retail Trade, Repair of Motor Vehicles and Motorcycles	283	22.0	53.0	155	22.9	29.0	63	19.0	11.8	33	17.7	6.2	534	21.5	100.0
	Transportation and storage	31	2.4	37.8	30	4.4	36.6	11	3.3	13.4	10	5.4	12.2	82	3.3	100.0
	Accommodation and Food Service Activities	190	14.8	53.4	91	13.5	25.6	56	16.9	15.7	19	10.2	5.3	356	14.4	100.0
	Information and Communication	104	8.1	55.0	49	7.3	25.9	23	7.0	12.2	13	7.0	6.9	189	7.6	100.0
	Financial and Insurance Activities	54	4.2	49.5	30	4.4	27.5	15	4.5	13.8	10	5.4	9.2	109	4.4	100.0
	Real Estate Activities	32	2.5	42.7	24	3.6	32.0	12	3.6	16.0	7	3.8	9.3	75	3.0	100.0
	Professional, Scientific, and Technical Activities	59	4.6	60.8	21	3.1	21.6	11	3.3	11.3	6	3.2	6.2	97	3.9	100.0
	Administrative and Support Service Activities	23	1.8	43.4	22	3.3	41.5	5	1.5	9.4	3	1.6	5.7	53	2.1	100.0
	Public Administration and Defense; Compulsory Social Security	–	–	–	–	–	–	–	–	–	1	0.5	100.0	1	0.0	100.0
	Education	19	1.5	61.3	6	0.9	19.4	1	0.3	3.2	5	2.7	16.1	31	1.3	100.0
	Human Health and Social Work Activities	9	0.7	60.0	2	0.3	13.3	3	0.9	20.0	1	0.5	6.7	15	0.6	100.0
	Arts, Entertainment and Recreation	30	2.3	52.6	19	2.8	33.3	1	0.3	1.8	7	3.8	12.3	57	2.3	100.0
	Other Service Activities	230	17.9	64.8	71	10.5	20.0	25	7.6	7.0	29	15.6	8.2	355	14.3	100.0
	Total	1,288	100.0	51.9	676	100.0	27.2	331	100.0	13.3	186	100.0	7.5	2,481	100.0	100.0
Location	National Capital Region	621	48.2	50.4	345	51.0	28.0	168	50.8	13.6	97	52.2	7.9	1,231	49.6	100.0
	Cordillera Administrative Region	18	1.4	78.3	2	0.3	8.7	3	0.9	13.0	–	–	–	23	0.9	100.0
	Region 1: Ilocos	18	1.4	69.2	5	0.7	19.2	3	0.9	11.5	–	–	–	26	1.1	100.0
	Region 2: Cagayan Valley	13	1.0	56.5	6	0.9	26.1	2	0.6	8.7	2	1.1	8.7	23	0.9	100.0
	Region 3: Central Luzon	127	9.9	55.2	62	9.2	27.0	20	6.0	8.7	21	11.3	9.1	230	9.3	100.0
	Region 4A: Calabarzon	183	14.2	52.7	84	12.4	24.2	48	14.5	13.8	32	17.2	9.2	347	14.0	100.0
	MIMAROPA	21	1.6	45.7	11	1.6	23.9	10	3.0	21.7	4	2.2	8.7	46	1.9	100.0
	Region 5: Bicol	29	2.3	56.9	13	1.9	25.5	7	2.1	13.7	2	1.1	3.9	51	2.1	100.0
	Region 6: Western Visayas	53	4.1	53.0	22	3.3	22.0	16	4.8	16.0	9	4.8	9.0	100	4.0	100.0
	Region 7: Central Visayas	87	6.8	47.0	60	8.9	32.4	27	8.2	14.6	11	5.9	5.9	185	7.5	100.0
	Region 8: Eastern Visayas	10	0.8	40.0	12	1.8	48.0	3	0.9	12.0	–	–	–	25	1.0	100.0
	Region 9: Zamboanga Peninsula	10	0.8	50.0	7	1.0	35.0	2	0.6	10.0	1	0.5	5.0	20	0.8	100.0
	Region 10: Northern Mindanao	24	1.9	50.0	15	2.2	31.3	6	1.8	12.5	3	1.6	6.3	48	1.9	100.0
	Region 11: Davao	50	3.9	58.8	23	3.4	27.1	9	2.7	10.6	3	1.6	3.5	85	3.4	100.0
	Region 12: SOCCSKSARGEN	9	0.7	45.0	7	1.0	35.0	4	1.2	20.0	–	–	–	20	0.8	100.0
	Region 13: Caraga	15	1.2	75.0	1	0.2	5.0	3	0.9	15.0	1	0.5	5.0	20	0.8	100.0
	BARMM (formerly ARMM)	–	–	–	1	0.2	100.0	–	–	–	–	–	–	1	0.0	100.0
	Total	1,288	100.0	51.9	676	100.0	27.2	331	100.0	13.3	186	100.0	7.5	2,481	100.0	100.0

– = no number; BARMM = Bangsamoro Autonomous Region in Muslim Mindanao; MIMAROPA = Mindoro, Marinduque, Romblon, and Palawan (Southwestern Tagalog Region); SOCCSKSARGEN = South Cotabato, Cotabato, Sultan Kudarat, Sarangani, and General Santos.

* Share of vertical column. ** Share of horizontal line.

Online Business/E-Commerce

		Part 1 q1.12: Are you engaged in online selling or e-commerce?								
		Yes			No			Total		
Item		No.	%*	%**	No.	%*	%**	No.	%*	%**
Firm size	Micro	205	58.1	15.9	1,083	50.9	84.1	1,288	51.9	100.0
	Small	79	22.4	11.7	597	28.1	88.3	676	27.3	100.0
	Medium-sized	36	10.2	10.9	295	13.9	89.1	331	13.3	100.0
	Large	33	9.4	17.7	153	7.2	82.3	186	7.5	100.0
	Total	353	100.0	14.2	2,128	100.0	85.8	2,481	100.0	100.0
Sector	Agriculture, Forestry, and Fishing	1	0.3	5.6	17	0.8	94.4	18	0.7	100.0
	Manufacturing	34	9.6	13.0	227	10.7	87.0	261	10.5	100.0
	Electricity, Gas, Steam, and Air Conditioning Supply	–	–	–	29	1.4	100.0	29	1.2	100.0
	Water Supply, Sewerage, Waste Management, and Remediation Activities	–	–	–	5	0.2	100.0	5	0.2	100.0
	Construction	9	2.6	4.2	205	9.6	95.8	214	8.6	100.0
	Wholesale and Retail Trade; Repair of Motor Vehicles and Motorcycles	111	31.4	20.8	423	19.9	79.2	534	21.5	100.0
	Transportation and storage	2	0.6	2.4	80	3.8	97.6	82	3.3	100.0
	Accommodation and Food Service Activities	89	25.2	25.0	267	12.6	75.0	356	14.4	100.0
	Information and Communication	39	11.1	20.6	150	7.1	79.4	189	7.6	100.0
	Financial and Insurance Activities	7	2.0	6.4	102	4.8	93.6	109	4.4	100.0
	Real Estate Activities	10	2.8	13.3	65	3.1	86.7	75	3.0	100.0
	Professional, Scientific, and Technical Activities	3	0.9	3.1	94	4.4	96.9	97	3.9	100.0
	Administrative and Support Service Activities	3	0.9	5.7	50	2.4	94.3	53	2.1	100.0
	Public Administration and Defense; Compulsory Social Security	–	–	–	1	0.1	100.0	1	0.0	100.0
	Education	1	0.3	3.2	30	1.4	96.8	31	1.3	100.0
	Human Health and Social Work Activities	–	–	–	15	0.7	100.0	15	0.6	100.0
	Arts, Entertainment, and Recreation	8	2.3	14.0	49	2.3	86.0	57	2.3	100.0
	Other Service Activities	36	10.2	10.1	319	15.0	89.9	355	14.3	100.0
	Total	353	100.0	14.2	2,128	100.0	85.8	2,481	100.0	100.0
Location	National Capital Region	193	54.7	15.7	1,038	48.8	84.3	1,231	49.6	100.0
	Cordillera Administrative Region	5	1.4	21.7	18	0.9	78.3	23	0.9	100.0
	Region 1: Ilocos	2	0.6	7.7	24	1.1	92.3	26	1.1	100.0
	Region 2: Cagayan Valley	3	0.9	13.0	20	0.9	87.0	23	0.9	100.0
	Region 3: Central Luzon	30	8.5	13.0	200	9.4	87.0	230	9.3	100.0
	Region 4A: Calabarzon	31	8.8	8.9	316	14.9	91.1	347	14.0	100.0
	MIMAROPA	14	4.0	30.4	32	1.5	69.6	46	1.9	100.0
	Region 5: Bicol	6	1.7	11.8	45	2.1	88.2	51	2.1	100.0
	Region 6: Western Visayas	14	4.0	14.0	86	4.0	86.0	100	4.0	100.0
	Region 7: Central Visayas	32	9.1	17.3	153	7.2	82.7	185	7.5	100.0
	Region 8: Eastern Visayas	2	0.6	8.0	23	1.1	92.0	25	1.0	100.0
	Region 9: Zamboanga Peninsula	1	0.3	5.0	19	0.9	95.0	20	0.8	100.0
	Region 10: Northern Mindanao	6	1.7	12.5	42	2.0	87.5	48	1.9	100.0
	Region 11: Davao	12	3.4	14.1	73	3.4	85.9	85	3.4	100.0
	Region 12: SOCCSKSARGEN	2	0.6	10.0	18	0.9	90.0	20	0.8	100.0
	Region 13: Caraga	–	–	–	20	0.9	100.0	20	0.8	100.0
	BARMM (formerly ARMM)	–	–	–	1	0.1	100.0	1	0.0	100.0
	Total	353	100.0	14.2	2,128	100.0	85.8	2,481	100.0	100.0

– = no number; BARMM = Bangsamoro Autonomous Region in Muslim Mindanao; MIMAROPA = Mindoro, Marinduque, Romblon, and Palawan (Southwestern Tagalog Region); SOCCSKSARGEN = South Cotabato, Cotabato, Sultan Kudarat, Sarangani, and General Santos.

* Share of vertical column. ** Share of horizontal line.

Source: Asian Development Bank, Philippine Enterprise Survey.

Export Business

Item		Part 1 q1.13: Do you export your products or services?								
		Yes			No			Total		
		No.	%*	%**	No.	%*	%**	No.	%*	%***
Firm size	Micro	68	35.2	5.3	1,220	53.3	94.7	1,288	51.9	100.0
	Small	54	28.0	8.0	622	27.2	92.0	676	27.3	100.0
	Medium-sized	49	25.4	14.8	282	12.3	85.2	331	13.3	100.0
	Large	22	11.4	11.8	164	7.2	88.2	186	7.5	100.0
	Total	193	100.0	7.8	2,288	100.0	92.2	2,481	100.0	100.0
Sector	Agriculture, Forestry, and Fishing	3	1.6	16.7	15	0.7	83.3	18	0.7	100.0
	Manufacturing	66	34.2	25.3	195	8.5	74.7	261	10.5	100.0
	Electricity, Gas, Steam, and Air Conditioning Supply	–	–	–	29	1.3	100.0	29	1.2	100.0
	Water Supply, Sewerage, Waste Management, and Remediation Activities	–	–	–	5	0.2	100.0	5	0.2	100.0
	Construction	1	0.5	0.5	213	9.3	99.5	214	8.6	100.0
	Wholesale and Retail Trade; Repair of Motor Vehicles and Motorcycles	20	10.4	3.7	514	22.5	96.3	534	21.5	100.0
	Transportation and storage	10	5.2	12.2	72	3.2	87.8	82	3.3	100.0
	Accommodation and Food Service Activities	12	6.2	3.4	344	15.0	96.6	356	14.4	100.0
	Information and Communication	51	26.4	27.0	138	6.0	73.0	189	7.6	100.0
	Financial and Insurance Activities	1	0.5	0.9	108	4.7	99.1	109	4.4	100.0
	Real Estate Activities	1	0.5	1.3	74	3.2	98.7	75	3.0	100.0
	Professional, Scientific, and Technical Activities	4	2.1	4.1	93	4.1	95.9	97	3.9	100.0
	Administrative and Support Service Activities	8	4.2	15.1	45	2.0	84.9	53	2.1	100.0
	Public Administration and Defense; Compulsory Social Security	–	–	–	1	0.0	100.0	1	0.0	100.0
	Education	–	–	–	31	1.4	100.0	31	1.3	100.0
	Human Health and Social Work Activities	–	–	–	15	0.7	100.0	15	0.6	100.0
	Arts, Entertainment, and Recreation	4	2.1	7.0	53	2.3	93.0	57	2.3	100.0
	Other Service Activities	12	6.2	3.4	343	15.0	96.6	355	14.3	100.0
	Total	193	100.0	7.8	2,288	100.0	92.2	2,481	100.0	100.0
Location	National Capital Region	95	49.2	7.7	1,136	49.7	92.3	1,231	49.6	100.0
	Cordillera Administrative Region	2	1.0	8.7	21	0.9	91.3	23	0.9	100.0
	Region 1: Ilocos	–	–	–	26	1.1	100.0	26	1.1	100.0
	Region 2: Cagayan Valley	2	1.0	8.7	21	0.9	91.3	23	0.9	100.0
	Region 3: Central Luzon	26	13.5	11.3	204	8.9	88.7	230	9.3	100.0
	Region 4A: Calabarzon	27	14.0	7.8	320	14.0	92.2	347	14.0	100.0
	MIMAROPA	–	–	–	46	2.0	100.0	46	1.9	100.0
	Region 5: Bicol	3	1.6	5.9	48	2.1	94.1	51	2.1	100.0
	Region 6: Western Visayas	4	2.1	4.0	96	4.2	96.0	100	4.0	100.0
	Region 7: Central Visayas	25	13.0	13.5	160	7.0	86.5	185	7.5	100.0
	Region 8: Eastern Visayas	–	–	–	25	1.1	100.0	25	1.0	100.0
	Region 9: Zamboanga Peninsula	2	1.0	10.0	18	0.8	90.0	20	0.8	100.0
	Region 10: Northern Mindanao	4	2.1	8.3	44	1.9	91.7	48	1.9	100.0
	Region 11: Davao	3	1.6	3.5	82	3.6	96.5	85	3.4	100.0
	Region 12: SOCCSKSARGEN	–	–	–	20	0.9	100.0	20	0.8	100.0
	Region 13: Caraga	–	–	–	20	0.9	100.0	20	0.8	100.0
	BARMM (formerly ARMM)	–	–	–	1	0.0	100.0	1	0.0	100.0
	Total	193	100.0	7.8	2,288	100.0	92.2	2,481	100.0	100.0

– = no number; BARMM = Bangsamoro Autonomous Region in Muslim Mindanao; MIMAROPA = Mindoro, Marinduque, Romblon, and Palawan (Southwestern Tagalog Region); SOCCSKSARGEN = South Cotabato, Cotabato, Sultan Kudarat, Sarangani, and General Santos.

* Share of vertical column. ** Share of horizontal line.

Source: Asian Development Bank, Philippine Enterprise Survey.

Share of Exports to Total Sales

Part 1

q1.13.1: What is the share of exports to your total sales as of the end of 2019?

Item		0% No.	%*	%**	1%–20% No.	%*	%**	21%–50% No.	%	%**	51%–70% No.	%*	%**	71%–90% No.	%*	%**	>90% No.	%*	%**	Total No.	%*	%**
Firm size	Micro	17	70.8	25.4	18	40.9	26.9	4	33.3	6.0	6	37.5	9.0	7	36.8	10.4	15	19.5	22.4	67	34.9	100.0
	Small	3	12.5	5.6	14	31.8	25.9	4	33.3	7.4	6	37.5	11.1	5	26.3	9.3	22	28.6	40.7	54	28.1	100.0
	Medium-sized	3	12.5	6.1	8	18.2	16.3	1	8.3	2.0	3	18.8	6.1	5	26.3	10.2	29	37.7	59.2	49	25.5	100.0
	Large	1	4.2	4.5	4	9.1	18.2	3	25.0	13.6	1	6.3	4.5	2	10.5	9.1	11	14.3	50.0	22	11.5	100.0
	Total	24	100.0	12.5	44	100.0	22.9	12	100.0	6.3	16	100.0	8.3	19	100.0	9.9	77	100.0	40.1	192	100.0	100.0
Sector	Agriculture, Forestry, and Fishing	1	4.2	33.3	1	2.3	33.3	–	–	–	–	–	–	1	5.3	33.3	–	–	–	3	1.6	100.0
	Manufacturing	3	12.5	4.6	14	31.8	21.5	5	41.7	7.7	5	31.3	7.7	6	31.6	9.2	32	41.6	49.2	65	33.9	100.0
	Electricity, Gas, Steam, and Air Conditioning Supply	–	–	–	–	–	–	–	–	–	–	–	–	–	–	–	–	–	–	–	–	–
	Water Supply, Sewerage, Waste Management, and Remediation Activities	–	–	–	–	–	–	–	–	–	–	–	–	–	–	–	–	–	–	–	–	–
	Construction	–	–	–	–	–	–	–	–	–	–	–	–	–	–	–	1	1.3	100.0	1	0.5	100.0
	Wholesale and Retail Trade; Repair of Motor Vehicles and Motorcycles	3	12.5	–	8	18.2	–	3	25.0	–	2	12.5	–	2	10.5	–	2	2.6	–	20	10.4	–
	Transportation and storage	1	4.2	10.0	4	9.1	40.0	1	8.3	10.0	1	6.3	10.0	2	10.5	20.0	1	1.3	10.0	10	5.2	100.0
	Accommodation and Food Service Activities	4	16.7	33.3	5	11.4	41.7	–	–	–	1	6.3	8.3	2	10.5	16.7	–	–	–	12	6.3	100.0
	Information and Communication	5	20.8	–	4	9.1	–	2	16.7	–	5	31.3	–	3	15.8	–	32	41.6	–	51	26.6	–
	Financial and Insurance Activities	1	4.2	100.0	–	–	–	–	–	–	–	–	–	–	–	–	–	–	–	1	0.5	100.0
	Real Estate Activities	1	4.2	100.0	–	–	–	–	–	–	–	–	–	–	–	–	–	–	–	1	0.5	100.0
	Professional, Scientific, and Technical Activities	–	–	–	2	4.6	50.0	–	–	–	–	–	–	1	5.3	25.0	1	1.3	25.0	4	2.1	100.0
	Administrative and Support Service Activities	–	–	–	1	2.3	12.5	–	–	–	1	6.3	12.5	1	5.3	12.5	5	6.5	62.5	8	4.2	100.0
	Public Administration and Defense; Compulsory Social Security	–	–	–	–	–	–	–	–	–	–	–	–	–	–	–	–	–	–	–	–	–

continued on next page

Share of Exports to Total Sales continued

		Part 1																				
		q1.13.1: What is the share of exports to your total sales as of the end of 2019?																				
Item		0%			1%–20%			21%–50%			51%–70%			71%–90%			>90%			Total		
		No.	%*	%**	No.	%*	%**	No.	%*	%**	No.	%*	%**	No.	%*	%**	No.	%*	%**	No.	%*	%**
	Education	–	–	–	–	–	–	–	–	–	–	–	–	–	–	–	–	–	–	–	–	–
	Human Health and Social Work Activities	–	–	–	–	–	–	–	–	–	–	–	–	–	–	–	–	–	–	–	–	–
	Arts, Entertainment, and Recreation	–	–	–	3	6.8	75.0	–	–	–	–	–	–	–	–	–	1	1.3	25.0	4	2.1	100.0
	Other Service Activities	5	20.8	41.7	2	4.6	16.7	1	8.3	8.3	1	6.3	8.3	1	5.3	8.3	2	2.6	16.7	12	6.3	100.0
	Total	24	100.0	12.5	44	100.0	22.9	12	100.0	6.3	16	100.0	8.3	19	100.0	9.9	77	100.0	40.1	192	100.0	100.0
Location	National Capital Region	10	41.7	10.5	28	63.6	29.5	6	50.0	6.3	10	62.5	10.5	8	42.1	8.4	33	42.9	34.7	95	49.5	100.0
	Cordillera Administrative Region	–	–	–	–	–	–	–	–	–	–	–	–	–	–	–	2	2.6	100.0	2	1.0	100.0
	Region 1: Ilocos	–	–	–	–	–	–	–	–	–	–	–	–	–	–	–	–	–	–	–	–	–
	Region 2: Cagayan Valley	–	–	–	1	2.3	50.0	–	–	–	–	–	–	–	–	–	1	1.3	50.0	2	1.0	100.0
	Region 3: Central Luzon	5	20.8	19.2	3	6.8	11.5	1	8.3	3.8	1	6.3	3.8	2	10.5	7.7	14	18.2	53.8	26	13.5	100.0
	Region 4A: Calabarzon	2	8.3	7.7	5	11.4	19.2	2	16.7	7.7	2	12.5	7.7	2	10.5	7.7	13	16.9	50.0	26	13.5	100.0
	MIMAROPA	–	–	–	–	–	–	–	–	–	–	–	–	–	–	–	–	–	–	–	–	–
	Region 5: Bicol	1	4.2	33.3	–	–	–	–	–	–	1	6.3	33.3	–	–	–	1	1.3	33.3	3	1.6	100.0
	Region 6: Western Visayas	2	8.3	50.0	–	–	–	–	–	–	–	–	–	1	5.3	25.0	1	1.3	25.0	4	2.1	100.0
	Region 7: Central Visayas	2	8.3	8.0	4	9.1	16.0	2	16.7	8.0	2	12.5	8.0	4	21.1	16.0	11	14.3	44.0	25	13.0	100.0
	Region 8: Eastern Visayas	–	–	–	–	–	–	–	–	–	–	–	–	–	–	–	–	–	–	–	–	–
	Region 9: Zamboanga Peninsula	1	4.2	50.0	–	–	–	–	–	–	–	–	–	1	5.3	50.0	–	–	–	2	1.0	100.0
	Region 10: Northern Mindanao	1	4.2	25.0	1	2.3	25.0	–	–	–	–	–	–	1	5.3	25.0	1	1.3	25.0	4	2.1	100.0
	Region 11: Davao	–	–	–	2	4.6	66.7	1	8.3	33.3	–	–	–	–	–	–	–	–	–	3	1.6	100.0
	Region 12: SOCCSKSARGEN	–	–	–	–	–	–	–	–	–	–	–	–	–	–	–	–	–	–	–	–	–
	Region 13: Caraga	–	–	–	–	–	–	–	–	–	–	–	–	–	–	–	–	–	–	–	–	–
	BARMM (formerly ARMM)	–	–	–	–	–	–	–	–	–	–	–	–	–	–	–	–	–	–	–	–	–
	Total	24	100.0	12.5	44	100.0	22.9	12	100.0	6.3	16	100.0	8.3	19	100.0	9.9	77	100.0	40.1	192	100.0	100.0

– = no number; BARMM = Bangsamoro Autonomous Region in Muslim Mindanao; MIMAROPA = Mindoro, Marinduque, Romblon, and Palawan (Southwestern Tagalog Region); SOCCSKSARGEN = South Cotabato, Cotabato, Sultan Kudarat, Sarangani, and General Santos.

Note: These correspond only to those who answered "Yes" in Question 13.

* Share of vertical column. ** Share of horizontal line.

Source: Asian Development Bank, Philippine Enterprise Survey.

Destination of Exports

Part 1
q.1.13.2: To which countries did you export your goods and services last year (2019)?

Item		People's Republic of China		Japan		Republic of Korea		Other Asian countries		United States		Europe		Latin America		Middle East and North Africa		Other Regions		Don't Know	
		No.	%	No.	%	No.	%	No.	%	No.	%	No.	%	No.	%	No.	%	No.	%	No.	%
Firm size	Micro	9	28.1	12	22.6	7	43.8	19	30.2	21	32.8	13	30.2	–	–	3	15.8	8	36.4	12	57.1
	Small	5	15.6	12	22.6	3	18.8	16	25.4	15	23.4	7	16.3	1	25.0	6	31.6	8	36.4	6	28.6
	Medium-sized	10	31.3	19	35.9	3	18.8	18	28.6	20	31.3	15	34.9	3	75.0	8	42.1	4	18.2	2	9.5
	Large	8	25.0	10	18.9	3	18.8	10	15.9	8	12.5	8	18.6	–	–	2	10.5	2	9.1	1	4.8
	Total	32	100.0	53	100.0	16	100.0	63	100.0	64	100.0	43	100.0	4	100.0	19	100.0	22	100.0	21	100.0
Industry	Agriculture, Forestry and Fishing	–	–	–	–	–	–	–	–	1	1.6	1	2.3	–	–	–	–	–	–	–	–
	Manufacturing	13	40.6	29	54.7	5	31.3	5	31.3	25	39.1	19	44.2	1	25.0	5	26.3	3	12.5	6	18.8
	Electricity, Gas, Steam, and Air Conditioning Supply	–	–	–	–	–	–	–	–	–	–	–	–	–	–	–	–	–	–	–	–
	Water Supply, Sewerage, Waste Management, and Remediation Activities	–	–	–	–	–	–	–	–	–	–	–	–	–	–	–	–	–	–	–	–
	Construction	–	–	–	–	–	–	–	–	–	–	–	–	–	–	1	5.3	3	12.5	–	–
	Wholesale and Retail Trade; Repair of Motor Vehicles and Motorcycles	6	18.8	2	3.8	2	12.5	2	12.5	5	7.8	2	4.7	–	–	–	–	11	45.8	6	18.8
	Transportation and storage	3	9.4	3	5.7	2	12.5	2	12.5	3	4.7	3	7.0	–	–	1	5.3	1	4.2	–	–
	Accommodation and Food Service Activities	3	9.4	3	5.7	3	18.8	3	18.8	–	–	–	–	–	–	1	5.3	2	8.3	10	31.3
	Information and Communication	4	12.5	12	22.6	1	6.3	1	6.3	24	37.5	9	20.9	1	25.0	2	10.5	–	–	2	6.3
	Financial and Insurance Activities	–	–	–	–	–	–	–	–	–	–	–	–	–	–	–	–	–	–	1	3.1
	Real Estate Activities	–	–	–	–	–	–	–	–	–	–	–	–	–	–	–	–	–	–	–	–
	Professional, Scientific, and Technical Activities	–	–	1	1.9	–	–	–	–	1	1.6	1	2.3	–	–	–	–	–	–	1	3.1
	Administrative and Support Service Activities	1	3.1	1	1.9	1	6.3	1	6.3	1	1.6	2	4.7	1	25.0	7	36.8	–	–	1	3.1
	Public Administration and Defense; Compulsory Social Security	–	–	–	–	–	–	–	–	–	–	–	–	–	–	–	–	–	–	–	–

continued on next page

Destination of Exports continued

Part 1

q.1.13.2: To which countries did you export your goods and services last year (2019)?

Item		People's Republic of China		Japan		Republic of Korea		Other Asian countries		United States		Europe		Latin America		Middle East and North Africa		Other Regions		Don't Know	
		No.	%	No.	%	No.	%	No.	%	No.	%	No.	%	No.	%	No.	%	No.	%	No.	%
Education		–	–	–	–	–	–	–	–	–	–	–	–	–	–	–	–	–	–	–	–
Human Health and Social Work Activities		–	–	–	–	–	–	–	–	–	–	–	–	–	–	–	–	–	–	–	–
Arts, Entertainment, and Recreation		1	3.1	1	1.9	1	6.3	1	6.3	2	3.1	2	4.7	–	–	–	–	–	–	1	3.1
Other Service Activities		1	3.1	1	1.9	1	6.3	1	6.3	2	3.1	4	9.3	1	25.0	2	10.5	4	16.7	4	12.5
Total		32	100.0	53	100.0	16	100.0	63	100.0	64	100.0	43	100.0	4	100.0	19	100.0	22	100.0	21	100.0
Location	National Capital Region	12	37.5	17	32.1	8	50.0	41	65.1	30	46.9	21	48.8	3	75.0	14	73.7	13	59.1	7	33.3
	Cordillera Administrative Region	1	3.1	1	1.9	–	–	–	–	2	3.1	1	2.3	–	–	–	–	–	–	–	–
	Region 1: Ilocos	–	–	–	–	–	–	–	–	–	–	–	–	–	–	–	–	–	–	–	–
	Region 2: Cagayan Valley	–	–	1	1.9	–	–	1	1.6	1	1.6	1	2.3	–	–	–	–	–	–	–	–
	Region 3: Central Luzon	7	21.9	8	15.1	4	25.0	7	11.1	8	12.5	6	14.0	–	–	2	10.5	2	9.1	6	28.6
	Region 4A: Calabarzon	7	21.9	13	24.5	–	–	8	12.7	4	6.3	5	11.6	–	–	–	–	4	18.2	1	4.8
	MIMAROPA	–	–	–	–	–	–	–	–	–	–	–	–	–	–	–	–	–	–	–	–
	Region 5: Bicol	1	3.1	1	1.9	–	–	–	–	1	1.6	1	2.3	–	–	–	–	1	4.6	–	–
	Region 6: Western Visayas	–	–	–	–	–	–	1	1.6	1	1.6	–	–	–	–	–	–	–	–	2	9.5
	Region 7: Central Visayas	2	6.3	10	18.9	1	6.3	2	3.2	14	21.9	7	16.3	1	25.0	2	10.5	1	4.6	3	14.3
	Region 8: Eastern Visayas	–	–	–	–	–	–	–	–	–	–	–	–	–	–	–	–	–	–	–	–
	Region 9: Zamboanga Peninsula	–	–	–	–	–	–	–	–	1	1.6	1	2.3	–	–	–	–	–	–	1	4.8
	Region 10: Northern Mindanao	1	3.1	1	1.9	1	6.3	2	3.2	2	3.1	–	–	–	–	1	5.3	–	–	–	–
	Region 11: Davao	1	3.1	1	1.9	2	12.5	1	1.6	–	–	–	–	–	–	–	–	1	4.6	1	4.8
	Region 12: SOCCSKSARGEN	–	–	–	–	–	–	–	–	–	–	–	–	–	–	–	–	–	–	–	–
	Region 13: Caraga	–	–	–	–	–	–	–	–	–	–	–	–	–	–	–	–	–	–	–	–
	BARMM (formerly ARMM)	–	–	–	–	–	–	–	–	–	–	–	–	–	–	–	–	–	–	–	–
	Total	32	100.0	53	100.0	16	100.0	63	100.0	64	100.0	43	100.0	4	100.0	19	100.0	22	100.0	21	100.0

– = no number; BARMM = Bangsamoro Autonomous Region in Muslim Mindanao; MIMAROPA = Mindoro, Marinduque, Romblon, and Palawan (Southwestern Tagalog Region); SOCCSKSARGEN = South Cotabato, Cotabato, Sultan Kudarat, Sarangani, and General Santos.

Source: Asian Development Bank, Philippine Enterprise Survey.

Import Business

Item		Part 1 q1.14: Do you import for your business?								
		Yes			No			Total		
		No.	%*	%**	No.	%*	%**	No.	%*	%**
Firm size	Micro	131	33.4	10.2	1,151	55.5	89.8	1,282	52.0	100.0
	Small	122	31.1	18.2	547	26.4	81.8	669	27.1	100.0
	Medium-sized	89	22.7	26.9	242	11.7	73.1	331	13.4	100.0
	Large	50	12.8	27.3	133	6.4	72.7	183	7.4	100.0
	Total	392	100.0	15.9	2,073	100.0	84.1	2,465	100.0	100.0
Sector	Agriculture, Forestry, and Fishing	5	1.3	27.8	13	0.6	72.2	18	0.7	100.0
	Manufacturing	87	22.2	33.7	171	8.3	66.3	258	10.5	100.0
	Electricity, Gas, Steam, and Air Conditioning Supply	5	1.3	17.2	24	1.2	82.8	29	1.2	100.0
	Water Supply, Sewerage, Waste Management, and Remediation Activities	2	0.5	40.0	3	0.1	60.0	5	0.2	100.0
	Construction	19	4.9	8.9	194	9.4	91.1	213	8.6	100.0
	Wholesale and Retail Trade; Repair of Motor Vehicles and Motorcycles	165	42.1	31.3	362	17.5	68.7	527	21.4	100.0
	Transportation and storage	13	3.3	15.9	69	3.3	84.1	82	3.3	100.0
	Accommodation and Food Service Activities	21	5.4	6.0	331	16.0	94.0	352	14.3	100.0
	Information and Communication	25	6.4	13.2	164	7.9	86.8	189	7.7	100.0
	Financial and Insurance Activities	1	0.3	0.9	108	5.2	99.1	109	4.4	100.0
	Real Estate Activities	1	0.3	1.3	74	3.6	98.7	75	3.0	100.0
	Professional, Scientific, and Technical Activities	4	1.0	4.2	92	4.4	95.8	96	3.9	100.0
	Administrative and Support Service Activities	2	0.5	3.8	51	2.5	96.2	53	2.2	100.0
	Public Administration and Defense; Compulsory Social Security	–	–	–	1	0.1	100.0	1	0.0	100.0
	Education	–	–	–	31	1.5	100.0	31	1.3	100.0
	Human Health and Social Work Activities	–	–	–	15	0.7	100.0	15	0.6	100.0
	Arts, Entertainment, and Recreation	8	2.0	14.0	49	2.4	86.0	57	2.3	100.0
	Other Service Activities	34	8.7	9.6	321	15.5	90.4	355	14.4	100.0
	Total	392	100.0	15.9	2,073	100.0	84.1	2,465	100.0	100.0
Location	National Capital Region	235	60.0	19.2	990	47.8	80.8	1,225	49.7	100.0
	Cordillera Administrative Region	1	0.3	4.3	22	1.1	95.7	23	0.9	100.0
	Region 1: Ilocos	1	0.3	3.8	25	1.2	96.2	26	1.1	100.0
	Region 2: Cagayan Valley	2	0.5	8.7	21	1.0	91.3	23	0.9	100.0
	Region 3: Central Luzon	37	9.4	16.2	191	9.2	83.8	228	9.3	100.0
	Region 4A: Calabarzon	62	15.8	18.1	281	13.6	81.9	343	13.9	100.0
	MIMAROPA	1	0.3	2.2	44	2.1	97.8	45	1.8	100.0
	Region 5: Bicol	2	0.5	3.9	49	2.4	96.1	51	2.1	100.0
	Region 6: Western Visayas	5	1.3	5.0	95	4.6	95.0	100	4.1	100.0
	Region 7: Central Visayas	24	6.1	13.1	159	7.7	86.9	183	7.4	100.0
	Region 8: Eastern Visayas	4	1.0	16.0	21	1.0	84.0	25	1.0	100.0
	Region 9: Zamboanga Peninsula	4	1.0	20.0	16	0.8	80.0	20	0.8	100.0
	Region 10: Northern Mindanao	5	1.3	10.6	42	2.0	89.4	47	1.9	100.0
	Region 11: Davao	9	2.3	10.6	76	3.7	89.4	85	3.5	100.0
	Region 12: SOCCSKSARGEN	–	–	–	20	1.0	100.0	20	0.8	100.0
	Region 13: Caraga	–	–	–	20	1.0	100.0	20	0.8	100.0
	BARMM (formerly ARMM)	–	–	–	1	0.1	100.0	1	0.0	100.0
	Total	392	100.0	15.9	2,073	100.0	84.1	2,465	100.0	100.0

– = no number; BARMM = Bangsamoro Autonomous Region in Muslim Mindanao; MIMAROPA = Mindoro, Marinduque, Romblon, and Palawan (Southwestern Tagalog Region); SOCCSKSARGEN = South Cotabato, Cotabato, Sultan Kudarat, Sarangani, and General Santos.

* Share of vertical column. ** Share of horizontal line.

Source: Asian Development Bank, Philippine Enterprise Survey.

Share of Imports to Total Inputs

Part 1

q1.14.1: What is the share of imports to your total inputs?

Item		0%			1%–20%			21%–50%			51%–70%			71%–90%			>90%			Total		
		No.	%*	%**	No.	%*	%**	No.	%*	%**	No.	%*	%**	No.	%*	%**	No.	%*	%**	No.	%*	%**
Firm size	Micro	10	35.7	7.3	42	39.6	30.7	24	35.8	17.5	18	26.9	13.1	16	23.9	11.7	27	37.0	19.7	137	33.6	100.0
	Small	8	28.6	6.2	40	37.7	31.0	19	28.4	14.7	20	29.9	15.5	25	37.3	19.4	17	23.3	13.2	129	31.6	100.0
	Medium-sized	3	10.7	3.4	14	13.2	15.7	15	22.4	16.9	19	28.4	21.3	18	26.9	20.2	20	27.4	22.5	89	21.8	100.0
	Large	7	25.0	13.2	10	9.4	18.9	9	13.4	17.0	10	14.9	18.9	8	11.9	15.1	9	12.3	17.0	53	13.0	100.0
	Total	28	100.0	6.9	106	100.0	26.0	67	100.0	16.4	67	100.0	16.4	67	100.0	16.4	73	100.0	17.9	408	100.0	100.0
Sector	Agriculture, Forestry, and Fishing	–	–	–	1	0.9	20.0	2	3.0	40.0	–	–	–	1	1.5	20.0	1	1.4	20.0	5	1.2	100.0
	Manufacturing	3	10.7	3.3	17	16.0	18.9	18	26.9	20.0	21	31.3	23.3	17	25.4	18.9	14	19.2	15.6	90	22.1	100.0
	Electricity, Gas, Steam, and Air Conditioning Supply	–	–	–	–	–	–	3	4.5	60.0	–	–	–	1	1.5	20.0	1	1.4	20.0	5	1.2	100.0
	Water Supply, Sewerage, Waste Management, and Remediation Activities	–	–	–	1	0.9	50.0	–	–	–	–	–	–	–	–	–	1	1.4	50.0	2	0.5	100.0
	Construction	–	–	–	12	11.3	60.0	3	4.5	15.0	4	6.0	20.0	1	1.5	5.0	–	–	–	20	4.9	100.0
	Wholesale and Retail Trade; Repair of Motor Vehicles and Motorcycles	7	25.0	4.1	32	30.2	18.6	25	37.3	14.5	25	37.3	14.5	31	46.3	18.0	52	71.2	30.2	172	42.2	100.0
	Transportation and storage	2	7.1	15.4	3	2.8	23.1	1	1.5	7.7	3	4.5	23.1	3	4.5	23.1	1	1.4	7.7	13	3.2	100.0
	Accommodation and Food Service Activities	6	21.4	24.0	11	10.4	44.0	2	3.0	8.0	2	3.0	8.0	4	6.0	16.0	–	–	–	25	6.1	100.0
	Information and Communication	2	7.1	8.0	8	7.6	32.0	3	4.5	12.0	5	7.5	20.0	6	9.0	24.0	1	1.4	4.0	25	6.1	100.0
	Financial and Insurance Activities	1	3.6	100.0	–	–	–	–	–	–	–	–	–	–	–	–	–	–	–	1	0.3	100.0
	Real Estate Activities	–	–	–	1	0.9	100.0	–	–	–	–	–	–	–	–	–	–	–	–	1	0.3	100.0
	Professional, Scientific, and Technical Activities	1	3.6	20.0	2	1.9	40.0	–	–	–	2	3.0	40.0	–	–	–	–	–	–	5	1.2	100.0
	Administrative and Support Service Activities	–	–	–	1	0.9	50.0	1	1.5	50.0	–	–	–	–	–	–	–	–	–	2	0.5	100.0
	Public Administration and Defense; Compulsory Social Security	–	–	–	–	–	–	–	–	–	–	–	–	–	–	–	–	–	–	–	–	–

continued on next page

Share of Imports to Total Inputs continued

Part 1

q1.14.1: What is the share of imports to your total inputs?

Item	0%			1%-20%			21%-50%			51%-70%			71%-90%			>90%			Total		
	No.	%*	%**	No.	%*	%**	No.	%*	%**	No.	%*	%**	No.	%*	%**	No.	%*	%**	No.	%*	%**
Education	–	–	–	–	–	–	–	–	–	–	–	–	–	–	–	–	–	–	–	–	–
Human Health and Social Work Activities	–	–	–	–	–	–	–	–	–	–	–	–	–	–	–	–	–	–	–	–	–
Arts, Entertainment, and Recreation	1	3.6	12.5	5	4.7	62.5	1	1.5	12.5	1	1.5	12.5	–	–	–	–	–	–	8	2.0	100.0
Other Service Activities	5	17.9	14.7	12	11.3	35.3	8	11.9	23.5	4	6.0	11.8	3	4.5	8.8	2	2.7	5.9	34	8.3	100.0
Total	28	100.0	6.9	106	100.0	26.0	67	100.0	16.4	67	100.0	16.4	67	100.0	16.4	73	100.0	17.9	408	100.0	100.0
Location																					
National Capital Region	15	53.6	6.2	63	59.4	26.1	38	56.7	15.8	36	53.7	14.9	41	61.2	17.0	48	65.8	19.9	241	59.1	100.0
Cordillera Administrative Region	–	–	–	–	–	–	1	1.5	100.0	–	–	–	–	–	–	–	–	–	1	0.3	100.0
Region 1: Ilocos	1	3.6	100.0	–	–	–	–	–	–	–	–	–	–	–	–	–	–	–	1	0.3	100.0
Region 2: Cagayan Valley	–	–	–	–	–	–	–	–	–	1	1.5	50.0	–	–	–	1	1.4	50.0	2	0.5	100.0
Region 3: Central Luzon	2	7.1	5.1	6	5.7	15.4	3	4.5	7.7	11	16.4	28.2	10	14.9	25.6	7	9.6	17.9	39	9.6	100.0
Region 4A: Calabarzon	3	10.7	4.5	18	17.0	27.3	15	22.4	22.7	11	16.4	16.7	8	11.9	12.1	11	15.1	16.7	66	16.2	100.0
MIMAROPA	1	3.6	50.0	–	–	–	–	–	–	–	–	–	1	1.5	50.0	–	–	–	2	0.5	100.0
Region 5: Bicol	1	3.6	50.0	–	–	–	–	–	–	–	–	–	–	–	–	1	1.4	50.0	2	0.5	100.0
Region 6: Western Visayas	–	–	–	3	2.8	60.0	–	–	–	1	1.5	20.0	1	1.5	20.0	–	–	–	5	1.2	100.0
Region 7: Central Visayas	2	7.1	7.7	8	7.6	30.8	5	7.5	19.2	4	6.0	15.4	3	4.5	11.5	4	5.5	15.4	26	6.4	100.0
Region 8: Eastern Visayas	1	3.6	25.0	–	–	–	3	4.5	75.0	–	–	–	–	–	–	–	–	–	4	1.0	100.0
Region 9: Zamboanga Peninsula	1	3.6	25.0	2	1.9	50.0	–	–	–	–	–	–	1	1.5	25.0	–	–	–	4	1.0	100.0
Region 10: Northern Mindanao	1	3.6	16.7	2	1.9	33.3	–	–	–	2	3.0	33.3	1	1.5	16.7	–	–	–	6	1.5	100.0
Region 11: Davao	–	–	–	4	3.8	44.4	2	3.0	22.2	1	1.5	11.1	1	1.5	11.1	1	1.4	11.1	9	2.2	88.9
Region 12: SOCCSKSARGEN	–	–	–	–	–	–	–	–	–	–	–	–	–	–	–	–	–	–	–	–	–
Region 13: Caraga	–	–	–	–	–	–	–	–	–	–	–	–	–	–	–	–	–	–	–	–	–
BARMM (formerly ARMM)	–	–	–	–	–	–	–	–	–	–	–	–	–	–	–	–	–	–	–	–	–
Total	28	100.0	6.9	106	100.0	26.0	67	100.0	16.4	67	100.0	16.4	67	100.0	16.4	73	100.0	17.9	408	100.0	100.0

– = no number; BARMM = Bangsamoro Autonomous Region in Muslim Mindanao; MIMAROPA = Mindoro, Marinduque, Romblon, and Palawan (Southwestern Tagalog Region); SOCCSKSARGEN = South Cotabato, Cotabato, Sultan Kudarat, Sarangani, and General Santos.

Note: These correspond only to those who provided responses.

* Share of vertical column. ** Share of horizontal line.

Source: Asian Development Bank, Philippine Enterprise Survey.

Importing Countries

Part 1

q1.14.2: From which countries did you import goods/materials last year (2019)?

Item		People's Republic of China		Japan		Republic of Korea		Other Asian countries		United States		Europe		Latin America		Middle East and North Africa		Other Regions		Don't Know	
		No.	%	No.	%	No.	%	No.	%	No.	%	No.	%	No.	%	No.	%	No.	%	No.	%
Firm size	Micro	74	30.2	19	30.2	20	29.0	41	29.1	28	31.1	20	21.7	–	–	3	27.3	9	37.5	9	28.1
	Small	72	29.4	12	19.1	26	37.7	46	32.6	25	27.8	29	31.5	2	28.6	2	18.2	11	45.8	11	34.4
	Medium-sized	67	27.4	19	30.2	13	18.8	33	23.4	21	23.3	29	31.5	2	28.6	5	45.5	3	12.5	5	15.6
	Large	32	13.1	13	20.6	10	14.5	21	14.9	16	17.8	14	15.2	3	42.9	1	9.1	1	4.2	7	21.9
	Total	245	100.0	63	100.0	69	100.0	141	100.0	90	100.0	92	100.0	7	100.0	11	100.0	24	100.0	32	100.0
Industry	Agriculture, Forestry, and Fishing	2	0.8	–	–	–	–	–	–	2	2.2	2	2.2	–	–	–	–	–	–	–	–
	Manufacturing	56	22.9	22	34.9	14	20.3	38	27.0	10	11.1	10	11.1	2	28.6	1	9.1	3	12.5	6	18.8
	Electricity, Gas, Steam, and Air Conditioning Supply	4	1.6	–	–	1	1.5	–	–	2	2.2	2	2.2	–	–	1	9.1	–	–	–	–
	Water Supply, Sewerage, Waste Management, and Remediation Activities	1	0.4	–	–	1	1.5	1	0.7	2	2.2	2	2.2	–	–	–	–	–	–	–	–
	Construction	12	4.9	2	3.2	5	7.3	5	3.6	2	2.2	2	2.2	–	–	–	–	3	12.5	–	–
	Wholesale and Retail Trade; Repair of Motor Vehicles and Motorcycles	115	46.9	28	44.4	32	46.4	61	43.3	42	46.7	42	46.7	4	57.1	6	54.6	11	45.8	6	18.8
	Transportation and storage	11	4.5	4	6.4	4	5.8	7	5.0	4	4.4	4	4.4	–	–	1	9.1	1	4.2	–	–
	Accommodation and Food Service Activities	9	3.7	4	6.4	7	10.1	7	5.0	3	3.3	3	3.3	–	–	1	9.1	2	8.3	10	31.3
	Information and Communication	13	5.3	–	–	–	–	10	7.1	10	11.1	10	11.1	–	–	–	–	–	–	2	6.3
	Financial and Insurance Activities	–	–	–	–	–	–	–	–	–	–	–	–	–	–	–	–	–	–	1	3.1
	Real Estate Activities	1	0.4	–	–	–	–	–	–	1	1.1	1	1.1	–	–	–	–	–	–	–	–
	Professional, Scientific, and Technical Activities	2	0.8	–	–	2	2.9	–	–	1	1.1	1	1.1	–	–	–	–	–	–	1	3.1
	Administrative and Support Service Activities	–	–	–	–	–	–	–	–	–	–	–	–	–	–	1	9.1	–	–	1	3.1
	Public Administration and Defense; Compulsory Social Security	–	–	–	–	–	–	–	–	–	–	–	–	–	–	–	–	–	–	–	–

continued on next page

Importing Countries continued

Part 1

q1.14.2: From which countries did you import goods/materials last year (2019)?

Item / Location	People's Republic of China		Japan		Republic of Korea		Other Asian countries		United States		Europe		Latin America		Middle East and North Africa		Other Regions		Don't Know	
	No.	%	No.	%	No.	%	No.	%	No.	%	No.	%	No.	%	No.	%	No.	%	No.	%
Item																				
Education	–	–	–	–	–	–	–	–	–	–	–	–	–	–	–	–	–	–	–	–
Human Health and Social Work Activities	–	–	–	–	–	–	–	–	–	–	–	–	–	–	–	–	–	–	–	–
Arts, Entertainment, and Recreation	5	2.0	–	–	–	–	1	0.7	3	3.3	3	3.3	1	14.3	–	–	–	–	1	3.1
Other Service Activities	14	5.7	3	4.8	3	4.4	11	7.8	8	8.9	8	8.9	–	–	–	–	4	16.7	4	12.5
Total	245	100.0	63	100.0	69	100.0	141	100.0	90	100.0	90	100.0	7	100.0	11	100.0	24	100.0	32	100.0
Location																				
National Capital Region	153	62.5	29	46.0	40	58.0	91	64.5	70	77.8	65	70.7	6	85.7	9	81.8	18	75.0	13	40.6
Cordillera Administrative Region	–	–	–	–	–	–	1	0.7	–	–	–	–	–	–	–	–	–	–	–	–
Region 1: Ilocos	–	–	–	–	–	–	–	–	–	–	–	–	–	–	–	–	–	–	1	3.1
Region 2: Cagayan Valley	2	0.8	–	–	–	–	–	–	–	–	–	–	–	–	–	–	–	–	–	–
Region 3: Central Luzon	23	9.4	4	6.4	10	14.5	12	8.5	3	3.3	8	8.7	–	–	1	9.1	1	4.2	3	9.4
Region 4A: Calabarzon	43	17.6	20	31.8	11	15.9	24	17.0	9	10.0	11	12.0	1	14.3	–	–	2	8.3	5	15.6
MIMAROPA	–	–	–	–	–	–	–	–	–	–	–	–	–	–	–	–	–	–	2	6.3
Region 5: Bicol	1	0.4	–	–	–	–	2	1.4	–	–	–	–	–	–	–	–	–	–	–	–
Region 6: Western Visayas	4	1.6	1	1.6	1	1.5	2	1.4	1	1.1	1	1.1	–	–	–	–	–	–	–	–
Region 7: Central Visayas	10	4.1	5	7.9	2	2.9	5	3.6	4	4.4	5	5.4	–	–	1	9.1	1	4.2	4	12.5
Region 8: Eastern Visayas	1	0.4	1	1.6	2	2.9	–	–	1	1.1	1	1.1	–	–	–	–	–	–	1	3.1
Region 9: Zamboanga Peninsula	3	1.2	–	–	–	–	–	–	1	1.1	–	–	–	–	–	–	–	–	–	–
Region 10: Northern Mindanao	1	0.4	–	–	1	1.5	2	1.4	1	1.1	–	–	–	–	–	–	–	–	3	9.4
Region 11: Davao	4	1.6	3	4.8	2	2.9	2	1.4	–	–	1	1.1	–	–	–	–	2	8.3	–	–
Region 12: SOCCSKSARGEN	–	–	–	–	–	–	–	–	–	–	–	–	–	–	–	–	–	–	–	–
Region 13: Caraga	–	–	–	–	–	–	–	–	–	–	–	–	–	–	–	–	–	–	–	–
BARMM (formerly ARMM)	–	–	–	–	–	–	–	–	–	–	–	–	–	–	–	–	–	–	–	–
Total	245	100.0	63	100.0	69	100.0	141	100.0	90	100.0	92	100.0	7	100.0	11	100.0	24	100.0	32	100.0

– = no number; BARMM = Bangsamoro Autonomous Region in Muslim Mindanao; MIMAROPA = Mindoro, Marinduque, Romblon, and Palawan (Southwestern Tagalog Region); SOCCSKSARGEN = South Cotabato, Cotabato, Sultan Kudarat, Sarangani, and General Santos.

Source: Asian Development Bank, Philippine Enterprise Survey.

Cost of Supplies

Part 1

q1.14.3: What has happened to the cost of supplies from abroad after the COVID-19 outbreak (15 March 2020)?

Item	Rather, cost decreased			No change			1%–5% increase			6%–10% increase			More than 10% increase			Total		
	No.	%*	%**	No.	%*	%**	No.	%*	%**	No.	%*	%**	No.	%*	%**	No.	%*	%**
Firm size																		
Micro	20.0	33.3	14.6	55.0	34.2	40.1	15.0	30.6	10.9	16.0	25.4	11.7	31.0	41.3	22.6	137.0	33.6	100.0
Small	20.0	33.3	15.5	46.0	28.6	35.7	20.0	40.8	15.5	19.0	30.2	14.7	24.0	32.0	18.6	129.0	31.6	100.0
Medium-sized	10.0	16.7	11.2	40.0	24.8	44.9	9.0	18.4	10.1	18.0	28.6	20.2	12.0	16.0	13.5	89.0	21.8	100.0
Large	10.0	16.7	18.9	20.0	12.4	37.7	5.0	10.2	9.4	10.0	15.9	18.9	8.0	10.7	15.1	53.0	13.0	100.0
Total	60.0	100.0	14.7	161.0	100.0	39.5	49.0	100.0	12.0	63.0	100.0	15.4	75.0	100.0	18.4	408.0	100.0	100.0
Sector																		
Agriculture, Forestry, and Fishing	–	–	–	3.0	1.9	60.0	–	–	–	1.0	1.6	20.0	1.0	1.3	20.0	5.0	1.2	100.0
Manufacturing	11.0	18.3	12.2	37.0	23.0	41.1	12.0	24.5	13.3	14.0	22.2	15.6	16.0	21.3	17.8	90.0	22.1	100.0
Electricity, Gas, Steam, and Air Conditioning Supply	–	–	–	2.0	1.2	40.0	1.0	2.0	20.0	1.0	1.6	20.0	1.0	1.3	20.0	5.0	1.2	100.0
Water Supply, Sewerage, Waste Management and Remediation Activities	–	–	–	2.0	1.2	100.0	–	–	–	–	–	–	–	–	–	2.0	0.5	100.0
Construction	3.0	5.0	15.0	8.0	5.0	40.0	2.0	4.1	10.0	4.0	6.4	20.0	3.0	4.0	15.0	20.0	4.9	100.0
Wholesale and Retail Trade; Repair of Motor Vehicles and Motorcycles	19.0	31.7	11.0	68.0	42.2	39.5	26.0	53.1	15.1	24.0	38.1	14.0	35.0	46.7	20.3	172.0	42.2	100.0
Transportation and storage	5.0	8.3	38.5	2.0	1.2	15.4	1.0	2.0	7.7	4.0	6.4	30.8	1.0	1.3	7.7	13.0	3.2	100.0
Accommodation and Food Service Activities	10.0	16.7	40.0	6.0	3.7	24.0	1.0	2.0	4.0	4.0	6.4	16.0	4.0	5.3	16.0	25.0	6.1	100.0
Information and Communication	3.0	5.0	12.0	11.0	6.8	44.0	2.0	4.1	8.0	4.0	6.4	16.0	5.0	6.7	20.0	25.0	6.1	100.0
Financial and Insurance Activities	1.0	1.7	100.0	–	–	–	–	–	–	–	–	–	–	–	–	1.0	0.3	100.0
Real Estate Activities	–	–	–	1.0	0.6	100.0	–	–	–	–	–	–	–	–	–	1.0	0.3	100.0
Professional, Scientific, and Technical Activities	–	–	–	4.0	2.5	80.0	–	–	–	–	–	–	1.0	1.3	20.0	5.0	1.2	100.0
Administrative and Support Service Activities	2.0	3.3	100.0	–	–	–	–	–	–	–	–	–	–	–	–	2.0	0.5	100.0
Public Administration and Defense; Compulsory Social Security	–	–	–	–	–	–	–	–	–	–	–	–	–	–	–	–	–	–
Education	–	–	–	–	–	–	–	–	–	–	–	–	–	–	–	–	–	–
Human Health and Social Work Activities	–	–	–	–	–	–	–	–	–	–	–	–	–	–	–	–	–	–
Arts, Entertainment, and Recreation	2.0	3.3	25.0	3.0	1.9	37.5	–	–	–	2.0	3.2	25.0	1.0	1.3	12.5	8.0	2.0	100.0
Other Service Activities	4.0	6.7	11.8	14.0	8.7	41.2	4.0	8.2	11.8	5.0	7.9	14.7	7.0	9.3	20.6	34.0	8.3	100.0
Total	60.0	100.0	14.7	161.0	100.0	39.5	49.0	100.0	12.0	63.0	100.0	15.4	75.0	100.0	18.4	408.0	100.0	100.0

continued on next page

Cost of Supplies continued

Part 1

q1.14.3: What has happened to the cost of supplies from abroad after the COVID-19 outbreak (15 March 2020)?

Item / Location	Rather, cost decreased			No change			1%–5% increase			6%–10% increase			More than 10% increase			Total		
	No.	%*	%**	No.	%*	%**	No.	%*	%**	No.	%*	%**	No.	%*	%**	No.	%*	%**
National Capital Region	32.0	53.3	13.3	103.0	64.0	42.7	24.0	49.0	10.0	38.0	60.3	15.8	44.0	58.7	18.3	241.0	59.1	100.0
Cordillera Administrative Region	–	–	–	–	–	–	–	–	–	–	–	–	1.0	1.3	100.0	1.0	0.3	100.0
Region 1: Ilocos	–	–	–	–	–	–	–	–	–	–	–	–	1.0	1.3	100.0	1.0	0.3	100.0
Region 2: Cagayan Valley	–	–	–	1.0	0.6	50.0	–	–	–	–	–	–	1.0	1.3	50.0	2.0	0.5	100.0
Region 3: Central Luzon	6.0	10.0	15.4	8.0	5.0	20.5	7.0	14.3	17.9	9.0	14.3	23.1	9.0	12.0	23.1	39.0	9.6	100.0
Region 4A: Calabarzon	10.0	16.7	15.2	24.0	14.9	36.4	11.0	22.5	16.7	11.0	17.5	16.7	10.0	13.3	15.2	66.0	16.2	100.0
MIMAROPA	2.0	3.3	100.0	–	–	–	–	–	–	–	–	–	–	–	–	2.0	0.5	100.0
Region 5: Bicol	–	–	–	1.0	0.6	50.0	–	–	–	1.0	1.6	50.0	–	–	–	2.0	0.5	100.0
Region 6: Western Visayas	1.0	1.7	20.0	–	–	–	–	–	–	–	–	–	4.0	5.3	80.0	5.0	1.2	100.0
Region 7: Central Visayas	5.0	8.3	19.2	13.0	8.1	50.0	3.0	6.1	11.5	2.0	3.2	7.7	3.0	4.0	11.5	26.0	6.4	100.0
Region 8: Eastern Visayas	1.0	1.7	25.0	3.0	1.9	75.0	–	–	–	–	–	–	–	–	–	4.0	1.0	100.0
Region 9: Zamboanga Peninsula	–	–	–	2.0	1.2	50.0	2.0	4.1	50.0	–	–	–	–	–	–	4.0	1.0	100.0
Region 10: Northern Mindanao	1.0	1.7	16.7	2.0	1.2	33.3	–	–	–	2.0	3.2	33.3	1.0	1.3	16.7	6.0	1.5	100.0
Region 11: Davao	2.0	3.3	22.2	4.0	2.5	44.4	2.0	4.1	22.2	–	–	–	1.0	1.3	11.1	9.0	2.2	100.0
Region 12: SOCCSKSARGEN	–	–	–	–	–	–	–	–	–	–	–	–	–	–	–	–	–	–
Region 13: Caraga	–	–	–	–	–	–	–	–	–	–	–	–	–	–	–	–	–	–
BARMM (formerly ARMM)	–	–	–	–	–	–	–	–	–	–	–	–	–	–	–	–	–	–
Total	60.0	100.0	14.7	161.0	100.0	39.5	49.0	100.0	12.0	63.0	100.0	15.4	75.0	100.0	18.4	408.0	100.0	100.0

– = no number; BARMM = Bangsamoro Autonomous Region in Muslim Mindanao; MIMAROPA = Mindoro, Marinduque, Romblon, and Palawan (Southwestern Tagalog Region); SOCCSKSARGEN = South Cotabato, Cotabato, Sultan Kudarat, Sarangani, and General Santos.

Note: These correspond only to those who provided responses.

* Share of vertical column. ** Share of horizontal line.

Source: Asian Development Bank, Philippine Enterprise Survey.

Buyers of Products and Services by Sector

Part 1

q.1.14.4: Buyers of your products and services are principally in which sectors?

Item		Individual		Agriculture, forestry and fisheries		Manufacturing – Food and beverages		Manufacturing – Electronics		Manufacturing – Garments		Manufacturing – Other manufacturing activities		Power and energy (e.g., electricity, gas, petrol stations)		Construction		Wholesale and retail trade	
		No.	%	No.	%	No.	%	No.	%	No.	%	No.	%	No.	%	No.	%	No.	%
Firm size	Micro	62	46.6	11	34.4	22	31.0	19	30.7	5	25.0	26	25.5	18	36.7	33	32.0	45	31.5
	Small	42	31.6	7	21.9	19	26.8	12	19.4	5	25.0	29	28.4	17	34.7	37	35.9	49	34.3
	Medium-sized	13	9.8	11	34.4	23	32.4	21	33.9	9	45.0	30	29.4	12	24.5	25	24.3	33	23.1
	Large	16	12.0	3	9.4	7	9.9	10	16.1	1	5.0	17	16.7	2	4.1	8	7.8	16	11.2
	Total	133	100.0	32	100.0	71	100.0	62	100.0	20	100.0	102	100.0	49	100.0	103	100.0	143	100.0
Location	National Capital Region	84	63.2	18	56.3	42	59.2	25	40.3	15	75.0	53	52.0	29	59.2	72	69.9	93	65.0
	Cordillera Administrative Region	1	0.8	–	–	–	–	–	–	–	–	–	–	–	–	–	–	–	–
	Region 1: Ilocos	–	–	–	–	–	–	–	–	–	–	–	–	–	–	1	1.0	–	–
	Region 2: Cagayan Valley	1	0.8	1	3.1	–	–	–	–	–	–	–	–	1	2.0	–	–	1	0.7
	Region 3: Central Luzon	15	11.3	1	3.1	3	4.2	4	6.5	1	5.0	7	6.9	3	6.1	9	8.7	11	7.7
	Region 4A: Calabarzon	13	9.8	5	15.6	19	26.8	26	41.9	4	20.0	33	32.4	11	22.5	10	9.7	17	11.9
	MIMAROPA	1	0.8	–	–	–	–	–	–	–	–	–	–	–	–	–	–	–	–
	Region 5: Bicol	–	–	–	–	1	1.4	–	–	–	–	–	–	–	–	–	–	2	1.4
	Region 6: Western Visayas	2	1.5	–	–	–	–	–	–	–	–	1	1.0	1	2.0	2	1.9	2	1.4
	Region 7: Central Visayas	9	6.8	3	9.4	2	2.8	5	8.1	–	–	6	5.9	1	2.0	6	5.8	10	7.0
	Region 8: Eastern Visayas	1	0.8	–	–	3	4.2	1	1.6	–	–	1	1.0	1	2.0	–	–	1	0.7
	Region 9: Zamboanga Peninsula	1	0.8	1	3.1	–	–	–	–	–	–	–	–	1	2.0	2	1.9	2	1.4
	Region 10: Northern Mindanao	2	1.5	1	3.1	–	–	–	–	–	–	–	–	–	–	1	1.0	2	1.4
	Region 11: Davao	3	2.3	2	6.3	1	1.4	1	1.6	–	–	1	1.0	1	2.0	–	–	2	1.4
	Region 12: SOCCSKSARGEN	–	–	–	–	–	–	–	–	–	–	–	–	–	–	–	–	–	–
	Region 13: Caraga	–	–	–	–	–	–	–	–	–	–	–	–	–	–	–	–	–	–
	BARMM (formerly ARMM)	–	–	–	–	–	–	–	–	–	–	–	–	–	–	–	–	–	–
	Total	133	100.0	32	100.0	71	100.0	62	100.0	20	100.0	102	100.0	49	100.0	103	100.0	143	100.0

continued on next page

Buyers of Products and Services by Sector continued

Part 1

q.1.14.4: Buyers of your products and services are principally in which sectors?

Item		Repair of motor vehicles and motorcycles		Transportation and storage		Tourism and accommodation services		Food service activities		Information and Communication technology – Business process outsourcing		Information and Communication technology – Others		Finance and insurance activities		Real estate activities		Arts, entertainment, and recreation	
		No.	%	No.	%	No.	%	No.	%	No.	%	No.	%	No.	%	No.	%	No.	%
Firm size	Micro	10	50.0	14	38.9	15	31.9	13	28.9	8	28.6	12	40.0	7	38.9	9	29.0	5	26.3
	Small	4	20.0	8	22.2	19	40.4	16	35.6	11	39.3	7	23.3	4	22.2	17	54.8	7	36.8
	Medium-sized	4	20.0	11	30.6	6	12.8	14	31.1	5	17.9	6	20.0	5	27.8	3	9.7	4	21.1
	Large	2	10.0	3	8.3	7	14.9	2	4.4	4	14.3	5	16.7	2	11.1	2	6.5	3	15.8
	Total	20	100.0	36	100.0	47	100.0	45	100.0	28	100.0	30	100.0	18	100.0	31	100.0	19	100.0
Location	National Capital Region	9	45.0	24	66.7	29	61.7	33	73.3	20	71.4	24	80.0	15	83.3	23	74.2	14	73.7
	Cordillera Administrative Region	–	–	–	–	–	–	–	–	–	–	–	–	–	–	–	–	–	–
	Region 1: Ilocos	–	–	–	–	–	–	–	–	–	–	–	–	–	–	–	–	–	–
	Region 2: Cagayan Valley	–	–	–	–	–	–	–	–	–	–	–	–	–	–	–	–	–	–
	Region 3: Central Luzon	4	20.0	4	11.1	4	8.5	2	4.4	1	3.6	3	10.0	–	–	–	–	–	–
	Region 4A: Calabarzon	3	15.0	6	16.7	4	8.5	3	6.7	3	10.7	2	6.7	1	5.6	3	9.7	1	5.3
	MIMAROPA	–	–	–	–	1	2.1	–	–	–	–	–	–	–	–	–	–	–	–
	Region 5: Bicol	–	–	–	–	–	–	1	2.2	–	–	–	–	–	–	–	–	–	–
	Region 6: Western Visayas	–	–	–	–	1	2.1	3	6.7	–	–	–	–	–	–	–	–	–	–
	Region 7: Central Visayas	3	15.0	2	5.6	5	10.6	3	6.7	3	10.7	1	3.3	2	11.1	4	12.9	3	15.8
	Region 8: Eastern Visayas	–	–	–	–	1	2.1	–	–	–	–	–	–	–	–	–	–	–	–
	Region 9: Zamboanga Peninsula	–	–	–	–	–	–	–	–	–	–	–	–	–	–	–	–	–	–
	Region 10: Northern Mindanao	1	5.0	–	–	–	–	–	–	–	–	–	–	–	–	–	–	–	–
	Region 11: Davao	–	–	–	–	2	4.3	–	–	1	3.6	–	–	–	–	1	3.2	1	5.3
	Region 12: SOCCSKSARGEN	–	–	–	–	–	–	–	–	–	–	–	–	–	–	–	–	–	–
	Region 13: Caraga	–	–	–	–	–	–	–	–	–	–	–	–	–	–	–	–	–	–
	BARMM (formerly ARMM)	–	–	–	–	–	–	–	–	–	–	–	–	–	–	–	–	–	–
	Total	20	100.0	36	100.0	47	100.0	45	100.0	28	100.0	30	100.0	18	100.0	31	100.0	19	100.0

– = no number; BARMM = Bangsamoro Autonomous Region in Muslim Mindanao; MIMAROPA = Mindoro, Marinduque, Romblon, and Palawan (Southwestern Tagalog Region); SOCCSKSARGEN = South Cotabato, Cotabato, Sultan Kudarat, Sarangani, and General Santos.

Source: Asian Development Bank, Philippine Enterprise Survey.

Sectors where Enterprises Buy Inputs

Part 1

q.1.14.5: From what sectors do you buy most of your business's inputs?

Item		Agriculture, forestry and fisheries		Manufacturing – Food and beverages		Manufacturing – Electronics		Manufacturing – Garments		Manufacturing – Other manufacturing activities		Power and energy (e.g., electricity, gas, petrol stations)		Construction		Wholesale and retail trade		Repair of motor vehicles and motorcycles	
		No.	%	No.	%	No.	%	No.	%	No.	%	No.	%	No.	%	No.	%	No.	%
Firm size	Micro	6	28.6	18	41.9	19	29.7	8	44.4	46	28.2	9	30.0	18	32.7	59	36.0	6	46.2
	Small	8	38.1	13	30.2	20	31.3	3	16.7	48	29.5	11	36.7	19	34.6	51	31.1	5	38.5
	Medium-sized	5	23.8	8	18.6	19	29.7	6	33.3	49	30.1	7	23.3	11	20.0	31	18.9	1	7.7
	Large	2	9.5	4	9.3	6	9.4	1	5.6	20	12.3	3	10.0	7	12.7	23	14.0	1	7.7
	Total	21	100.0	43	100.0	64	100.0	18	100.0	163	100.0	30	100.0	55	100.0	164	100.0	13	100.0
Location	National Capital Region	13	61.9	19	44.2	34	53.1	9	50.0	88	54.0	16	53.3	33	60.0	108	65.9	7	53.9
	Cordillera Administrative Region	–	–	1	2.3	–	–	–	–	–	–	–	–	–	–	1	0.6	–	–
	Region 1: Ilocos	–	–	–	–	1	1.6	–	–	1	0.6	–	–	1	1.8	–	–	–	–
	Region 2: Cagayan Valley	–	–	–	–	–	–	–	–	1	0.6	–	–	–	–	1	0.6	–	–
	Region 3: Central Luzon	2	9.5	6	14.0	4	6.3	2	11.1	18	11.0	2	6.7	6	10.9	16	9.8	3	23.1
	Region 4A: Calabarzon	2	9.5	8	18.6	15	23.4	3	16.7	34	20.9	10	33.3	8	14.6	21	12.8	1	7.7
	MIMAROPA	–	–	–	–	–	–	–	–	–	–	–	–	–	–	–	–	–	–
	Region 5: Bicol	–	–	1	2.3	–	–	–	–	–	–	–	–	–	–	1	0.6	–	–
	Region 6: Western Visayas	–	–	2	4.7	1	1.6	1	5.6	1	0.6	1	3.3	1	1.8	3	1.8	–	–
	Region 7: Central Visayas	1	4.8	2	4.7	4	6.3	2	11.1	14	8.6	–	–	5	9.1	8	4.9	1	7.7
	Region 8: Eastern Visayas	–	–	2	4.7	1	1.6	–	–	2	1.2	1	3.3	–	–	–	–	–	–
	Region 9: Zamboanga Peninsula	1	4.8	–	–	–	–	–	–	2	1.2	–	–	–	–	2	1.2	–	–
	Region 10: Northern Mindanao	–	–	1	2.3	2	3.1	–	–	1	0.6	–	–	–	–	2	1.2	1	7.7
	Region 11: Davao	2	9.5	1	2.3	2	3.1	1	5.6	1	0.6	–	–	1	1.8	1	0.6	–	–
	Region 12: SOCCSKSARGEN	–	–	–	–	–	–	–	–	–	–	–	–	–	–	–	–	–	–
	Region 13: Caraga	–	–	–	–	–	–	–	–	–	–	–	–	–	–	–	–	–	–
	BARMM (formerly ARMM)	–	–	–	–	–	–	–	–	–	–	–	–	–	–	–	–	–	–
	Total	21	100.0	43	100.0	64	100.0	18	100.0	163	100.0	30	100.0	55	100.0	164	100.0	13	100.0

continued on next page

Sectors where Enterprises Buy Inputs continued

Part 1

q.1.14.5: From what sectors do you buy most of your business's inputs?

Item		Transportation and storage		Tourism and accommodation services		Food service activities		Information and Communication technology – Business process outsourcing		Information and Communication technology – Others		Finance and insurance activities		Real estate activities		Arts, entertainment, and recreation	
		No.	%	No.	%	No.	%	No.	%	No.	%	No.	%	No.	%	No.	%
Firm size	Micro	10	41.7	4	28.6	5	27.8	2	28.6	9	31.0	1	16.7	1	50.0	1	20.0
	Small	8	33.3	5	35.7	7	38.9	5	71.4	11	37.9	2	33.3	–	–	2	40.0
	Medium-sized	5	20.8	4	28.6	4	22.2	–	–	3	10.3	2	33.3	1	50.0	1	20.0
	Large	1	4.2	1	7.1	2	11.1	–	–	6	20.7	1	16.7	–	–	1	20.0
	Total	24	100.0	14	100.0	18	100.0	7	100.0	29	100.0	6	100.0	2	100.0	5	100.0
Location	National Capital Region	17	70.8	7	50.0	10	55.6	5	71.4	21	72.4	5	83.3	2	100.0	4	80.0
	Cordillera Administrative Region	–	–	–	–	–	–	–	–	–	–	–	–	–	–	–	–
	Region 1: Ilocos	–	–	–	–	–	–	–	–	–	–	–	–	–	–	–	–
	Region 2: Cagayan Valley	–	–	–	–	–	–	–	–	–	–	–	–	–	–	–	–
	Region 3: Central Luzon	3	12.5	1	7.1	3	16.7	–	–	3	10.3	–	–	–	–	–	–
	Region 4A: Calabarzon	3	12.5	2	14.3	2	11.1	1	14.3	1	3.5	1	16.7	–	–	–	–
	MIMAROPA	–	–	2	14.3	–	–	–	–	–	–	–	–	–	–	–	–
	Region 5: Bicol	–	–	–	–	–	–	–	–	–	–	–	–	–	–	1	–
	Region 6: Western Visayas	–	–	–	–	1	5.6	–	–	2	6.9	–	–	–	–	–	–
	Region 7: Central Visayas	1	4.2	1	7.1	1	5.6	1	14.3	1	3.5	–	–	–	–	–	–
	Region 8: Eastern Visayas	–	–	–	–	–	–	–	–	–	–	–	–	–	–	–	–
	Region 9: Zamboanga Peninsula	–	–	–	–	–	–	–	–	–	–	–	–	–	–	–	–
	Region 10: Northern Mindanao	–	–	–	–	1	5.6	–	–	1	3.5	–	–	–	–	–	–
	Region 11: Davao	–	–	1	7.1	–	–	–	–	–	–	–	–	–	–	1	20.0
	Region 12: SOCCSKSARGEN	–	–	–	–	–	–	–	–	–	–	–	–	–	–	–	–
	Region 13: Caraga	–	–	–	–	–	–	–	–	–	–	–	–	–	–	–	–
	BARMM (formerly ARMM)	–	–	–	–	–	–	–	–	–	–	–	–	–	–	–	–
	Total	24	100.0	14	100.0	18	100.0	7	100.0	29	100.0	6	100.0	2	100.0	5	100.0

– = no number; BARMM = Bangsamoro Autonomous Region in Muslim Mindanao; MIMAROPA = Mindoro, Marinduque, Romblon, and Palawan (Southwestern Tagalog Region); SOCCSKSARGEN = South Cotabato, Cotabato, Sultan Kudarat, Sarangani, and General Santos.

Source: Asian Development Bank, Philippine Enterprise Survey.

Location of Domestic Input/Raw Material Suppliers

Part 1

q1.14.6: Where is the location of your domestic input/raw material supplier?

Item		Within the same municipality			In a different municipality/region, easily substitutable			In a different municipality/region, not easily substitutable			Not Applicable, only use import inputs			Total		
		No.	%*	%**	No.	%*	%**	No.	%*	%**	No.	%*	%***	No.	%*	%**
Firm size	Micro	30	36.1	21.9	41	33.3	29.9	20	25.0	14.6	46	38.3	33.6	137	33.7	100.0
	Small	31	37.4	24.2	35	28.5	27.3	30	37.5	23.4	32	26.7	25.0	128	31.5	100.0
	Medium-sized	15	18.1	17.0	30	24.4	34.1	18	22.5	20.5	25	20.8	28.4	88	21.7	100.0
	Large	7	8.4	13.2	17	13.8	32.1	12	15.0	22.6	17	14.2	32.1	53	13.1	100.0
	Total	83	100.0	20.4	123	100.0	30.3	80	100.0	19.7	120	100.0	29.6	406	100.0	100.0
Industry	Agriculture, Forestry, and Fishing	2	2.4	40.0	1	0.8	20.0	1	1.3	20.0	1	0.8	20.0	5	1.2	100.0
	Manufacturing	14	16.9	15.7	35	28.5	39.3	20	25.0	22.5	20	16.7	22.5	89	21.9	100.0
	Electricity, Gas, Steam, and Air Conditioning Supply	1	1.2	20.0	2	1.6	40.0	1	1.3	20.0	1	0.8	20.0	5	1.2	100.0
	Water Supply, Sewerage, Waste Management, and Remediation Activities	–	–	–	–	–	–	–	–	–	2	1.7	100.0	2	0.5	100.0
	Construction	7	8.4	35.0	11	8.9	55.0	–	–	–	2	1.7	10.0	20	4.9	100.0
	Wholesale and Retail Trade; Repair of Motor Vehicles and Motorcycles	31	37.4	18.0	41	33.3	23.8	33	41.3	19.2	67	55.8	39.0	172	42.4	100.0
	Transportation and storage	3	3.6	23.1	2	1.6	15.4	3	3.8	23.1	5	4.2	38.5	13	3.2	100.0
	Accommodation and Food Service Activities	8	9.6	33.3	9	7.3	37.5	6	7.5	25.0	1	0.8	4.2	24	5.9	100.0
	Information and Communication	3	3.6	12.0	7	5.7	28.0	5	6.3	20.0	10	8.3	40.0	25	6.2	100.0
	Financial and Insurance Activities	–	–	–	1	0.8	100.0	–	–	–	–	–	–	1	0.3	100.0
	Real Estate Activities	–	–	–	1	0.8	100.0	–	–	–	–	–	–	1	0.3	100.0
	Professional, Scientific, and Technical Activities	2	2.4	40.0	1	0.8	20.0	–	–	–	2	1.7	40.0	5	1.2	100.0
	Administrative and Support Service Activities	–	–	–	1	0.8	50.0	–	–	–	1	0.8	50.0	2	0.5	100.0
	Public Administration and Defense; Compulsory Social Security	–	–	–	–	–	–	–	–	–	–	–	–	–	–	–
	Education	–	–	–	–	–	–	–	–	–	–	–	–	–	–	–
	Human Health and Social Work Activities	–	–	–	–	–	–	–	–	–	–	–	–	–	–	–
	Arts, Entertainment, and Recreation	5	6.0	62.5	2	1.6	25.0	1	1.3	12.5	–	–	–	8	2.0	100.0
	Other Service Activities	7	8.4	20.6	9	7.3	26.5	10	12.5	29.4	8	6.7	23.5	34	8.4	100.0
	Total	83	100.0	20.4	123	100.0	30.3	80	100.0	19.7	120	100.0	29.6	406	100.0	100.0
Location	National Capital Region	54	65.1	22.5	64	52.0	26.7	43	53.8	17.9	79	65.8	32.9	240	59.1	100.0
	Cordillera Administrative Region	–	–	–	–	–	–	1	1.3	100.0	–	–	–	1	0.3	100.0
	Region 1: Ilocos	–	–	–	–	–	–	1	1.3	100.0	–	–	–	1	0.3	100.0
	Region 2: Cagayan Valley	1	1.2	50.0	–	–	–	–	–	–	1	0.8	50.0	2	0.5	100.0
	Region 3: Central Luzon	9	10.8	23.1	10	8.1	25.6	6	7.5	15.4	14	11.7	35.9	39	9.6	100.0
	Region 4A: Calabarzon	6	7.2	9.1	32	26.0	48.5	18	22.5	27.3	10	8.3	15.2	66	16.3	100.0
	MIMAROPA	1	1.2	50.0	1	0.8	50.0	–	–	–	–	–	–	2	0.5	100.0
	Region 5: Bicol	–	–	–	1	0.8	50.0	–	–	–	1	0.8	50.0	2	0.5	100.0
	Region 6: Western Visayas	3	3.6	60.0	–	–	–	1	1.3	20.0	1	0.8	20.0	5	1.2	100.0
	Region 7: Central Visayas	2	2.4	8.0	10	8.1	40.0	6	7.5	24.0	7	5.8	28.0	25	6.2	100.0
	Region 8: Eastern Visayas	–	–	–	2	1.6	50.0	–	–	–	2	1.7	50.0	4	1.0	100.0
	Region 9: Zamboanga Peninsula	–	–	–	2	1.6	50.0	2	2.5	50.0	–	–	–	4	1.0	100.0
	Region 10: Northern Mindanao	2	2.4	33.3	–	–	–	–	–	–	4	3.3	66.7	6	1.5	100.0
	Region 11: Davao	5	6.0	55.6	1	0.8	11.1	2	2.5	22.2	1	0.8	11.1	9	2.2	100.0
	Region 12: SOCCSKSARGEN	–	–	–	–	–	–	–	–	–	–	–	–	–	–	–
	Region 13: Caraga	–	–	–	–	–	–	–	–	–	–	–	–	–	–	–
	BARMM (formerly ARMM)	–	–	–	–	–	–	–	–	–	–	–	–	–	–	–
	Total	83	100.0	20.4	123	100.0	30.3	80	100.0	19.7	120	100.0	29.6	406	100.0	100.0

– = no number; BARMM = Bangsamoro Autonomous Region in Muslim Mindanao; MIMAROPA = Mindoro, Marinduque, Romblon, and Palawan (Southwestern Tagalog Region); SOCCSKSARGEN = South Cotabato, Cotabato, Sultan Kudarat, Sarangani, and General Santos.

Note: These correspond only to those who provided responses.

* Share of vertical column. ** Share of horizontal line.

Part 2: COVID-19 Impact on Business
Business Conditions after the ECQ Implemented

Part 2

q2.1: What is the status of your business after the Enhanced Community Quarantine (ECQ) (15 March 2020)?

Item		Open			Open but limited operations			Temporarily closed			Permanently closed (will not reopen)			Total		
		No.	%*	%**	No.	%*	%**	No.	%*	%**	No.	%*	%**	No.	%*	%**
Firm size	Micro	43	43.9	3.3	311	43.1	24.1	917	56.1	71.2	17	63.0	1.3	1,288	51.9	100.0
	Small	25	25.5	3.7	220	30.5	32.5	427	26.1	63.2	4	14.8	0.6	676	27.3	100.0
	Medium-sized	17	17.4	5.1	120	16.6	36.3	190	11.6	57.4	4	14.8	1.2	331	13.3	100.0
	Large	13	13.3	7.0	71	9.8	38.2	100	6.1	53.8	2	7.4	1.1	186	7.5	100.0
	Total	98	100.0	4.0	722	100.0	29.1	1,634	100.0	65.9	27	100.0	1.1	2,481	100.0	100.0
Industry	Agriculture, Forestry, and Fishing	–	–	–	10	1.4	55.6	8	0.5	44.4	–	–	–	18	0.7	100.0
	Manufacturing	12	12.2	4.6	68	9.4	26.1	180	11.0	69.0	1	3.7	0.4	261	10.5	100.0
	Electricity, Gas, Steam, and Air Conditioning Supply	3	3.1	10.3	16	2.2	55.2	10	0.6	34.5	–	–	–	29	1.2	100.0
	Water Supply, Sewerage, Waste Management, and Remediation Activities	1	1.0	20.0	3	0.4	60.0	1	0.1	20.0	–	–	–	5	0.2	100.0
	Construction	15	15.3	7.0	35	4.9	16.4	162	9.9	75.7	2	7.4	0.9	214	8.6	100.0
	Wholesale and Retail Trade; Repair of Motor Vehicles and Motorcycles	16	16.3	3.0	155	21.5	29.0	356	21.8	66.7	7	25.9	1.3	534	21.5	100.0
	Transportation and storage	3	3.1	3.7	40	5.5	48.8	39	2.4	47.6	–	–	–	82	3.3	100.0
	Accommodation and Food Service Activities	5	5.1	1.4	69	9.6	19.4	276	16.9	77.5	6	22.2	1.7	356	14.4	100.0
	Information and Communication	16	16.3	8.5	83	11.5	43.9	87	5.3	46.0	3	11.1	1.6	189	7.6	100.0
	Financial and Insurance Activities	6	6.1	5.5	33	4.6	30.3	69	4.2	63.3	1	3.7	0.9	109	4.4	100.0
	Real Estate Activities	6	6.1	8.0	21	2.9	28.0	47	2.9	62.7	1	3.7	1.3	75	3.0	100.0
	Professional, Scientific, and Technical Activities	6	6.1	6.2	35	4.9	36.1	56	3.4	57.7	–	–	–	97	3.9	100.0
	Administrative and Support Service Activities	2	2.0	3.8	22	3.1	41.5	28	1.7	52.8	1	3.7	1.9	53	2.1	100.0
	Public Administration and Defense; Compulsory Social Security	–	–	–	1	0.1	100.0	–	–	–	–	–	–	1	0.0	100.0
	Education	–	–	–	7	1.0	22.6	23	1.4	74.2	1	3.2	3.2	31	1.3	100.0
	Human Health and Social Work Activities	–	–	–	5	0.7	33.3	9	0.6	60.0	1	6.7	6.7	15	0.6	100.0
	Arts, Entertainment, and Recreation	–	–	–	13	1.8	22.8	43	2.6	75.4	1	3.7	1.8	57	2.3	100.0
	Other Service Activities	7	7.1	2.0	106	14.7	29.9	240	14.7	67.6	2	7.4	0.6	355	14.3	100.0
	Total	98	100.0	4.0	722	100.0	29.1	1,634	100.0	65.9	27	100.0	1.1	2,481	100.0	100.0
Location	National Capital Region	60	61.2	4.9	343	47.5	27.9	816	49.9	66.3	12	44.4	1.0	1,231	49.6	100.0
	Cordillera Administrative Region	–	–	–	7	1.0	30.4	15	0.9	65.2	1	3.7	4.3	23	0.9	100.0
	Region 1: Ilocos	1	1.0	3.8	8	1.1	30.8	17	1.0	65.4	–	–	–	26	1.1	100.0
	Region 2: Cagayan Valley	–	–	–	6	0.8	26.1	15	0.9	65.2	2	7.4	8.7	23	0.9	100.0
	Region 3: Central Luzon	10	10.2	4.3	57	7.9	24.8	159	9.7	69.1	4	14.8	1.7	230	9.3	100.0
	Region 4A: Calabarzon	15	15.3	4.3	97	13.4	28.0	233	14.3	67.1	2	7.4	0.6	347	14.0	100.0
	MIMAROPA	1	1.0	2.2	10	1.4	21.7	35	2.1	76.1	–	–	–	46	1.9	100.0
	Region 5: Bicol	–	–	–	14	1.9	27.5	35	2.1	68.6	2	7.4	3.9	51	2.1	100.0
	Region 6: Western Visayas	2	2.0	2.0	35	4.9	35.0	63	3.9	63.0	–	–	–	100	4.0	100.0
	Region 7: Central Visayas	7	7.1	3.8	58	8.0	31.4	118	7.2	63.8	2	7.4	1.1	185	7.5	100.0
	Region 8: Eastern Visayas	1	1.0	4.0	14	1.9	56.0	9	0.6	36.0	1	3.7	4.0	25	1.0	100.0
	Region 9: Zamboanga Peninsula	–	–	–	9	1.3	45.0	11	0.7	55.0	–	–	–	20	0.8	100.0
	Region 10: Northern Mindanao	–	–	–	18	2.5	37.5	30	1.8	62.5	–	–	–	48	1.9	100.0
	Region 11: Davao	1	1.0	1.2	26	3.6	30.6	57	3.5	67.1	1	3.7	1.2	85	3.4	100.0
	Region 12: SOCCSKSARGEN	–	–	–	9	1.3	45.0	11	0.7	55.0	–	–	–	20	0.8	100.0
	Region 13: Caraga	–	–	–	11	1.5	55.0	9	0.6	45.0	–	–	–	20	0.8	100.0
	BARMM (formerly ARMM)	–	–	–	–	–	–	1	0.1	100.0	–	–	–	1	0.0	100.0
	Total	98	100.0	4.0	722	100.0	29.1	1,634	100.0	65.9	27	100.0	1.1	2,481	100.0	100.0

– = no number; BARMM = Bangsamoro Autonomous Region in Muslim Mindanao; COVID-19 = coronavirus disease; MIMAROPA = Mindoro, Marinduque, Romblon, and Palawan (Southwestern Tagalog Region); SOCCSKSARGEN = South Cotabato, Cotabato, Sultan Kudarat, Sarangani, and General Santos.

* Share of vertical column. ** Share of horizontal line.

Source: Asian Development Bank, Philippine Enterprise Survey.

Status of Business Operation after the ECQ Implemented

		Part 2														
		q2.1.1: If you have faced limited operations, what is the status?														
		Less than 25% operational			25%-50% operational			51%-75% operational			More than 75% operational			Total		
Item		No.	%*	%**	No.	%*	%**	No.	%*	%**	No.	%*	%**	No.	%*	%**
Firm size	Micro	116	45.1	37.3	132	42.7	42.4	50	41.0	16.1	13	38.2	4.2	311	43.1	100.0
	Small	67	26.1	30.5	104	33.7	47.3	38	31.2	17.3	11	32.4	5.0	220	30.5	100.0
	Medium-sized	47	18.3	39.2	44	14.2	36.7	24	19.7	20.0	5	14.7	4.2	120	16.6	100.0
	Large	27	10.5	38.0	29	9.4	40.8	10	8.2	14.1	5	14.7	7.0	71	9.8	100.0
	Total	257	100.0	35.6	309	100.0	42.8	122	100.0	16.9	34	100.0	4.7	722	100.0	100.0
Industry	Agriculture, Forestry, and Fishing	3	1.2	30.0	5	1.6	50.0	1	0.8	10.0	1	2.9	10.0	10	1.4	100.0
	Manufacturing	26	10.1	38.2	35	11.3	51.5	7	5.7	10.3	–	–	–	68	9.4	100.0
	Electricity, Gas, Steam, and Air Conditioning Supply	7	2.7	43.8	7	2.3	43.8	2	1.6	12.5	–	–	–	16	2.2	100.0
	Water Supply, Sewerage, Waste Management, and Remediation Activities	1	0.4	33.3	–	–	–	2	1.6	66.7	–	–	–	3	0.4	100.0
	Construction	17	6.6	48.6	15	4.9	42.9	2	1.6	5.7	1	2.9	2.9	35	4.9	100.0
	Wholesale and Retail Trade; Repair of Motor Vehicles and Motorcycles	66	25.7	42.6	58	18.8	37.4	27	22.1	17.4	4	11.8	2.6	155	21.5	100.0
	Transportation and storage	12	4.7	30.0	22	7.1	55.0	3	2.5	7.5	3	8.8	7.5	40	5.5	100.0
	Accommodation and Food Service Activities	31	12.1	44.9	31	10.0	44.9	6	4.9	8.7	1	2.9	1.4	69	9.6	100.0
	Information and Communication	18	7.0	21.7	35	11.3	42.2	21	17.2	25.3	9	26.5	10.8	83	11.5	100.0
	Financial and Insurance Activities	3	1.2	9.1	19	6.2	57.6	10	8.2	30.3	1	2.9	3.0	33	4.6	100.0
	Real Estate Activities	11	4.3	52.4	6	1.9	28.6	3	2.5	14.3	1	2.9	4.8	21	2.9	100.0
	Professional, Scientific, and Technical Activities	13	5.1	37.1	15	4.9	42.9	5	4.1	14.3	2	5.9	5.7	35	4.9	100.0
	Administrative and Support Service Activities	10	3.9	45.5	7	2.3	31.8	4	3.3	18.2	1	2.9	4.5	22	3.1	100.0
	Public Administration and Defense; Compulsory Social Security	–	–	–	–	–	–	–	–	–	1	100.0	100.0	1	0.1	100.0
	Education	5	2.0	71.4	2	0.7	28.6	–	–	–	–	–	–	7	1.0	100.0
	Human Health and Social Work Activities	1	0.4	20.0	2	0.7	40.0	2	1.6	40.0	–	–	–	5	0.7	100.0
	Arts, Entertainment, and Recreation	5	2.0	38.5	5	1.6	38.5	3	2.5	23.1	–	–	–	13	1.8	100.0
	Other Service Activities	28	10.9	26.4	45	14.6	42.5	24	19.7	22.6	9	26.5	8.5	106	14.7	100.0
	Total	257	100.0	35.6	309	100.0	42.8	122	100.0	16.9	34	100.0	4.7	722	100.0	100.0
Location	National Capital Region	131	51.0	38.2	118	38.2	34.4	71	58.2	20.7	23	67.7	6.7	343	47.5	100.0
	Cordillera Administrative Region	2	0.8	28.6	4	1.3	57.1	1	0.8	14.3	–	–	–	7	1.0	100.0
	Region 1: Ilocos	1	0.4	12.5	4	1.3	50.0	2	1.6	25.0	1	2.9	12.5	8	1.1	100.0
	Region 2: Cagayan Valley	1	0.4	16.7	4	1.3	66.7	1	0.8	16.7	–	–	–	6	0.8	100.0
	Region 3: Central Luzon	17	6.6	29.8	27	8.7	47.4	11	9.0	19.3	2	5.9	3.5	57	7.9	100.0
	Region 4A: Calabarzon	39	15.2	40.2	48	15.5	49.5	8	6.6	8.2	2	5.9	2.1	97	13.4	100.0
	MIMAROPA	5	2.0	50.0	4	1.3	40.0	1	0.8	10.0	–	–	–	10	1.4	100.0
	Region 5: Bicol	5	2.0	35.7	6	1.9	42.9	3	2.5	21.4	–	–	–	14	1.9	100.0
	Region 6: Western Visayas	10	3.9	28.6	22	7.1	62.9	2	1.6	5.7	1	2.9	2.9	35	4.9	100.0
	Region 7: Central Visayas	20	7.8	34.5	29	9.4	50.0	7	5.7	12.1	2	5.9	3.4	58	8.0	100.0
	Region 8: Eastern Visayas	5	2.0	35.7	6	1.9	42.9	2	1.6	14.3	1	2.9	7.1	14	1.9	100.0
	Region 9: Zamboanga Peninsula	2	0.8	22.2	3	1.0	33.3	3	2.5	33.3	1	2.9	11.1	9	1.3	100.0
	Region 10: Northern Mindanao	4	1.6	22.2	12	3.9	66.7	2	1.6	11.1	–	–	–	18	2.5	100.0
	Region 11: Davao	8	3.1	30.8	15	4.9	57.7	2	1.6	7.7	1	2.9	3.8	26	3.6	100.0
	Region 12: SOCCSKSARGEN	2	0.8	22.2	3	1.0	33.3	4	3.3	44.4	–	–	–	9	1.3	100.0
	Region 13: Caraga	5	2.0	45.5	4	1.3	36.4	2	1.6	18.2	–	–	–	11	1.5	100.0
	BARMM (formerly ARMM)	–	–	–	–	–	–	–	–	–	–	–	–	–	–	–
	Total	257	100.0		309	100.0		122	100.0		34	100.0		722	100.0	100.0

– = no number; BARMM = Bangsamoro Autonomous Region in Muslim Mindanao; ECQ = Enhanced Community Quarantine; MIMAROPA = Mindoro, Marinduque, Romblon, and Palawan (Southwestern Tagalog Region); SOCCSKSARGEN = South Cotabato, Cotabato, Sultan Kudarat, Sarangani, and General Santos.

Note: These correspond only to those who provided responses.

* Share of vertical column. ** Share of horizontal line.

Source: Asian Development Bank, Philippine Enterprise Survey.

Time Frame on Business Recovery

Part 2

q2.2: What is the expected timeframe on your business recovery from the end of the Enhanced Community Quarantine?

Item		Within 2 weeks			1 month			1 to 3 months			More than 3 months			Unable to judge			Total		
		No.	%*	%**	No.	%*	%**	No.	%*	%**	No.	%*	%**	No.	%*	%**	No.	%*	%**
Firm size	Micro	23	52.3	1.8	27	50.0	2.1	176	48.5	13.7	396	53.4	30.8	664	52.0	51.6	1,286	51.9	100.0
	Small	15	34.1	2.2	14	25.9	2.1	102	28.1	15.1	195	26.3	28.8	350	27.4	51.8	676	27.3	100.0
	Medium-sized	4	9.1	1.2	5	9.3	1.5	56	15.4	16.9	98	13.2	29.6	168	13.2	50.8	331	13.4	100.0
	Large	2	4.6	1.1	8	14.8	4.3	29	8.0	15.6	53	7.1	28.5	94	7.4	50.5	186	7.5	100.0
	Total	44	100.0	1.8	54	100.0	2.2	363	100.0	14.6	742	100.0	29.9	1,276	100.0	51.5	2,479	100.0	100.0
Industry	Agriculture, Forestry, and Fishing	–	–	–	–	–	–	3	0.8	16.7	8	1.1	44.4	7	0.6	38.9	18	0.7	100.0
	Manufacturing	4	9.1	1.5	2	3.7	0.8	48	13.2	18.4	68	9.2	26.1	139	10.9	53.3	261	10.5	100.0
	Electricity, Gas, Steam, and Air Conditioning Supply	–	–	–	–	–	–	4	1.1	13.8	12	1.6	41.4	13	1.0	44.8	29	1.2	100.0
	Water Supply, Sewerage, Waste Management, and Remediation Activities	–	–	–	–	–	–	–	–	–	2	0.3	40.0	3	0.2	60.0	5	0.2	100.0
	Construction	5	11.4	2.3	5	9.3	2.3	42	11.6	19.6	64	8.6	29.9	98	7.7	45.8	214	8.6	100.0
	Wholesale and Retail Trade; Repair of Motor Vehicles and Motorcycles	5	11.4	0.9	13	24.1	2.4	78	21.5	14.6	154	20.8	28.8	284	22.3	53.2	534	21.5	100.0
	Transportation and storage	2	4.6	2.5	1	1.9	1.2	16	4.4	19.8	26	3.5	32.1	36	2.8	44.4	81	3.3	100.0
	Accommodation and Food Service Activities	5	11.4	1.4	7	13.0	2.0	30	8.3	8.4	102	13.8	28.7	212	16.6	59.6	356	14.4	100.0
	Information and Communication	5	11.4	2.6	4	7.4	2.1	35	9.6	18.5	52	7.0	27.5	93	7.3	49.2	189	7.6	100.0
	Financial and Insurance Activities	2	4.6	1.8	2	3.7	1.8	13	3.6	11.9	43	5.8	39.4	49	3.8	45.0	109	4.4	100.0
	Real Estate Activities	3	6.8	4.0	4	7.4	5.3	16	4.4	21.3	20	2.7	26.7	32	2.5	42.7	75	3.0	100.0
	Professional, Scientific, and Technical Activities	2	4.6	2.1	7	13.0	7.2	13	3.6	13.4	25	3.4	25.8	50	3.9	51.5	97	3.9	100.0
	Administrative and Support Service Activities	2	4.6	3.8	1	1.9	1.9	9	2.5	17.0	21	2.8	39.6	20	1.6	37.7	53	2.1	100.0
	Public Administration and Defense; Compulsory Social Security	–	–	–	–	–	–	–	–	–	–	–	–	1	0.1	100.0	1	0.0	100.0
	Education	–	–	–	–	–	–	2	0.6	6.5	7	0.9	22.6	22	1.7	71.0	31	1.3	100.0
	Human Health and Social Work Activities	–	–	–	–	–	–	2	0.6	13.3	3	0.4	20.0	10	0.8	66.7	15	0.6	100.0
	Arts, Entertainment, and Recreation	1	2.3	1.8	–	–	–	3	0.8	5.3	18	2.4	31.6	35	2.7	61.4	57	2.3	100.0
	Other Service Activities	8	18.2	2.3	8	14.8	2.3	49	13.5	13.8	117	15.8	33.1	172	13.5	48.6	354	14.3	100.0
	Total	44	100.0	1.8	54	100.0	2.2	363	100.0	14.6	742	100.0	29.9	1,276	100.0	51.5	2,479	100.0	100.0

continued on next page

Time Frame on Business Recovery continued

Part 2

q2.2: What is the expected timeframe on your business recovery from the end of the Enhanced Community Quarantine?

Item	Location	Within 2 weeks			1 month			1 to 3 months			More than 3 months			Unable to judge			Total		
		No.	%*	%**	No.	%*	%**	No.	%*	%**	No.	%*	%**	No.	%*	%**	No.	%*	%**
Location	National Capital Region	23	52.3	1.9	24	44.4	2.0	190	52.3	15.5	361	48.7	29.4	631	49.5	51.3	1,229	49.6	100.0
	Cordillera Administrative Region	1	2.3	4.3	–	–	–	3	0.8	13.0	10	1.4	43.5	9	0.7	39.1	23	0.9	100.0
	Region 1: Ilocos	1	2.3	3.8	2	3.7	7.7	3	0.8	11.5	7	0.9	26.9	13	1.0	50.0	26	1.1	100.0
	Region 2: Cagayan Valley	–	–	–	–	–	–	5	1.4	21.7	5	0.7	21.7	13	1.0	56.5	23	0.9	100.0
	Region 3: Central Luzon	6	13.6	2.6	10	18.5	4.3	35	9.6	15.2	69	9.3	30.0	110	8.6	47.8	230	9.3	100.0
	Region 4A: Calabarzon	6	13.6	1.7	6	11.1	1.7	52	14.3	15.0	115	15.5	33.1	168	13.2	48.4	347	14.0	100.0
	MIMAROPA	–	–	–	2	3.7	4.3	5	1.4	10.9	15	2.0	32.6	24	1.9	52.2	46	1.9	100.0
	Region 5: Bicol	1	2.3	2.0	–	–	–	7	1.9	13.7	19	2.6	37.3	24	1.9	47.1	51	2.1	100.0
	Region 6: Western Visayas	3	6.8	3.0	1	1.9	1.0	12	3.3	12.0	37	5.0	37.0	47	3.7	47.0	100	4.0	100.0
	Region 7: Central Visayas	2	4.6	1.1	6	11.1	3.2	26	7.2	14.1	42	5.7	22.7	109	8.5	58.9	185	7.5	100.0
	Region 8: Eastern Visayas	–	–	–	2	3.7	8.0	4	1.1	16.0	4	0.5	16.0	15	1.2	60.0	25	1.0	100.0
	Region 9: Zamboanga Peninsula	–	–	–	–	–	–	1	0.3	5.0	6	0.8	30.0	13	1.0	65.0	20	0.8	100.0
	Region 10: Northern Mindanao	1	2.3	2.1	–	–	–	9	2.5	18.8	12	1.6	25.0	26	2.0	54.2	48	1.9	100.0
	Region 11: Davao	–	–	–	1	1.9	1.2	5	1.4	5.9	26	3.5	30.6	53	4.2	62.4	85	3.4	100.0
	Region 12: SOCCSKSARGEN	–	–	–	–	–	–	4	1.1	20.0	6	0.8	30.0	10	0.8	50.0	20	0.8	100.0
	Region 13: Caraga	–	–	–	–	–	–	2	0.6	10.0	7	0.9	35.0	11	0.9	55.0	20	0.8	100.0
	BARMM (formerly ARMM)	–	–	–	–	–	–	–	–	–	1	0.1	100.0	–	–	–	1	0.0	100.0
	Total	44	100.0	1.8	54	100.0	2.2	363	100.0	14.6	742	100.0	29.9	1,276	100.0	51.5	2,479	100.0	100.0

– = no number; BARMM = Bangsamoro Autonomous Region in Muslim Mindanao; MIMAROPA = Mindoro, Marinduque, Romblon, and Palawan (Southwestern Tagalog Region); SOCCSKSARGEN = South Cotabato, Cotabato, Sultan Kudarat, Sarangani, and General Santos.

Note: Business recovery means one of the following conditions: return to profitability, return to previous production level, return to previous workforce level.

* Share of vertical column. ** Share of horizontal line.

Source: Asian Development Bank, Philippine Enterprise Survey.

Status of Sales (1)

Part 2

q2.3: What is the status of your sales (value) in April 2020 as compared to March 2020?

Item		Increased			Decreased			Remain the same			Total		
		No.	%*	%***	No.	%*	%***	No.	%*	%***	No.	%*	%**
Firm size	Micro	15	51.7	1.2	987	51.9	76.7	284	51.9	22.1	1,286	51.9	100.0
	Small	5	17.2	0.7	520	27.3	76.9	151	27.6	22.3	676	27.3	100.0
	Medium-sized	6	20.7	1.8	254	13.4	76.7	71	13.0	21.5	331	13.4	100.0
	Large	3	10.3	1.6	142	7.5	76.3	41	7.5	22.0	186	7.5	100.0
	Total	29	100.0	1.2	1,903	100.0	76.8	547	100.0	22.1	2,479	100.0	100.0
Industry	Agriculture, Forestry, and Fishing	–	–	–	15	0.8	83.3	3	0.6	16.7	18	0.7	100.0
	Manufacturing	3	10.3	1.1	207	10.9	79.3	51	9.3	19.5	261	10.5	100.0
	Electricity, Gas, Steam, and Air Conditioning Supply	1	3.5	3.4	23	1.2	79.3	5	0.9	17.2	29	1.2	100.0
	Water Supply, Sewerage, Waste Management, and Remediation Activities	–	–	–	4	0.2	80.0	1	0.2	20.0	5	0.2	100.0
	Construction	2	6.9	0.9	142	7.5	66.4	70	12.8	32.7	214	8.6	100.0
	Wholesale and Retail Trade; Repair of Motor Vehicles and Motorcycles	11	37.9	2.1	426	22.4	79.8	97	17.7	18.2	534	21.5	100.0
	Transportation and storage	–	–	–	65	3.4	80.2	16	2.9	19.8	81	3.3	100.0
	Accommodation and Food Service Activities	1	3.5	0.3	300	15.8	84.3	55	10.1	15.4	356	14.4	100.0
	Information and Communication	5	17.2	2.6	138	7.3	73.0	46	8.4	24.3	189	7.6	100.0
	Financial and Insurance Activities	2	6.9	1.8	72	3.8	66.1	35	6.4	32.1	109	4.4	100.0
	Real Estate Activities	1	3.5	1.3	52	2.7	69.3	22	4.0	29.3	75	3.0	100.0
	Professional, Scientific, and Technical Activities	–	–	–	73	3.8	75.3	24	4.4	24.7	97	3.9	100.0
	Administrative and Support Service Activities	–	–	–	43	2.3	81.1	10	1.8	18.9	53	2.1	100.0
	Public Administration and Defense; Compulsory Social Security	–	–	–	1	0.1	100.0	–	–	–	1	0.0	100.0
	Education	–	–	–	23	1.2	74.2	8	1.5	25.8	31	1.3	100.0
	Human Health and Social Work Activities	–	–	–	10	0.5	66.7	5	0.9	33.3	15	0.6	100.0
	Arts, Entertainment, and Recreation	1	3.5	1.8	40	2.1	70.2	16	2.9	28.1	57	2.3	100.0
	Other Service Activities	2	6.9	0.6	269	14.1	76.0	83	15.2	23.4	354	14.3	100.0
	Total	29	100.0	1.2	1,903	100.0	76.8	547	100.0	22.1	2,479	100.0	100.0
Location	National Capital Region	13	44.8	1.1	923	48.5	75.1	293	53.6	23.8	1,229	49.6	100.0
	Cordillera Administrative Region	–	–	–	20	1.1	87.0	3	0.6	13.0	23	0.9	100.0
	Region 1: Ilocos	1	3.5	3.8	20	1.1	76.9	5	0.9	19.2	26	1.1	100.0
	Region 2: Cagayan Valley	–	–	–	19	1.0	82.6	4	0.7	17.4	23	0.9	100.0
	Region 3: Central Luzon	1	3.5	0.4	185	9.7	80.4	44	8.0	19.1	230	9.3	100.0
	Region 4A: Calabarzon	6	20.7	1.7	242	12.7	69.7	99	18.1	28.5	347	14.0	100.0
	MIMAROPA	–	–	–	41	2.2	89.1	5	0.9	10.9	46	1.9	100.0
	Region 5: Bicol	–	–	–	38	2.0	74.5	13	2.4	25.5	51	2.1	100.0
	Region 6: Western Visayas	3	10.3	3.0	82	4.3	82.0	15	2.7	15.0	100	4.0	100.0
	Region 7: Central Visayas	4	13.8	2.2	152	8.0	82.2	29	5.3	15.7	185	7.5	100.0
	Region 8: Eastern Visayas	1	3.5	4.0	19	1.0	76.0	5	0.9	20.0	25	1.0	100.0
	Region 9: Zamboanga Peninsula	–	–	–	15	0.8	75.0	5	0.9	25.0	20	0.8	100.0
	Region 10: Northern Mindanao	–	–	–	39	2.1	81.3	9	1.7	18.8	48	1.9	100.0
	Region 11: Davao	–	–	–	70	3.7	82.4	15	2.7	17.6	85	3.4	100.0
	Region 12: SOCCSKSARGEN	–	–	–	18	1.0	90.0	2	0.4	10.0	20	0.8	100.0
	Region 13: Caraga	–	–	–	19	1.0	95.0	1	0.2	5.0	20	0.8	100.0
	BARMM (formerly ARMM)	–	–	–	1	0.1	100.0	–	–	–	1	0.0	100.0
	Total	29	100.0	1.2	1,903	100.0	76.8	547	100.0	22.1	2,479	100.0	100.0

– = no number; BARMM = Bangsamoro Autonomous Region in Muslim Mindanao; MIMAROPA = Mindoro, Marinduque, Romblon, and Palawan (Southwestern Tagalog Region); SOCCSKSARGEN = South Cotabato, Cotabato, Sultan Kudarat, Sarangani, and General Santos.

* Share of vertical column. ** Share of horizontal line.

Source: Asian Development Bank, Philippine Enterprise Survey.

Status of Sales (2)

Item		Part2 q2.3.1 and q2.3.2: Sales value increased/decreased by % in April 2020 from March 2020:									
		Sales increased					Sales decreased				
			Range		# of responses			Range		# of responses	
		Average	Min	Max	No.	%	Average	Min	Max	No.	%
Firm size	Micro	20.2	1	100	15	55.6	81.5	0	200	856	51.3
	Small	29.0	5	70	5	18.5	82.0	0	500	460	27.6
	Medium–sized	37.5	10	100	4	14.8	76.4	0	150	227	13.6
	Large	15.0	10	20	3	11.1	74.9	0	100	126	7.5
	Total	23.8	1	100	27	100.0	80.4	0	500	1,669	100.0
Industry	Agriculture, Forestry, and Fishing	–	–	–	–	–	78.0	50	100	12	0.7
	Manufacturing	41.7	10	100	3	11.1	80.7	–	200	180	10.8
	Electricity, Gas, Steam, and Air Conditioning Supply	10.0	10	10	1	3.7	65.5	–	100	22	1.3
	Water Supply, Sewerage, Waste Management, and Remediation Activities	–	–	–	–	–	90.0	80	100	3	0.2
	Construction	15.9	2	30	2	7.4	81.8	–	100	124	7.4
	Wholesale and Retail Trade; Repair of Motor Vehicles and Motorcycles	20.9	5	100	11	40.7	80.8	–	230	375	22.5
	Transportation and storage	–	–	–	–	–	70.3	–	100	51	3.1
	Accommodation and Food Service Activities	5.0	5	5	1	3.7	88.0	–	500	266	15.9
	Information and Communication	30.3	20	56	4	14.8	69.9	–	100	119	7.1
	Financial and Insurance Activities	70.0	70	70	1	3.7	77.5	15	100	59	3.5
	Real Estate Activities	1.0	1	1	1	3.7	75.5	–	100	43	2.6
	Professional, Scientific, and Technical Activities	–	–	–	–	–	74.4	–	100	68	4.1
	Administrative and Support Service Activities	–	–	–	–	–	74.3	–	200	38	2.3
	Public Administration and Defense; Compulsory Social Security	–	–	–	–	–	30.0	30	30	1	0.1
	Education	–	–	–	–	–	84.9	20	100	17	1.0
	Human Health and Social Work Activities	–	–	–	–	–	95.0	75	100	9	0.5
	Arts, Entertainment, and Recreation	10.0	10	10	1	3.7	93.4	50	100	35	2.1
	Other Service Activities	20.0	20	20	2	7.4	81.2	–	100	247	14.8
	Total	23.8	1	100	27	100.0	80.4	–	500	1,669	100.0
Location	National Capital Region	18.1	2	56	12	44.4	81.9	–	300	813	48.7
	Cordillera Administrative Region	–	–	–	–	–	68.6	–	100	18	1.1
	Region 1: Ilocos	20.0	20	20	1	3.7	85.0	50	100	18	1.1
	Region 2: Cagayan Valley	–	–	–	–	–	82.3	25	100	15	0.9
	Region 3: Central Luzon	10.0	10	10	1	3.7	82.0	–	100	157	9.4
	Region 4A: Calabarzon	45.2	1	100	5	18.5	82.2	–	500	215	12.9
	MIMAROPA	–	–	–	–	–	81.9	1	100	37	2.2
	Region 5: Bicol	–	–	–	–	–	84.9	10	100	33	2.0
	Region 6: Western Visayas	28.3	5	70	3	11.1	78.8	–	100	76	4.6
	Region 7: Central Visayas	15.0	5	30	4	14.8	73.7	–	150	135	8.1
	Region 8: Eastern Visayas	25.0	25	25	1	3.7	64.4	5	100	16	1.0
	Region 9: Zamboanga Peninsula	–	–	–	–	–	71.0	–	100	14	0.8
	Region 10: Northern Mindanao	–	–	–	–	–	70.9	15	100	33	2.0
	Region 11: Davao	–	–	–	–	–	79.7	–	100	53	3.2
	Region 12: SOCCSKSARGEN	–	–	–	–	–	81.8	25	150	17	1.0
	Region 13: Caraga	–	–	–	–	–	71.1	25	100	18	1.1
	BARMM (formerly ARMM)	–	–	–	–	–	70.0	70	70	1	0.1
	Total	23.8	1	100	27	100.0	80.4	–	500	1,669	100.0

– = no number; BARMM = Bangsamoro Autonomous Region in Muslim Mindanao; MIMAROPA = Mindoro, Marinduque, Romblon, and Palawan (Southwestern Tagalog Region); SOCCSKSARGEN = South Cotabato, Cotabato, Sultan Kudarat, Sarangani, and General Santos.

Source: Asian Development Bank, Philippine Enterprise Survey.

Full-Time Regular Workers in April 2020

Part 2

q2.4: As of the end of April 2020, how many full-time regular workers were/have been:

Item		Hired				Laid off				Granted leave				Reduced salary/wages/benefit				Reduced working hours			
			Range		# of		Range		# of		Range		# of		Range		# of		Range		# of
		Avg	Min	Max	Resp	Avg	Min	Max	Resp	Avg	Min	Max	Resp	Avg	Min	Max	Resp	Avg	Min	Max	Resp
Firm size	Micro	1.5	–	231	1,272	1.3	–	150	1,272	3.7	–	1,515	1,272	3.8	–	700	1,272	3.7	–	377	1,272
	Small	3.2	–	188	671	2.5	–	280	671	6.8	–	200	671	7.5	–	313	671	9.3	–	600	671
	Medium-sized	3.7	–	156	320	3.4	–	200	320	16.4	–	450	320	9.8	–	445	320	14.6	–	508	320
	Large	7.5	–	353	181	3.1	–	138	181	29.4	–	750	181	15.2	–	512	181	50.6	–	4,355	181
	Total	2.7	–	353	2,444	2.0	–	280	2,444	8.1	–	1,515	2,444	6.4	–	700	2,444	10.1	–	4,355	2,444
Industry	Agriculture, Forestry, and Fishing	1.1	–	16	18	0.4	–	5	18	8.7	–	70	18	4.7	–	65	18	11.1	–	73	18
	Manufacturing	4.2	–	191	254	2.8	–	200	254	12.4	–	320	254	10.3	–	321	254	11.6	–	321	254
	Electricity, Gas, Steam, and Air Conditioning Supply	1.1	–	16	29	0.9	–	10	29	2.2	–	15	29	5.8	–	30	29	3.8	–	16	29
	Water Supply, Sewerage, Waste Management, and Remediation Activities	0.8	–	4	5	–	–	–	5	17.0	–	62	5	4.0	–	20	5	16.8	–	62	5
	Construction	2.7	–	154	211	4.5	–	138	211	7.9	–	486	211	3.9	–	148	211	6.5	–	211	211
	Wholesale and Retail Trade; Repair of Motor Vehicles and Motorcycles	1.8	–	188	528	0.7	–	89	528	5.3	–	212	528	4.1	–	133	528	8.1	–	957	528
	Transportation and storage	4.9	–	119	81	1.7	–	50	81	13.9	–	750	81	5.2	–	55	81	12.2	–	400	81
	Accommodation and Food Service Activities	2.4	–	125	353	2.4	–	120	353	5.1	–	120	353	5.1	–	125	353	5.0	–	100	353
	Information and Communication	3.4	–	100	187	2.0	–	80	187	11.7	–	500	187	10.5	–	700	187	10.9	–	445	187
	Financial and Insurance Activities	5.5	–	353	109	0.6	–	55	109	10.5	–	496	109	2.5	–	30	109	46.6	–	4,355	109
	Real Estate Activities	1.3	–	22	73	0.8	–	23	73	1.5	–	16	73	8.3	–	402	73	2.7	–	22	73
	Professional, Scientific, and Technical Activities	1.2	–	53	96	2.1	–	111	96	4.5	–	53	96	4.3	–	53	96	5.9	–	53	96
	Administrative and Support Service Activities	4.1	–	56	52	1.8	–	50	52	12.1	–	450	52	12.5	–	377	52	24.7	–	600	52
	Public Administration and Defense; Compulsory Social Security	–	–	–	1	–	–	–	1	–	–	–	1	–	–	–	1	–	–	–	1

continued on next page

Full-Time Regular Workers in April 2020 continued

Part 2

q2.4: As of the end of April 2020, how many full-time regular workers were/have been:

Item		Hired				Laid off				Granted leave				Reduced salary/wages/benefit				Reduced working hours			
		Avg	Range Min	Range Max	# of Resp	Avg	Range Min	Range Max	# of Resp	Avg	Range Min	Range Max	# of Resp	Avg	Range Min	Range Max	# of Resp	Avg	Range Min	Range Max	# of Resp
	Education	0.4	–	8	31	1.5	–	25	31	2.7	–	20	31	2.8	–	24	31	2.1	–	21	31
	Human Health and Social Work Activities	0.8	–	10	15	–	–	–	15	5.1	–	30	15	2.3	–	10	15	2.2	–	10	15
	Arts, Entertainment, and Recreation	2.1	–	26	56	1.1	–	33	56	4.2	–	90	56	3.1	–	50	56	2.7	–	50	56
	Other Service Activities	2.8	–	231	345	2.8	–	280	345	12.0	–	1,515	345	9.9	–	512	345	10.5	–	508	345
	Total	2.7	–	353	2,444	2.0	–	280	2,444	8.1	–	1,515	2,444	6.4	–	700	2,444	10.1	–	4,355	2,444
Location	National Capital Region	2.8	–	353	1,218	1.8	–	280	1,218	10.0	–	1,515	1,218	5.8	–	500	1,218	11.9	–	4,355	1,218
	Cordillera Administrative Region	1.5	–	18	23	2.5	–	48	23	12.0	–	155	23	22.1	–	445	23	22.1	–	445	23
	Region 1: Ilocos	11.6	–	188	25	2.1	–	42	25	11.1	–	200	25	18.0	–	350	25	21.8	–	350	25
	Region 2: Cagayan Valley	0.7	–	5	23	0.6	–	5	23	4.4	–	39	23	3.8	–	35	23	4.9	–	35	23
	Region 3: Central Luzon	1.8	–	79	229	2.0	–	150	229	3.7	–	89	229	4.1	–	106	229	6.9	–	600	229
	Region 4A: Calabarzon	3.3	–	191	337	2.5	–	120	337	6.3	–	185	337	8.9	–	512	337	8.7	–	377	337
	MIMAROPA	2.2	–	40	46	3.2	–	35	46	7.7	–	114	46	5.9	–	56	46	8.3	–	90	46
	Region 5: Bicol	1.0	–	22	50	1.4	–	20	50	9.3	–	254	50	1.6	–	16	50	9.4	–	175	50
	Region 6: Western Visayas	4.2	–	156	97	0.9	–	20	97	4.4	–	95	97	2.9	–	57	97	5.2	–	75	97
	Region 7: Central Visayas	2.5	–	62	183	3.8	–	200	183	7.5	–	200	183	7.5	–	402	183	9.9	–	400	183
	Region 8: Eastern Visayas	2.3	–	24	23	2.0	–	37	23	1.0	–	11	23	31.6	–	700	23	5.0	–	21	23
	Region 9: Zamboanga Peninsula	0.5	–	4	20	0.1	–	1	20	4.0	–	70	20	7.9	–	148	20	6.6	–	64	20
	Region 10: Northern Mindanao	0.7	–	8	46	2.5	–	58	46	13.8	–	486	46	2.5	–	31	46	11.3	–	211	46
	Region 11: Davao	3.0	–	119	84	1.5	–	25	84	6.8	–	200	84	5.8	–	85	84	5.7	–	85	84
	Region 12: SOCCSKSARGEN	0.6	–	12	19	1.6	–	15	19	6.5	–	35	19	10.8	–	150	19	6.4	–	70	19
	Region 13: Caraga	1.1	–	6	20	0.6	–	8	20	1.5	–	8	20	2.1	–	23	20	4.0	–	28	20
	BARMM (formerly ARMM)	–	–	–	1	–	–	–	1	–	–	–	1	–	–	–	1	9.0	9	9	1
	Total	2.7	–	353	2,444	2.0	–	280	2,444	8.1	–	1,515	2,444	6.4	–	700	2,444	10.1	–	4,355	2,444

– = no number; BARMM = Bangsamoro Autonomous Region in Muslim Mindanao; MIMAROPA = Mindoro, Marinduque, Romblon, and Palawan (Southwestern Tagalog Region); SOCCSKSARGEN = South Cotabato, Cotabato, Sultan Kudarat, Sarangani, and General Santos.

Note: Use absolute values (number of workers), more than one condition may apply to the same worker (e.g., salary and hours reduced).

Source: Asian Development Bank, Philippine Enterprise Survey.

Part-Time or Contractual Workers in April 2020

Part 2

q2.5: As of the end of April 2020, how many part-time or contractual workers were/have been:

Item		Hired Avg	Hired Min	Hired Max	Hired # of Resp	Laid off Avg	Laid off Min	Laid off Max	Laid off # of Resp	Granted leave Avg	Granted leave Min	Granted leave Max	Granted leave # of Resp	Reduced salary/wages/benefit Avg	Reduced salary Min	Reduced salary Max	Reduced salary # of Resp	Reduced working hours Avg	Reduced w.h. Min	Reduced w.h. Max	Reduced w.h. # of Resp
Firm size	Micro	0.5	–	38	1,272	1.2	–	200	1,272	4.2	–	2,626	1,272	3.1	–	754	1,272	2.7	–	754	1,272
	Small	1.2	–	90	671	1.7	–	116	671	2.5	–	200	671	3.7	–	268	671	4.6	–	270	671
	Medium-sized	1.3	–	68	320	1.1	–	96	320	5.4	–	408	320	4.0	–	455	320	7.1	–	508	320
	Large	3.1	–	300	181	1.5	–	103	181	9.6	–	700	181	7.0	–	512	181	6.5	–	250	181
	Total	1.0	–	300	2,444	1.4	–	200	2,444	4.3	–	2,626	2,444	3.7	–	754	2,444	4.1	–	754	2,444
Industry	Agriculture, Forestry, and Fishing	0.6	–	8	18	0.9	–	5	18	0.7	–	8	18	0.6	–	5	18	0.6	–	5	18
	Manufacturing	1.0	–	47	254	0.7	–	24	254	2.6	–	100	254	2.2	–	71	254	3.0	–	75	254
	Electricity, Gas, Steam, and Air Conditioning Supply	–	–	1	29	–	–	1	29	0.2	–	2	29	0.2	–	3	29	0.3	–	3	29
	Water Supply, Sewerage, Waste Management, and Remediation Activities	–	–	–	5	–	–	–	5	2.4	–	12	5	–	–	–	5	2.2	–	11	5
	Construction	3.0	–	300	211	5.3	–	103	211	5.4	–	300	211	3.8	–	125	211	6.4	–	270	211
	Wholesale and Retail Trade; Repair of Motor Vehicles and Motorcycles	0.5	–	80	528	0.5	–	60	528	1.7	–	80	528	1.6	–	100	528	2.6	–	160	528
	Transportation and storage	2.5	–	60	81	1.7	–	30	81	33.8	–	2,626	81	1.8	–	28	81	2.6	–	40	81
	Accommodation and Food Service Activities	0.5	–	50	353	1.3	–	116	353	1.5	–	100	353	1.9	–	100	353	2.2	–	100	353
	Information and Communication	0.6	–	40	187	1.0	–	30	187	6.0	–	700	187	8.0	–	700	187	5.8	–	455	187
	Financial and Insurance Activities	1.6	–	105	109	0.1	–	5	109	1.8	–	120	109	0.6	–	30	109	3.4	–	120	109
	Real Estate Activities	0.2	–	9	73	0.5	–	11	73	0.2	–	8	73	6.2	–	404	73	2.0	–	50	73
	Professional, Scientific, and Technical Activities	0.2	–	7	96	1.6	–	100	96	0.8	–	27	96	4.4	–	200	96	2.9	–	100	96
	Administrative and Support Service Activities	3.3	–	90	52	1.3	–	50	52	2.8	–	50	52	20.2	–	754	52	20.3	–	754	52
	Public Administration and Defense; Compulsory Social Security	–	–	–	1	–	–	–	1	–	–	–	1	–	–	–	1	–	–	–	1

continued on next page

Part-Time or Contractual Workers in April 2020 continued

Part 2

q2.5: As of the end of April 2020, how many part-time or contractual workers were/have been:

Item		Hired Avg	Hired # of Resp	Hired Range Min	Hired Range Max	Laid off Avg	Laid off # of Resp	Laid off Range Min	Laid off Range Max	Granted leave Avg	Granted leave # of Resp	Granted leave Range Min	Granted leave Range Max	Reduced salary/wages/benefit Avg	Reduced salary/wages/benefit # of Resp	Reduced salary/wages/benefit Range Min	Reduced salary/wages/benefit Range Max	Reduced working hours Avg	Reduced working hours # of Resp	Reduced working hours Range Min	Reduced working hours Range Max
	Education	0.7	31	–	8	1.1	31	–	11	1.1	31	–	11	2.5	31	–	30	1.6	31	–	10
	Human Health and Social Work Activities	5.3	15	–	80	1.3	15	–	20	2.0	15	–	20	4.3	15	–	50	4.6	15	–	50
	Arts, Entertainment, and Recreation	0.2	56	–	4	0.9	56	–	33	2.9	56	–	90	1.5	56	–	20	1.4	56	–	15
	Other Service Activities	0.6	345	–	35	1.9	345	–	200	8.1	345	–	1,515	6.6	345	–	512	6.7	345	–	508
	Total	1.0	2,444	–	300	1.4	2,444	–	200	4.3	2,444	–	2,626	3.7	2,444	–	754	4.1	2,444	–	754
Location	National Capital Region	0.9	1,218	–	105	1.5	1,218	–	200	6.5	1,218	–	2,626	2.4	1,218	–	200	3.5	1,218	–	508
	Cordillera Administrative Region	0.4	23	–	8	0.1	23	–	2	9.6	23	–	155	19.9	23	–	455	20.4	23	–	455
	Region 1: Ilocos	2.0	25	–	38	–	25	–	1	0.3	25	–	4	2.8	25	–	47	3.3	25	–	40
	Region 2: Cagayan Valley	0.4	23	–	5	0.7	23	–	11	2.1	23	–	18	1.8	23	–	35	3.5	23	–	35
	Region 3: Central Luzon	0.8	229	–	52	1.5	229	–	100	1.7	229	–	50	1.6	229	–	64	1.9	229	–	64
	Region 4A: Calabarzon	1.8	337	–	300	0.7	337	–	26	2.6	337	–	300	7.6	337	–	754	8.1	337	–	754
	MIMAROPA	1.4	46	–	45	1.7	46	–	35	0.9	46	–	8	1.5	46	–	17	2.1	46	–	23
	Region 5: Bicol	0.5	50	–	7	2.9	50	–	116	2.6	50	–	42	1.4	50	–	48	2.1	50	–	48
	Region 6: Western Visayas	1.1	97	–	60	1.0	97	–	30	1.4	97	–	36	0.6	97	–	15	2.2	97	–	75
	Region 7: Central Visayas	0.6	183	–	24	1.4	183	–	80	1.9	183	–	45	5.4	183	–	404	3.6	183	–	260
	Region 8: Eastern Visayas	0.5	23	–	8	2.8	23	–	40	0.6	23	–	10	34.4	23	–	700	3.7	23	–	42
	Region 9: Zamboanga Peninsula	0.2	20	–	4	0.4	20	–	6	0.3	20	–	7	0.2	20	–	4	0.2	20	–	4
	Region 10: Northern Mindanao	0.5	46	–	10	1.0	46	–	18	1.8	46	–	53	6.3	46	–	268	3.5	46	–	125
	Region 11: Davao	0.7	84	–	35	2.3	84	–	75	3.7	84	–	200	2.5	84	–	36	5.0	84	–	270
	Region 12: SOCCSKSARGEN	–	19	–	–	1.4	19	–	25	2.4	19	–	35	2.9	19	–	35	2.3	19	–	30
	Region 13: Caraga	1.1	20	–	6	0.7	20	–	8	1.4	20	–	8	0.9	20	–	7	1.9	20	–	10
	BARMM (formerly ARMM)	–	1	–	–	–	1	–	–	–	1	–	–	–	1	–	–	–	1	–	–
	Total	1.0	2,444	–	300	1.4	2,444	–	200	4.3	2,444	–	2,626	3.7	2,444	–	754	4.1	2,444	–	754

– = no number; BARMM = Bangsamoro Autonomous Region in Muslim Mindanao; MIMAROPA = Mindoro, Marinduque, Romblon, and Palawan (Southwestern Tagalog Region); SOCCSKSARGEN = South Cotabato, Cotabato, Sultan Kudarat, Sarangani, and General Santos.

Note: Use absolute values (number of workers), more than one condition may apply to the same worker (e.g., salary and hours reduced).

Source: Asian Development Bank, Philippine Enterprise Survey.

Total Wage Payments after the COVID-19 Outbreak (15 March 2020)

Part 2

q2.6: Changes in total wage payments to employees after the COVID-19 outbreak (15 March 2020):

Item		Temporarily no payment			More than 50% decrease			31%–50% decrease			11%–30% decrease			1%–10% decrease			No change		
		No.	%*	%**	No.	%*	%**	No.	%*	%**	No.	%*	%**	No.	%*	%**	No.	%*	%**
Firm size	Micro	719	58.7	55.8	146	44.2	11.3	105	43.4	8.2	40	35.7	3.1	15	46.9	1.2	246	49.9	19.1
	Small	297	24.3	43.9	105	31.8	15.5	75	31.0	11.1	37	33.0	5.5	7	21.9	1.0	141	28.6	20.9
	Medium-sized	124	10.1	37.5	54	16.4	16.3	48	19.8	14.5	29	25.9	8.8	7	21.9	2.1	59	12.0	17.8
	Large	84	6.9	45.2	25	7.6	13.4	14	5.8	7.5	6	5.4	3.2	3	9.4	1.6	47	9.5	25.3
	Total	1,224	100.0	49.3	330	100.0	13.3	242	100.0	9.8	112	100.0	4.5	32	100.0	1.3	493	100.0	19.9
Industry	Agriculture, Forestry and Fishing	6	0.5	33.3	5	1.5	27.8	3	1.2	16.7	3	2.7	16.7	–	–	–	1	0.2	5.6
	Manufacturing	138	11.3	52.9	37	11.2	14.2	19	7.9	7.3	8	7.1	3.1	4	12.5	1.5	51	10.3	19.5
	Electricity, Gas, Steam and Air Conditioning Supply	7	0.6	24.1	4	1.2	13.8	7	2.9	24.1	2	1.8	6.9	–	–	–	9	1.8	31.0
	Water Supply; Sewerage, Waste Management and Remediation Activities	2	0.2	40.0	–	–	–	–	–	–	2	1.8	40.0	–	–	–	1	0.2	20.0
	Construction	118	9.6	55.1	30	9.1	14.0	22	9.1	10.3	5	4.5	2.3	3	9.4	1.4	34	6.9	15.9
	Wholesale and Retail Trade; Repair of Motor Vehicles and Motorcycles	250	20.4	46.8	66	20.0	12.4	51	21.1	9.6	21	18.8	3.9	6	18.8	1.1	133	27.0	24.9
	Transportation and storage	30	2.5	36.6	22	6.7	26.8	10	4.1	12.2	6	5.4	7.3	–	–	–	13	2.6	15.9
	Accommodation and Food Service Activities	212	17.3	59.6	47	14.2	13.2	30	12.4	8.4	10	8.9	2.8	3	9.4	0.8	45	9.1	12.6
	Information and Communication	64	5.2	33.9	19	5.8	10.1	27	11.2	14.3	20	17.9	10.6	7	21.9	3.7	44	8.9	23.3
	Financial and Insurance Activities	50	4.1	45.9	10	3.0	9.2	12	5.0	11.0	3	2.7	2.8	2	6.3	1.8	31	6.3	28.4
	Real Estate Activities	39	3.2	52.0	10	3.0	13.3	12	5.0	16.0	–	–	–	1	3.1	1.3	11	2.2	14.7
	Professional, Scientific and Technical Activities	43	3.5	44.3	15	4.6	15.5	9	3.7	9.3	6	5.4	6.2	2	6.3	2.1	19	3.9	19.6
	Administrative and Support Service Activities	24	2.0	45.3	13	3.9	24.5	4	1.7	7.5	1	0.9	1.9	2	6.3	3.8	8	1.6	15.1

continued on next page

Total Wage Payments after the COVID-19 Outbreak (15 March 2020) continued

Part 2

q2.6: Changes in total wage payments to employees after the COVID-19 outbreak (15 March 2020):

Item		Temporarily no payment			More than 50% decrease			31%–50% decrease			11%–30% decrease			1%–10% decrease			No change		
		No.	%*	%**	No.	%*	%**	No.	%*	%**	No.	%*	%**	No.	%*	%**	No.	%*	%**
	Public Administration and Defense; Compulsory Social Security	–	–	–	–	–	–	–	–	–	–	–	–	–	–	–	1	0.2	100.0
	Education	14	1.1	45.2	4	1.2	12.9	3	1.2	9.7	1	0.9	3.2	–	–	–	8	1.6	25.8
	Human Health and Social Work Activities	9	0.7	60.0	1	0.3	6.7	2	0.8	13.3	1	0.9	6.7	–	–	–	2	0.4	13.3
	Arts, Entertainment, and Recreation	33	2.7	57.9	9	2.7	15.8	4	1.7	7.0	1	0.9	1.8	1	3.1	1.8	8	1.6	14.0
	Other Service Activities	185	15.1	52.1	38	11.5	10.7	27	11.2	7.6	22	19.6	6.2	1	3.1	0.3	74	15.0	20.8
	Total	1,224	100.0	49.3	330	100.0	13.3	242	100.0	9.8	112	100.0	4.5	32	100.0	1.3	493	100.0	19.9
Location	National Capital Region	587	48.0	47.7	176	53.3	14.3	106	43.8	8.6	58	51.8	4.7	15	46.9	1.2	265	53.8	21.5
	Cordillera Administrative Region	11	0.9	47.8	7	2.1	30.4	3	1.2	13.0	–	–	–	1	3.1	4.3	1	0.2	4.3
	Region 1: Ilocos	13	1.1	50.0	6	1.8	23.1	2	0.8	7.7	1	0.9	3.8	–	–	–	4	0.8	15.4
	Region 2: Cagayan Valley	13	1.1	56.5	2	0.6	8.7	2	0.8	8.7	–	–	–	–	–	–	4	0.8	17.4
	Region 3: Central Luzon	135	11.0	58.7	24	7.3	10.4	19	7.9	8.3	5	4.5	2.2	3	9.4	1.3	42	8.5	18.3
	Region 4A: Calabarzon	193	15.8	55.6	37	11.2	10.7	37	15.3	10.7	7	6.3	2.0	6	18.8	1.7	59	12.0	17.0
	MIMAROPA	26	2.1	56.5	6	1.8	13.0	6	2.5	13.0	–	–	–	1	3.1	2.2	6	1.2	13.0
	Region 5: Bicol	32	2.6	62.7	8	2.4	15.7	3	1.2	5.9	2	1.8	3.9	–	–	–	6	1.2	11.8
	Region 6: Western Visayas	45	3.7	45.0	13	3.9	13.0	9	3.7	9.0	10	8.9	10.0	–	–	–	20	4.1	20.0
	Region 7: Central Visayas	76	6.2	41.1	19	5.8	10.3	29	12.0	15.7	13	11.6	7.0	4	12.5	2.2	39	7.9	21.1
	Region 8: Eastern Visayas	7	0.6	28.0	4	1.2	16.0	2	0.8	8.0	4	3.6	16.0	–	–	–	7	1.4	28.0
	Region 9: Zamboanga Peninsula	8	0.7	40.0	2	0.6	10.0	1	0.4	5.0	2	1.8	10.0	–	–	–	7	1.4	35.0
	Region 10: Northern Mindanao	18	1.5	37.5	6	1.8	12.5	9	3.7	18.8	3	2.7	6.3	1	3.1	2.1	10	2.0	20.8
	Region 11: Davao	42	3.4	49.4	13	3.9	15.3	9	3.7	10.6	6	5.4	7.1	–	–	–	14	2.8	16.5
	Region 12: SOCCSKSARGEN	11	0.9	55.0	5	1.5	25.0	1	0.4	5.0	–	–	–	1	3.1	5.0	2	0.4	10.0
	Region 13: Caraga	6	0.5	30.0	2	0.6	10.0	4	1.7	20.0	1	0.9	5.0	–	–	–	7	1.4	35.0
	BARMM (formerly ARMM)	1	0.1	100.0	–	–	–	–	–	–	–	–	–	–	–	–	–	–	–
	Total	1,224	100.0	49.3	330	100.0	13.3	242	100.0	9.8	112	100.0	4.5	32	100.0	1.3	493	100.0	19.9

continued on next page

Total Wage Payments after the COVID-19 Outbreak (15 March 2020) continued

Part 2

q2.6: Changes in total wage payments to employees after the COVID-19 outbreak (15 March 2020):

Item		Less than 10% increase			10%–30% increase			31%–50% increase			More than 50% increase			Total		
		No.	%*	%**	No.	%*	%**	No.	%*	%**	No.	%*	%**	No.	%*	%**
Firm size	Micro	1	10.0	0.1	6	35.3	0.5	4	44.4	0.3	6	50.0	0.5	1,288	51.9	100.0
	Small	4	40.0	0.6	5	29.4	0.7	3	33.3	0.4	2	16.7	0.3	676	27.3	100.0
	Medium-sized	4	40.0	1.2	4	23.5	1.2	1	11.1	0.3	1	8.3	0.3	331	13.3	100.0
	Large	1	10.0	0.5	2	11.8	1.1	1	11.1	0.5	3	25.0	1.6	186	7.5	100.0
	Total	10	100.0	0.4	17	100.0	0.7	9	100.0	0.4	12	100.0	0.5	2,481	100.0	100.0
Industry	Agriculture, Forestry, and Fishing	–	–	–	–	–	–	–	–	–	–	–	–	18	0.7	100.0
	Manufacturing	1	10.0	0.4	1	5.9	0.4	–	–	–	2	16.7	0.8	261	10.5	100.0
	Electricity, Gas, Steam, and Air Conditioning Supply	–	–	–	–	–	–	–	–	–	–	–	–	29	1.2	100.0
	Water Supply, Sewerage, Waste Management, and Remediation Activities	–	–	–	–	–	–	–	–	–	–	–	–	5	0.2	100.0
	Construction	–	–	–	1	5.9	0.5	–	–	–	1	8.3	0.5	214	8.6	100.0
	Wholesale and Retail Trade; Repair of Motor Vehicles and Motorcycles	–	–	–	4	23.5	0.7	2	22.2	0.4	1	8.3	0.2	534	21.5	100.0
	Transportation and storage	–	–	–	–	–	–	–	–	–	1	8.3	1.2	82	3.3	100.0
	Accommodation and Food Service Activities	1	10.0	0.3	3	17.7	0.8	2	22.2	0.6	3	25.0	0.8	356	14.4	100.0
	Information and Communication	2	20.0	1.1	2	11.8	1.1	3	33.3	1.6	1	8.3	0.5	189	7.6	100.0
	Financial and Insurance Activities	1	10.0	0.9	–	–	–	–	–	–	–	–	–	109	4.4	100.0
	Real Estate Activities	1	10.0	1.3	1	5.9	1.3	–	–	–	–	–	–	75	3.0	100.0
	Professional, Scientific, and Technical Activities	–	–	–	1	5.9	1.0	1	11.1	1.0	1	8.3	1.0	97	3.9	100.0
	Administrative and Support Service Activities	1	10.0	1.9	–	–	–	–	–	–	–	–	–	53	2.1	100.0
	Public Administration and Defense; Compulsory Social Security	–	–	–	–	–	–	–	–	–	–	–	–	1	0.0	100.0
	Education	–	–	–	–	–	–	1	11.1	3.2	–	–	–	31	1.3	100.0
	Human Health and Social Work Activities	–	–	–	–	–	–	–	–	–	–	–	–	15	0.6	100.0
	Arts, Entertainment, and Recreation	1	10.0	1.8	–	–	–	–	–	–	–	–	–	57	2.3	100.0
	Other Service Activities	2	20.0	0.6	4	23.5	1.1	–	–	–	2	16.7	0.6	355	14.3	100.0
	Total	10	100.0	0.4	17	100.0	0.7	9	100.0	0.4	12	100.0	0.5	2,481	100.0	100.0

continued on next page

Total Wage Payments after the COVID-19 Outbreak (15 March 2020) continued

Part 2

q2.6: Changes in total wage payments to employees after the COVID-19 outbreak (15 March 2020):

Item	Location	Less than 10% increase			10%–30% increase			31%–50% increase			More than 50% increase			Total		
		No.	%*	%**	No.	%*	%**	No.	%*	%**	No.	%*	%**	No.	%*	%**
Location	National Capital Region	5	50.0	0.4	8	47.1	0.6	3	33.3	0.2	8	66.7	0.6	1,231	49.6	100.0
	Cordillera Administrative Region	–	–	–	–	–	–	–	–	–	–	–	–	23	0.9	100.0
	Region 1: Ilocos	–	–	–	–	–	–	–	–	–	–	–	–	26	1.1	100.0
	Region 2: Cagayan Valley	–	–	–	1	5.9	4.3	1	11.1	4.3	–	–	–	23	0.9	100.0
	Region 3: Central Luzon	–	–	–	1	5.9	0.4	–	–	–	1	8.3	0.4	230	9.3	100.0
	Region 4A: Calabarzon	3	30.0	0.9	2	11.8	0.6	3	33.3	0.9	–	–	–	347	14.0	100.0
	MIMAROPA	–	–	–	–	–	–	–	–	–	1	8.3	2.2	46	1.9	100.0
	Region 5: Bicol	–	–	–	–	–	–	–	–	–	–	–	–	51	2.1	100.0
	Region 6: Western Visayas	–	–	–	2	11.8	2.0	1	11.1	1.0	–	–	–	100	4.0	100.0
	Region 7: Central Visayas	2	20.0	1.1	1	5.9	0.5	–	–	–	2	16.7	1.1	185	7.5	100.0
	Region 8: Eastern Visayas	–	–	–	1	5.9	4.0	–	–	–	–	–	–	25	1.0	100.0
	Region 9: Zamboanga Peninsula	–	–	–	–	–	–	–	–	–	–	–	–	20	0.8	100.0
	Region 10: Northern Mindanao	–	–	–	1	5.9	2.1	–	–	–	–	–	–	48	1.9	100.0
	Region 11: Davao	–	–	–	–	–	–	1	11.1	1.2	–	–	–	85	3.4	100.0
	Region 12: SOCCSKSARGEN	–	–	–	–	–	–	–	–	–	–	–	–	20	0.8	100.0
	Region 13: Caraga	–	–	–	–	–	–	–	–	–	–	–	–	20	0.8	100.0
	BARMM (formerly ARMM)	–	–	–	–	–	–	–	–	–	–	–	–	1	0.0	100.0
	Total	10	100.0	0.4	17	100.0	0.7	9	100.0	0.4	12	100.0	0.5	2,481	100.0	100.0

– = no number; BARMM = Bangsamoro Autonomous Region in Muslim Mindanao; COVID-19 = coronavirus disease; MIMAROPA = Mindoro, Marinduque, Romblon, and Palawan (Southwestern Tagalog Region); SOCCSKSARGEN = South Cotabato, Cotabato, Sultan Kudarat, Sarangani, and General Santos.

* Share of vertical column. ** Share of horizontal line.

Source: Asian Development Bank, Philippine Enterprise Survey.

Status of Work From Home

Part 2

q2.8: What percentage of your workers can work from home without major disruption in your operations?

Item		Work from home not possible for any workers			More than 50%			26%-50%			6%-25%			1%-5%			Total		
		No.	%*	%**	No.	%*	%**	No.	%*	%**	No.	%*	%**	No.	%*	%**	No.	%*	%**
Firm size	Micro	811	57.3	63.0	146	54.5	11.3	86	55.1	6.7	82	40.0	6.4	163	37.3	12.7	1,288	51.9	100.0
	Small	354	25.0	52.4	64	23.9	9.5	35	22.4	5.2	69	33.7	10.2	154	35.2	22.8	676	27.3	100.0
	Medium-sized	157	11.1	47.4	32	11.9	9.7	21	13.5	6.3	35	17.1	10.6	86	19.7	26.0	331	13.3	100.0
	Large	93	6.6	50.0	26	9.7	14.0	14	9.0	7.5	19	9.3	10.2	34	7.8	18.3	186	7.5	100.0
	Total	1,415	100.0	57.0	268	100.0	10.8	156	100.0	6.3	205	100.0	8.3	437	100.0	17.6	2,481	100.0	100.0
Industry	Agriculture, Forestry, and Fishing	11	0.8	61.1	2	0.8	11.1	1	0.6	5.6	2	1.0	11.1	2	0.5	11.1	18	0.7	100.0
	Manufacturing	167	11.8	64.0	11	4.1	4.2	7	4.5	2.7	18	8.8	6.9	58	13.3	22.2	261	10.5	100.0
	Electricity, Gas, Steam, and Air Conditioning Supply	20	1.4	69.0	–			1	0.6	3.4	3	1.5	10.3	5	1.1	17.2	29	1.2	100.0
	Water Supply, Sewerage, Waste Management, and Remediation Activities	2	0.1	40.0	1	0.4	20.0	–			–			2	0.5	40.0	5	0.2	100.0
	Construction	128	9.1	59.8	8	3.0	3.7	5	3.2	2.3	18	8.8	8.4	55	12.6	25.7	214	8.6	100.0
	Wholesale and Retail Trade; Repair of Motor Vehicles and Motorcycles	317	22.4	59.4	44	16.4	8.2	29	18.6	5.4	52	25.4	9.7	92	21.1	17.2	534	21.5	100.0
	Transportation and storage	44	3.1	53.7	9	3.4	11.0	3	1.9	3.7	9	4.4	11.0	17	3.9	20.7	82	3.3	100.0
	Accommodation and Food Service Activities	267	18.9	75.0	8	3.0	2.2	12	7.7	3.4	18	8.8	5.1	51	11.7	14.3	356	14.4	100.0
	Information and Communication	45	3.2	23.8	78	29.1	41.3	21	13.5	11.1	19	9.3	10.1	26	6.0	13.8	189	7.6	100.0
	Financial and Insurance Activities	59	4.2	54.1	14	5.2	12.8	13	8.3	11.9	14	6.8	12.8	9	2.1	8.3	109	4.4	100.0
	Real Estate Activities	39	2.8	52.0	12	4.5	16.0	5	3.2	6.7	4	2.0	5.3	15	3.4	20.0	75	3.0	100.0
	Professional, Scientific, and Technical Activities	27	1.9	27.8	31	11.6	32.0	20	12.8	20.6	7	3.4	7.2	12	2.8	12.4	97	3.9	100.0
	Administrative and Support Service Activities	19	1.3	35.8	9	3.4	17.0	5	3.2	9.4	5	2.4	9.4	15	3.4	28.3	53	2.1	100.0
	Public Administration and Defense; Compulsory Social Security	–			1	0.4	100.0	–			–			–			1	0.0	100.0
	Education	13	0.9	41.9	8	3.0	25.8	3	1.9	9.7	3	1.5	9.7	4	0.9	12.9	31	1.3	100.0
	Human Health and Social Work Activities	11	0.8	73.3	–			–			2	1.0	13.3	2	0.5	13.3	15	0.6	100.0

continued on next page

Status of Work From Home continued

Part 2

q2.8: What percentage of your workers can work from home without major disruption in your operations?

Item		Work from home not possible for any workers			More than 50%			26%–50%			6%–25%			1%–5%			Total		
		No.	%*	%**	No.	%*	%**	No.	%*	%**	No.	%*	%**	No.	%*	%**	No.	%*	%**
	Arts, Entertainment, and Recreation	32	2.3	56.1	6	2.2	10.5	5	3.2	8.8	5	2.4	8.8	9	2.1	15.8	57	2.3	100.0
	Other Service Activities	214	15.1	60.3	26	9.7	7.3	26	16.7	7.3	26	12.7	7.3	63	14.4	17.7	355	14.3	100.0
	Total	1,415	100.0	57.0	268	100.0	10.8	156	100.0	6.3	205	100.0	8.3	437	100.0	17.6	2,481	100.0	100.0
Location	National Capital Region	608	43.0	49.4	186	69.4	15.1	101	64.7	8.2	120	58.5	9.7	216	49.4	17.5	1,231	49.6	100.0
	Cordillera Administrative Region	13	0.9	56.5	2	0.8	8.7	–	–	–	1	0.5	4.3	7	1.6	30.4	23	0.9	100.0
	Region 1: Ilocos	13	0.9	50.0	1	0.4	3.8	2	1.3	7.7	2	1.0	7.7	8	1.8	30.8	26	1.1	100.0
	Region 2: Cagayan Valley	14	1.0	60.9	1	0.4	4.3	2	1.3	8.7	1	0.5	4.3	5	1.1	21.7	23	0.9	100.0
	Region 3: Central Luzon	148	10.5	64.3	13	4.9	5.7	7	4.5	3.0	13	6.3	5.7	49	11.2	21.3	230	9.3	100.0
	Region 4A: Calabarzon	210	14.8	60.5	24	9.0	6.9	21	13.5	6.1	29	14.2	8.4	63	14.4	18.2	347	14.0	100.0
	MIMAROPA	33	2.3	71.7	1	0.4	2.2	1	0.6	2.2	2	1.0	4.3	9	2.1	19.6	46	1.9	100.0
	Region 5: Bicol	34	2.4	66.7	–	–	–	1	0.6	2.0	4	2.0	7.8	12	2.8	23.5	51	2.1	100.0
	Region 6: Western Visayas	71	5.0	71.0	7	2.6	7.0	3	1.9	3.0	7	3.4	7.0	12	2.8	12.0	100	4.0	100.0
	Region 7: Central Visayas	116	8.2	62.7	18	6.7	9.7	10	6.4	5.4	15	7.3	8.1	26	6.0	14.1	185	7.5	100.0
	Region 8: Eastern Visayas	16	1.1	64.0	3	1.1	12.0	1	0.6	4.0	3	1.5	12.0	2	0.5	8.0	25	1.0	100.0
	Region 9: Zamboanga Peninsula	17	1.2	85.0	–	–	–	1	0.6	5.0	1	0.5	5.0	1	0.2	5.0	20	0.8	100.0
	Region 10: Northern Mindanao	32	2.3	66.7	5	1.9	10.4	4	2.6	8.3	2	1.0	4.2	5	1.1	10.4	48	1.9	100.0
	Region 11: Davao	56	4.0	65.9	6	2.2	7.1	2	1.3	2.4	3	1.5	3.5	18	4.1	21.2	85	3.4	100.0
	Region 12: SOCCSKSARGEN	17	1.2	85.0	–	–	–	–	–	–	1	0.5	5.0	2	0.5	10.0	20	0.8	100.0
	Region 13: Caraga	16	1.1	80.0	1	0.4	5.0	–	–	–	1	0.5	5.0	2	0.5	10.0	20	0.8	100.0
	BARMM (formerly ARMM)	1	0.1	100.0	–	–	–	–	–	–	–	–	–	–	–	–	1	0.0	100.0
	Total	1,415	100.0	57.0	268	100.0	10.8	156	100.0	6.3	205	100.0	8.3	437	100.0	17.6	2,481	100.0	100.0

* Share of vertical column. ** Share of horizontal line.

Source: Asian Development Bank, Philippine Enterprise Survey.

Enterprise Assistance to Employees during the ECQ

Part 2

q2.9: What assistance has your company provided to employees during the Enhanced Community Quarantine (ECQ)?

Item		Shuttle service to and from home or designated pick-up points No.	%	Accommodation near the workplace No.	%	Additional leave credits No.	%	Internet/data allowance No.	%	Personal protective equipment (PPE; e.g, face masks) No.	%	Vitamins and hygiene products (e.g., alcohol-based) No.	%
Firm size	Micro	115	33.8	143	37.9	159	46.9	150	45.5	342	41.9	416	47.1
	Small	102	30.0	127	33.7	99	29.2	101	30.6	266	32.6	258	29.2
	Medium-sized	71	20.9	71	18.8	58	17.1	54	16.4	136	16.7	140	15.8
	Large	52	15.3	36	9.6	23	6.8	25	7.6	72	8.8	70	7.9
	Total	340	100.0	377	100.0	339	100.0	330	100.0	816	100.0	884	100.0
Industry	Agriculture, Forestry, and Fishing	3	0.9	1	0.3	2	0.6	1	0.3	8	1.0	6	0.7
	Manufacturing	58	17.1	46	12.2	25	7.4	17	5.2	106	13.0	107	12.1
	Electricity, Gas, Steam, and Air Conditioning Supply	8	2.4	9	2.4	4	1.2	2	0.6	16	2.0	17	1.9
	Water Supply, Sewerage, Waste Management, and Remediation Activities	2	0.6	–	–	1	0.3	1	0.3	1	0.1	1	0.1
	Construction	31	9.1	54	14.3	23	6.8	25	7.6	74	9.1	69	7.8
	Wholesale and Retail Trade; Repair of Motor Vehicles and Motorcycles	72	21.2	64	17.0	81	23.9	63	19.1	191	23.4	196	22.2
	Transportation and storage	18	5.3	17	4.5	10	3.0	12	3.6	41	5.0	39	4.4
	Accommodation and Food Service Activities	33	9.7	53	14.1	41	12.1	26	7.9	98	12.0	127	14.4
	Information and Communication	25	7.4	30	8.0	36	10.6	56	17.0	42	5.2	54	6.1
	Financial and Insurance Activities	20	5.9	15	4.0	18	5.3	17	5.2	40	4.9	49	5.5
	Real Estate Activities	11	3.2	18	4.8	6	1.8	9	2.7	24	2.9	31	3.5
	Professional, Scientific, and Technical Activities	10	2.9	10	2.7	19	5.6	22	6.7	26	3.2	29	3.3
	Administrative and Support Service Activities	11	3.2	8	2.1	12	3.5	16	4.9	22	2.7	18	2.0
	Public Administration and Defense; Compulsory Social Security	1	0.3	–	–	–	–	–	–	1	0.1	1	0.1
	Education	–	–	1	0.3	6	1.8	–	–	6	0.7	10	1.1
	Human Health and Social Work Activities	–	–	1	0.3	1	0.3	2	0.6	5	0.6	6	0.7
	Arts, Entertainment, and Recreation	3	0.9	7	1.9	12	3.5	5	1.5	9	1.1	10	1.1
	Other Service Activities	33	9.7	43	11.4	42	12.4	56	17.0	106	13.0	114	12.9
	Total	340	100.0	377	100.0	339	100.0	330	100.0	816	100.0	884	100.0
Location	National Capital Region	150	44.1	3	0.8	189	55.8	196	59.4	382	46.8	398	45.0
	Cordillera Administrative Region	3	0.9	3	0.8	3	0.9	4	1.2	7	0.9	8	0.9
	Region 1: Ilocos	5	1.5	5	1.3	2	0.6	2	0.6	12	1.5	9	1.0
	Region 2: Cagayan Valley	4	1.2	25	6.6	4	1.2	1	0.3	11	1.4	9	1.0
	Region 3: Central Luzon	33	9.7	63	16.7	28	8.3	20	6.1	83	10.2	97	11.0
	Region 4A: Calabarzon	63	18.5	7	1.9	39	11.5	41	12.4	116	14.2	130	14.7
	MIMAROPA	4	1.2	3	0.8	10	3.0	3	0.9	10	1.2	16	1.8
	Region 5: Bicol	2	0.6	19	5.0	5	1.5	3	0.9	13	1.6	14	1.6
	Region 6: Western Visayas	15	4.4	26	6.9	17	5.0	18	5.5	34	4.2	49	5.5
	Region 7: Central Visayas	29	8.5	5	1.3	22	6.5	25	7.6	62	7.6	70	7.9
	Region 8: Eastern Visayas	4	1.2	2	0.5	–	–	3	0.9	11	1.4	9	1.0
	Region 9: Zamboanga Peninsula	–	–	4	1.1	–	–	1	0.3	7	0.9	4	0.5
	Region 10: Northern Mindanao	5	1.5	14	3.7	9	2.7	6	1.8	16	2.0	22	2.5
	Region 11: Davao	13	3.8	1	0.3	9	2.7	5	1.5	33	4.0	33	3.7
	Region 12: SOCCSKSARGEN	2	0.6	–	–	1	0.3	1	0.3	6	0.7	4	0.5
	Region 13: Caraga	7	2.1	–	–	1	0.3	1	0.3	12	1.5	11	1.2
	BARMM (formerly ARMM)	1	0.3	–	–	–	–	–	–	1	0.1	1	0.1
	Total	340	100.0	377	100.0	339	100.0	330	100.0	816	100.0	884	100.0

– = no number; BARMM = Bangsamoro Autonomous Region in Muslim Mindanao; MIMAROPA = Mindoro, Marinduque, Romblon, and Palawan (Southwestern Tagalog Region); SOCCSKSARGEN = South Cotabato, Cotabato, Sultan Kudarat, Sarangani, and General Santos.

Source: Asian Development Bank, Philippine Enterprise Survey.

Bottlenecks in Supply Chain

Part 2

Item		q2.10: Have you experienced or are you expecting to experience any bottlenecks in your supply chain?												
		Yes, minor bottlenecks			Yes, severe bottlenecks			No			Total		
		No.	%*	%**	No.	%*	%**	No.	%*	%**	No.	%*	%**
Firm size	Micro	307	46.4	23.8	525	54.1	40.8	456	53.8	35.4	1,288	51.9	100.0
	Small	189	28.6	28.0	270	27.8	39.9	217	25.6	32.1	676	27.3	100.0
	Medium-sized	118	17.8	35.6	122	12.6	36.9	91	10.7	27.5	331	13.3	100.0
	Large	48	7.3	25.8	54	5.6	29.0	84	9.9	45.2	186	7.5	100.0
	Total	662	100.0	26.7	971	100.0	39.1	848	100.0	34.2	2,481	100.0	100.0
Industry	Agriculture, Forestry, and Fishing	7	1.1	38.9	9	0.9	50.0	2	0.2	11.1	18	0.7	100.0
	Manufacturing	100	15.1	38.3	117	12.1	44.8	44	5.2	16.9	261	10.5	100.0
	Electricity, Gas, Steam, and Air Conditioning Supply	9	1.4	31.0	11	1.1	37.9	9	1.1	31.0	29	1.2	100.0
	Water Supply, Sewerage, Waste Management, and Remediation Activities	3	0.5	60.0	–	–	–	2	0.2	40.0	5	0.2	100.0
	Construction	49	7.4	22.9	105	10.8	49.1	60	7.1	28.0	214	8.6	100.0
	Wholesale and Retail Trade; Repair of Motor Vehicles and Motorcycles	162	24.5	30.3	268	27.6	50.2	104	12.3	19.5	534	21.5	100.0
	Transportation and storage	26	3.9	31.7	25	2.6	30.5	31	3.7	37.8	82	3.3	100.0
	Accommodation and Food Service Activities	102	15.4	28.7	149	15.4	41.9	105	12.4	29.5	356	14.4	100.0
	Information and Communication	38	5.7	20.1	55	5.7	29.1	96	11.3	50.8	189	7.6	100.0
	Financial and Insurance Activities	25	3.8	22.9	20	2.1	18.3	64	7.6	58.7	109	4.4	100.0
	Real Estate Activities	14	2.1	18.7	10	1.0	13.3	51	6.0	68.0	75	3.0	100.0
	Professional, Scientific, and Technical Activities	15	2.3	15.5	22	2.3	22.7	60	7.1	61.9	97	3.9	100.0
	Administrative and Support Service Activities	10	1.5	18.9	18	1.9	34.0	25	3.0	47.2	53	2.1	100.0
	Public Administration and Defense; Compulsory Social Security	–	–	–	–	–	–	1	0.1	100.0	1	0.0	100.0
	Education	5	0.8	16.1	9	0.9	29.0	17	2.0	54.8	31	1.3	100.0
	Human Health and Social Work Activities	3	0.5	20.0	8	0.8	53.3	4	0.5	26.7	15	0.6	100.0
	Arts, Entertainment, and Recreation	14	2.1	24.6	20	2.1	35.1	23	2.7	40.4	57	2.3	100.0
	Other Service Activities	80	12.1	22.5	125	12.9	35.2	150	17.7	42.3	355	14.3	100.0
	Total	662	100.0	26.7	971	100.0	39.1	848	100.0	34.2	2,481	100.0	100.0
Location	National Capital Region	320	48.3	26.0	450	46.3	36.6	461	54.4	37.4	1,231	49.6	100.0
	Cordillera Administrative Region	8	1.2	34.8	8	0.8	34.8	7	0.8	30.4	23	0.9	100.0
	Region 1: Ilocos	8	1.2	30.8	10	1.0	38.5	8	0.9	30.8	26	1.1	100.0
	Region 2: Cagayan Valley	6	0.9	26.1	12	1.2	52.2	5	0.6	21.7	23	0.9	100.0
	Region 3: Central Luzon	70	10.6	30.4	87	9.0	37.8	73	8.6	31.7	230	9.3	100.0
	Region 4A: Calabarzon	104	15.7	30.0	135	13.9	38.9	108	12.7	31.1	347	14.0	100.0
	MIMAROPA	9	1.4	19.6	26	2.7	56.5	11	1.3	23.9	46	1.9	100.0
	Region 5: Bicol	14	2.1	27.5	21	2.2	41.2	16	1.9	31.4	51	2.1	100.0
	Region 6: Western Visayas	24	3.6	24.0	40	4.1	40.0	36	4.3	36.0	100	4.0	100.0
	Region 7: Central Visayas	43	6.5	23.2	81	8.3	43.8	61	7.2	33.0	185	7.5	100.0
	Region 8: Eastern Visayas	5	0.8	20.0	9	0.9	36.0	11	1.3	44.0	25	1.0	100.0
	Region 9: Zamboanga Peninsula	6	0.9	30.0	7	0.7	35.0	7	0.8	35.0	20	0.8	100.0
	Region 10: Northern Mindanao	9	1.4	18.8	25	2.6	52.1	14	1.7	29.2	48	1.9	100.0
	Region 11: Davao	23	3.5	27.1	44	4.5	51.8	18	2.1	21.2	85	3.4	100.0
	Region 12: SOCCSKSARGEN	6	0.9	30.0	8	0.8	40.0	6	0.7	30.0	20	0.8	100.0
	Region 13: Caraga	7	1.1	35.0	7	0.7	35.0	6	0.7	30.0	20	0.8	100.0
	BARMM (formerly ARMM)	–	–	–	1	0.1	100.0	–	–	–	1	0.0	100.0
	Total	662	100.0	26.7	971	100.0	39.1	848	100.0	34.2	2,481	100.0	100.0

– = no number; BARMM = Bangsamoro Autonomous Region in Muslim Mindanao; MIMAROPA = Mindoro, Marinduque, Romblon, and Palawan (Southwestern Tagalog Region); SOCCSKSARGEN = South Cotabato, Cotabato, Sultan Kudarat, Saranggani, and General Santos.

* Share of vertical column. ** Share of horizontal line.

Source: Asian Development Bank, Philippine Enterprise Survey.

Main Reasons for Bottlenecks in Supply Chain

Part 2

q2.10.1: What are the main reasons for bottlenecks in supply chain?

Item	Delay in importing goods/raw materials because of international suppliers' problems — No.	%	Delay in importing goods/raw materials because of slow customs clearance — No.	%	Local suppliers or distributors have ceased or have reduced operations — No.	%	Delayed logistics because of checkpoints or border shutdown — No.	%	Delayed logistics because limited availability of trucks/drivers — No.	%	Prices of goods/raw materials have become too expensive — No.	%
Firm size												
Micro	118	41.8	558	50.3	384	49.7	231	47.1	299	53.6	113	46.1
Small	85	30.1	324	29.2	222	28.7	147	29.9	157	28.1	79	32.2
Medium-sized	55	19.5	164	14.8	117	15.1	75	15.3	70	12.5	32	13.1
Large	24	8.5	63	5.7	50	6.5	38	7.7	32	5.7	21	8.6
Total	282	100.0	1,109	100.0	773	100.0	491	100.0	558	100.0	245	100.0
Industry												
Agriculture, Forestry, and Fishing	3	0.7	3	1.1	11	1.0	9	1.2	7	1.4	3	0.5
Manufacturing	78	19.3	62	22.0	176	15.9	98	12.7	69	14.1	84	15.1
Electricity, Gas, Steam, and Air Conditioning Supply	3	0.7	1	0.4	12	1.1	8	1.0	7	1.4	4	0.7
Water Supply, Sewerage, Waste Management, and Remediation Activities	3	0.7	–	–	2	0.2	1	0.1	–	–	1	0.2
Construction	35	8.6	23	8.2	126	11.4	72	9.3	51	10.4	69	12.4
Wholesale and Retail Trade; Repair of Motor Vehicles and Motorcycles	154	38.0	111	39.4	327	29.5	264	34.2	192	39.1	152	27.2
Transportation and storage	15	3.7	14	5.0	29	2.6	25	3.2	20	4.1	8	1.4
Accommodation and Food Service Activities	31	7.7	13	4.6	161	14.5	114	14.8	56	11.4	106	19.0
Information and Communication	16	4.0	16	5.7	54	4.9	35	4.5	16	3.3	18	3.2
Financial and Insurance Activities	1	0.3	–	–	15	1.4	17	2.2	5	1.0	4	0.7
Real Estate Activities	5	1.2	5	1.8	12	1.1	13	1.7	6	1.2	5	0.9
Professional, Scientific, and Technical Activities	8	2.0	6	2.1	20	1.8	14	1.8	8	1.6	8	1.4
Administrative and Support Service Activities	2	0.5	–	–	12	1.1	7	0.9	3	0.6	7	1.3
Public Administration and Defense; Compulsory Social Security	–	–	–	–	–	–	–	–	–	–	–	–
Education	–	–	–	–	7	0.6	3	0.4	2	0.4	3	0.5
Human Health and Social Work Activities	3	0.7	1	0.4	7	0.6	6	0.8	5	1.0	6	1.1
Arts, Entertainment, and Recreation	4	1.0	2	0.7	19	1.7	14	1.8	3	0.6	13	2.3
Other Service Activities	44	10.9	25	8.9	119	10.7	73	9.4	41	8.4	67	12.0
Total	405	100.0	282	100.0	1,109	100.0	773	100.0	491	100.0	558	100.0
Location												
National Capital Region	148	52.5	505	45.5	336	43.5	214	43.6	242	43.4	113	46.1
Cordillera Administrative Region	2	0.7	13	1.2	9	1.2	8	1.6	9	1.6	1	0.4
Region 1: Ilocos	–	–	15	1.4	9	1.2	6	1.2	7	1.3	3	1.2
Region 2: Cagayan Valley	2	0.7	11	1.0	10	1.3	7	1.4	7	1.3	4	1.6
Region 3: Central Luzon	34	12.1	106	9.6	79	10.2	53	10.8	71	12.7	28	11.4
Region 4A: Calabarzon	43	15.3	171	15.4	114	14.8	64	13.0	89	16.0	33	13.5
MIMAROPA	5	1.8	27	2.4	18	2.3	13	2.7	13	2.3	2	0.8
Region 5: Bicol	5	1.8	20	1.8	22	2.9	15	3.1	11	2.0	10	4.1
Region 6: Western Visayas	7	2.5	49	4.4	36	4.7	25	5.1	17	3.1	7	2.9
Region 7: Central Visayas	19	6.7	90	8.1	55	7.1	35	7.1	46	8.2	18	7.4
Region 8: Eastern Visayas	–	–	10	0.9	11	1.4	5	1.0	7	1.3	1	0.4
Region 9: Zamboanga Peninsula	2	0.7	8	0.7	10	1.3	4	0.8	3	0.5	1	0.4
Region 10: Northern Mindanao	4	1.4	22	2.0	16	2.1	9	1.8	10	1.8	9	3.7
Region 11: Davao	8	2.8	41	3.7	30	3.9	21	4.3	18	3.2	12	4.9
Region 12: SOCCSKSARGEN	2	0.7	7	0.6	7	0.9	3	0.6	3	0.5	1	0.4
Region 13: Caraga	1	0.4	13	1.2	10	1.3	8	1.6	5	0.9	2	0.8
BARMM (formerly ARMM)	–	–	1	0.1	1	0.1	1	0.2	–	–	–	–
Total	282	100.0	1,109	100.0	773	100.0	491	100.0	558	100.0	245	100.0

– = no number; BARMM = Bangsamoro Autonomous Region in Muslim Mindanao; MIMAROPA = Mindoro, Marinduque, Romblon, and Palawan (Southwestern Tagalog Region); SOCCSKSARGEN = South Cotabato, Cotabato, Sultan Kudarat, Sarangani, and General Santos.

Source: Asian Development Bank, Philippine Enterprise Survey.

Cost of Supplies/Raw Materials during the ECQ

Part 2

q2.11: How have your cost of supplies/raw materials changed since imposition of the Enhanced Community Quarantine (ECQ) in April 2020 against March 2020?

Item		Increased			Decreased			No change			Total		
		No.	%*	%**	No.	%*	%**	No.	%*	%**	No.	%*	%**
Firm size	Micro	317	49.1	24.6	288	54.6	22.4	683	52.3	53.0	1,288	52.0	100.0
	Small	181	28.0	26.8	137	26.0	20.3	357	27.4	52.9	675	27.2	100.0
	Medium-sized	105	16.3	31.8	55	10.4	16.7	170	13.0	51.5	330	13.3	100.0
	Large	43	6.7	23.1	48	9.1	25.8	95	7.3	51.1	186	7.5	100.0
	Total	646	100.0	26.1	528	100.0	21.3	1,305	100.0	52.6	2,479	100.0	100.0
Industry	Agriculture, Forestry, and Fishing	6	0.9	33.3	4	0.8	22.2	8	0.6	44.4	18	0.7	100.0
	Manufacturing	88	13.6	33.7	44	8.3	16.9	129	9.9	49.4	261	10.5	100.0
	Electricity, Gas, Steam, and Air Conditioning Supply	5	0.8	17.2	16	3.0	55.2	8	0.6	27.6	29	1.2	100.0
	Water Supply, Sewerage, Waste Management, and Remediation Activities	1	0.2	20.0	–	–	–	4	0.3	80.0	5	0.2	100.0
	Construction	76	11.8	35.7	46	8.7	21.6	91	7.0	42.7	213	8.6	100.0
	Wholesale and Retail Trade; Repair of Motor Vehicles and Motorcycles	169	26.2	31.7	110	20.8	20.6	254	19.5	47.7	533	21.5	100.0
	Transportation and storage	22	3.4	26.8	27	5.1	32.9	33	2.5	40.2	82	3.3	100.0
	Accommodation and Food Service Activities	100	15.5	28.1	85	16.1	23.9	171	13.1	48.0	356	14.4	100.0
	Information and Communication	36	5.6	19.0	29	5.5	15.3	124	9.5	65.6	189	7.6	100.0
	Financial and Insurance Activities	13	2.0	11.9	28	5.3	25.7	68	5.2	62.4	109	4.4	100.0
	Real Estate Activities	10	1.6	13.3	14	2.7	18.7	51	3.9	68.0	75	3.0	100.0
	Professional, Scientific, and Technical Activities	14	2.2	14.4	18	3.4	18.6	65	5.0	67.0	97	3.9	100.0
	Administrative and Support Service Activities	7	1.1	13.2	18	3.4	34.0	28	2.2	52.8	53	2.1	100.0
	Public Administration and Defense; Compulsory Social Security	–	–	–	1	0.2	100.0	–	–	–	1	0.0	100.0
	Education	2	0.3	6.5	7	1.3	22.6	22	1.7	71.0	31	1.3	100.0
	Human Health and Social Work Activities	8	1.2	53.3	1	0.2	6.7	6	0.5	40.0	15	0.6	100.0
	Arts, Entertainment, and Recreation	11	1.7	19.3	12	2.3	21.1	34	2.6	59.6	57	2.3	100.0
	Other Service Activities	78	12.1	22.0	68	12.9	19.2	209	16.0	58.9	355	14.3	100.0
	Total	646	100.0	26.1	528	100.0	21.3	1,305	100.0	52.6	2,479	100.0	100.0
Location	National Capital Region	318	49.2	25.9	197	37.3	16.0	715	54.8	58.1	1,230	49.6	100.0
	Cordillera Administrative Region	11	1.7	47.8	3	0.6	13.0	9	0.7	39.1	23	0.9	100.0
	Region 1: Ilocos	8	1.2	30.8	5	1.0	19.2	13	1.0	50.0	26	1.1	100.0
	Region 2: Cagayan Valley	6	0.9	26.1	5	1.0	21.7	12	0.9	52.2	23	0.9	100.0
	Region 3: Central Luzon	63	9.8	27.4	64	12.1	27.8	103	7.9	44.8	230	9.3	100.0
	Region 4A: Calabarzon	92	14.2	26.6	81	15.3	23.4	173	13.3	50.0	346	14.0	100.0
	MIMAROPA	9	1.4	19.6	18	3.4	39.1	19	1.5	41.3	46	1.9	100.0
	Region 5: Bicol	15	2.3	29.4	11	2.1	21.6	25	1.9	49.0	51	2.1	100.0
	Region 6: Western Visayas	24	3.7	24.0	32	6.1	32.0	44	3.4	44.0	100	4.0	100.0
	Region 7: Central Visayas	51	7.9	27.6	50	9.5	27.0	84	6.4	45.4	185	7.5	100.0
	Region 8: Eastern Visayas	8	1.2	32.0	6	1.1	24.0	11	0.8	44.0	25	1.0	100.0
	Region 9: Zamboanga Peninsula	5	0.8	25.0	2	0.4	10.0	13	1.0	65.0	20	0.8	100.0
	Region 10: Northern Mindanao	10	1.6	20.8	16	3.0	33.3	22	1.7	45.8	48	1.9	100.0
	Region 11: Davao	18	2.8	21.2	25	4.7	29.4	42	3.2	49.4	85	3.4	100.0
	Region 12: SOCCSKSARGEN	5	0.8	25.0	7	1.3	35.0	8	0.6	40.0	20	0.8	100.0
	Region 13: Caraga	3	0.5	15.0	5	1.0	25.0	12	0.9	60.0	20	0.8	100.0
	BARMM (formerly ARMM)	–	–	–	1	0.2	100.0	–	–	–	1	0.0	100.0
	Total	646	100.0	26.1	528	100.0	21.3	1,305	100.0	52.6	2,479	100.0	100.0

– = no number; BARMM = Bangsamoro Autonomous Region in Muslim Mindanao; MIMAROPA = Mindoro, Marinduque, Romblon, and Palawan (Southwestern Tagalog Region); SOCCSKSARGEN = South Cotabato, Cotabato, Sultan Kudarat, Sarangani, and General Santos.

* Share of vertical column. ** Share of horizontal line.

Source: Asian Development Bank, Philippine Enterprise Survey.

Financial Condition after the COVID-19 Outbreak (15 March 2020)

Part 2

q2.12: Financial condition after the COVID-19 outbreak (15 March 2020):

Item		Enough savings, liquid assets, and other contingency budget to maintain business for more than 6 months			Cash/funds covering operation costs to be run out in 3–6 months			Cash/funds covering operation costs to be run out in 1–3 months			Already no cash and savings			Others			Total		
		No.	%*	%**	No.	%*	%**	No.	%*	%**	No.	%*	%**	No.	%*	%**	No.	%*	%**
Firm size	Micro	68	29.7	5.3	180	42.0	14.1	464	51.6	36.3	526	63.5	41.1	41	50.6	3.2	1,279	51.8	100.0
	Small	78	34.1	11.6	141	32.9	20.9	253	28.1	37.5	180	21.7	26.7	22	27.2	3.3	674	27.3	100.0
	Medium-sized	52	22.7	15.8	72	16.8	21.8	125	13.9	37.9	72	8.7	21.8	9	11.1	2.7	330	13.4	100.0
	Large	31	13.5	16.8	36	8.4	19.5	58	6.4	31.4	51	6.2	27.6	9	11.1	4.9	185	7.5	100.0
	Total	229	100.0	9.3	429	100.0	17.4	900	100.0	36.5	829	100.0	33.6	81	100.0	3.3	2,468	100.0	100.0
Industry	Agriculture, Forestry, and Fishing	3	1.3	16.7	4	0.9	22.2	6	0.7	33.3	5	0.6	27.8	–	–	–	18	0.7	100.0
	Manufacturing	31	13.5	12.0	62	14.5	23.9	84	9.3	32.4	71	8.6	27.4	11	13.6	4.2	259	10.5	100.0
	Electricity, Gas, Steam, and Air Conditioning Supply	7	3.1	24.1	9	2.1	31.0	9	1.0	31.0	4	0.5	13.8	–	–	–	29	1.2	100.0
	Water Supply, Sewerage, Waste Management, and Remediation Activities	–	–	–	1	0.2	20.0	3	0.3	60.0	1	0.1	20.0	–	–	–	5	0.2	100.0
	Construction	11	4.8	5.1	25	5.8	11.7	84	9.3	39.3	83	10.0	38.8	11	13.6	5.1	214	8.7	100.0
	Wholesale and Retail Trade; Repair of Motor Vehicles and Motorcycles	58	25.3	10.9	109	25.4	20.5	217	24.1	40.9	131	15.8	24.7	16	19.8	3.0	531	21.5	100.0
	Transportation and storage	6	2.6	7.3	16	3.7	19.5	28	3.1	34.1	29	3.5	35.4	3	3.7	3.7	82	3.3	100.0
	Accommodation and Food Service Activities	19	8.3	5.4	46	10.7	13.0	135	15.0	38.1	147	17.7	41.5	7	8.6	2.0	354	14.3	100.0
	Information and Communication	17	7.4	9.0	29	6.8	15.4	75	8.3	39.9	63	7.6	33.5	4	4.9	2.1	188	7.6	100.0
	Financial and Insurance Activities	25	10.9	23.1	17	4.0	15.7	42	4.7	38.9	20	2.4	18.5	4	4.9	3.7	108	4.4	100.0
	Real Estate Activities	20	8.7	26.7	19	4.4	25.3	23	2.6	30.7	11	1.3	14.7	2	2.5	2.7	75	3.0	100.0
	Professional, Scientific, and Technical Activities	5	2.2	5.2	19	4.4	19.8	27	3.0	28.1	38	4.6	39.6	7	8.6	7.3	96	3.9	100.0
	Administrative and Support Service Activities	6	2.6	11.3	11	2.6	20.8	16	1.8	30.2	18	2.2	34.0	2	2.5	3.8	53	2.2	100.0
	Public Administration and Defense; Compulsory Social Security	–	–	–	–	–	–	–	–	–	–	–	–	1	1.2	100.0	1	0.0	100.0

continued on next page

Financial Condition after the COVID-19 Outbreak (15 March 2020) continued

Part 2

q2.12: Financial condition after the COVID-19 outbreak (15 March 2020):

Item		Enough savings, liquid assets, and other contingency budget to maintain business for more than 6 months			Cash/funds covering operation costs to be run out in 3–6 months			Cash/funds covering operation costs to be run out in 1–3 months			Already no cash and savings			Others			Total		
		No.	%*	%**	No.	%*	%**	No.	%*	%**	No.	%*	%**	No.	%*	%**	No.	%*	%**
	Education	1	0.4	3.2	1	0.2	3.2	12	1.3	38.7	17	2.1	54.8	–	–	–	31	1.3	100.0
	Human Health and Social Work Activities	–	–	–	2	0.5	13.3	7	0.8	46.7	6	0.7	40.0	–	–	–	15	0.6	100.0
	Arts, Entertainment, and Recreation	4	1.8	7.0	10	2.3	17.5	20	2.2	35.1	21	2.5	36.8	2	2.5	3.5	57	2.3	100.0
	Other Service Activities	16	7.0	4.5	49	11.4	13.9	112	12.4	31.8	164	19.8	46.6	11	13.6	3.1	352	14.3	100.0
	Total	229	100.0	9.3	429	100.0	17.4	900	100.0	36.5	829	100.0	33.6	81	100.0	3.3	2,468	100.0	100.0
Location	National Capital Region	123	53.7	10.0	215	50.1	17.6	447	49.7	36.5	399	48.1	32.6	41	50.6	3.3	1,225	49.6	100.0
	Cordillera Administrative Region	1	0.4	4.5	5	1.2	22.7	9	1.0	40.9	7	0.8	31.8	–	–	–	22	0.9	100.0
	Region 1: Ilocos	1	0.4	3.8	3	0.7	11.5	8	0.9	30.8	14	1.7	53.8	–	–	–	26	1.1	100.0
	Region 2: Cagayan Valley	4	1.8	17.4	3	0.7	13.0	7	0.8	30.4	7	0.8	30.4	2	2.5	8.7	23	0.9	100.0
	Region 3: Central Luzon	20	8.7	8.8	39	9.1	17.2	88	9.8	38.8	72	8.7	31.7	8	9.9	3.5	227	9.2	100.0
	Region 4A: Calabarzon	22	9.6	6.4	64	14.9	18.6	130	14.4	37.7	114	13.8	33.0	15	18.5	4.3	345	14.0	100.0
	MIMAROPA	2	0.9	4.3	7	1.6	15.2	14	1.6	30.4	23	2.8	50.0	–	–	–	46	1.9	100.0
	Region 5: Bicol	6	2.6	11.8	6	1.4	11.8	13	1.4	25.5	26	3.1	51.0	–	–	–	51	2.1	100.0
	Region 6: Western Visayas	7	3.1	7.0	20	4.7	20.0	37	4.1	37.0	35	4.2	35.0	1	1.2	1.0	100	4.1	100.0
	Region 7: Central Visayas	20	8.7	10.9	37	8.6	20.1	66	7.3	35.9	57	6.9	31.0	4	4.9	2.2	184	7.5	100.0
	Region 8: Eastern Visayas	4	1.8	16.0	4	0.9	16.0	8	0.9	32.0	9	1.1	36.0	–	–	–	25	1.0	100.0
	Region 9: Zamboanga Peninsula	5	2.2	25.0	4	0.9	20.0	4	0.4	20.0	6	0.7	30.0	1	1.2	5.0	20	0.8	100.0
	Region 10: Northern Mindanao	3	1.3	6.3	6	1.4	12.5	18	2.0	37.5	18	2.2	37.5	3	3.7	6.3	48	1.9	100.0
	Region 11: Davao	9	3.9	10.6	12	2.8	14.1	31	3.4	36.5	28	3.4	32.9	5	6.2	5.9	85	3.4	100.0
	Region 12: SOCCSKSARGEN	1	0.4	5.0	1	0.2	5.0	10	1.1	50.0	8	1.0	40.0	–	–	–	20	0.8	100.0
	Region 13: Caraga	1	0.4	5.0	3	0.7	15.0	9	1.0	45.0	6	0.7	30.0	1	1.2	5.0	20	0.8	100.0
	BARMM (formerly ARMM)	–	–	–	–	–	–	1	0.1	100.0	–	–	–	–	–	–	1	0.0	100.0
	Total	229	100.0	9.3	429	100.0	17.4	900	100.0	36.5	829	100.0	33.6	81	100.0	3.3	2,468	100.0	100.0

– = no number; BARMM = Bangsamoro Autonomous Region in Muslim Mindanao; COVID-19 = coronavirus disease; MIMAROPA = Mindoro, Marinduque, Romblon, and Palawan (Southwestern Tagalog Region); SOCCSKSARGEN = South Cotabato, Cotabato, Sultan Kudarat, Sarangani, and General Santos.

* Share of vertical column. ** Share of horizontal line.

Source: Asian Development Bank, Philippine Enterprise Survey.

Most Significant Financial Problems during the COVID-19 Pandemic

Part 2

q2.13: What are the most significant financial problems for your company during the COVID-19 outbreak?

Item		Staff wages and social security charges			Rent			Repayment of loans			Payments of invoices			Other expenses			No specific problem			Total		
		No.	%*	%**	No.	%*	%**	No.	%*	%**	No.	%*	%**	No.	%*	%**	No.	%*	%**	No.	%*	%**
Firm size	Micro	483	52.4	37.6	269	65.0	21.0	215	51.3	16.8	162	43.7	12.6	121	49.6	9.4	33	33.7	2.6	1,283	52.0	100.0
	Small	276	29.9	41.1	83	20.1	12.4	117	27.9	17.4	112	30.2	16.7	58	23.8	8.6	25	25.5	3.7	671	27.2	100.0
	Medium-sized	101	11.0	30.7	39	9.4	11.9	57	13.6	17.3	67	18.1	20.4	41	16.8	12.5	24	24.5	7.3	329	13.3	100.0
	Large	62	6.7	33.5	23	5.6	12.4	30	7.2	16.2	30	8.1	16.2	24	9.8	13.0	16	16.3	8.6	185	7.5	100.0
	Total	922	100.0	37.4	414	100.0	16.8	419	100.0	17.0	371	100.0	15.0	244	100.0	9.9	98	100.0	4.0	2,468	100.0	100.0
Industry	Agriculture, Forestry, and Fishing	8	0.9	44.4	–	–	–	5	1.2	27.8	2	0.5	11.1	1	0.4	5.6	2	2.0	11.1	18	0.7	100.0
	Manufacturing	86	9.3	33.3	34	8.2	13.2	44	10.5	17.1	43	11.6	16.7	33	13.5	12.8	18	18.4	7.0	258	10.5	100.0
	Electricity, Gas, Steam, and Air Conditioning Supply	8	0.9	28.6	2	0.5	7.1	5	1.2	17.9	8	2.2	28.6	3	1.2	10.7	2	2.0	7.1	28	1.1	100.0
	Water Supply, Sewerage, Waste Management, and Remediation Activities	–	–	–	2	0.5	40.0	1	0.2	20.0	1	0.3	20.0	1	0.4	20.0	–	–	–	5	0.2	100.0
	Construction	94	10.2	43.9	10	2.4	4.7	46	11.0	21.5	40	10.8	18.7	18	7.4	8.4	6	6.1	2.8	214	8.7	100.0
	Wholesale and Retail Trade; Repair of Motor Vehicles and Motorcycles	145	15.7	27.3	86	20.8	16.2	102	24.3	19.2	138	37.2	25.9	41	16.8	7.7	20	20.4	3.8	532	21.6	100.0
	Transportation and storage	33	3.6	40.2	8	1.9	9.8	24	5.7	29.3	5	1.4	6.1	11	4.5	13.4	1	1.0	1.2	82	3.3	100.0
	Accommodation and Food Service Activities	126	13.7	35.5	103	24.9	29.0	60	14.3	16.9	27	7.3	7.6	33	13.5	9.3	6	6.1	1.7	355	14.4	100.0
	Information and Communication	91	9.9	48.4	29	7.0	15.4	17	4.1	9.0	22	5.9	11.7	18	7.4	9.6	11	11.2	5.9	188	7.6	100.0
	Financial and Insurance Activities	52	5.6	48.1	11	2.7	10.2	19	4.5	17.6	2	0.5	1.9	15	6.2	13.9	9	9.2	8.3	108	4.4	100.0
	Real Estate Activities	24	2.6	32.4	7	1.7	9.5	16	3.8	21.6	10	2.7	13.5	8	3.3	10.8	9	9.2	12.2	74	3.0	100.0
	Professional, Scientific, and Technical Activities	50	5.4	52.1	15	3.6	15.6	10	2.4	10.4	12	3.2	12.5	7	2.9	7.3	2	2.0	2.1	96	3.9	100.0
	Administrative and Support Service Activities	22	2.4	41.5	9	2.2	17.0	4	1.0	7.5	6	1.6	11.3	11	4.5	20.8	1	1.0	1.9	53	2.2	100.0
	Public Administration and Defense; Compulsory Social Security	–	–	–	–	–	–	–	–	–	–	–	–	–	–	–	1	1.0	100.0	1	0.0	100.0

continued on next page

Most Significant Financial Problems during the COVID-19 Pandemic continued

Part 2

q2.13: What are the most significant financial problems for your company during the COVID-19 outbreak?

Item		Staff wages and social security charges			Rent			Repayment of loans			Payments of invoices			Other expenses			No specific problem			Total		
		No.	%*	%**	No.	%*	%**	No.	%*	%**	No.	%*	%**	No.	%*	%**	No.	%*	%**	No.	%*	%**
	Education	13	1.4	41.9	8	1.9	25.8	7	1.7	22.6	–	–	–	1	0.4	3.2	2	2.0	6.5	31	1.3	100.0
	Human Health and Social Work Activities	3	0.3	20.0	4	1.0	26.7	3	0.7	20.0	3	0.8	20.0	2	0.8	13.3	–	–	–	15	0.6	100.0
	Arts, Entertainment, and Recreation	23	2.5	40.4	16	3.9	28.1	5	1.2	8.8	4	1.1	7.0	4	1.6	7.0	5	5.1	8.8	57	2.3	100.0
	Other Service Activities	144	15.6	40.8	70	16.9	19.8	51	12.2	14.4	48	12.9	13.6	37	15.2	10.5	3	3.1	0.8	353	14.3	100.0
	Total	922	100.0	37.4	414	100.0	16.8	419	100.0	17.0	371	100.0	15.0	244	100.0	9.9	98	100.0	4.0	2,468	100.0	100.0
Location	National Capital Region	488	52.9	39.9	224	54.1	18.3	178	42.5	14.5	181	48.8	14.8	101	41.4	8.3	52	53.1	4.2	1,224	49.6	100.0
	Cordillera Administrative Region	10	1.1	43.5	3	0.7	13.0	6	1.4	26.1	3	0.8	13.0	1	0.4	4.3	–	–	–	23	0.9	100.0
	Region 1: Ilocos	9	1.0	34.6	3	0.7	11.5	6	1.4	23.1	3	0.8	11.5	4	1.6	15.4	1	1.0	3.8	26	1.1	100.0
	Region 2: Cagayan Valley	4	0.4	17.4	7	1.7	30.4	4	1.0	17.4	4	1.1	17.4	3	1.2	13.0	1	1.0	4.3	23	0.9	100.0
	Region 3: Central Luzon	71	7.7	31.0	36	8.7	15.7	55	13.1	24.0	37	10.0	16.2	21	8.6	9.2	9	9.2	3.9	229	9.3	100.0
	Region 4A: Calabarzon	113	12.3	32.8	40	9.7	11.6	62	14.8	18.0	62	16.7	18.0	56	23.0	16.2	12	12.2	3.5	345	14.0	100.0
	MIMAROPA	17	1.8	37.8	10	2.4	22.2	5	1.2	11.1	5	1.4	11.1	7	2.9	15.6	1	1.0	2.2	45	1.8	100.0
	Region 5: Bicol	17	1.8	33.3	4	1.0	7.8	18	4.3	35.3	6	1.6	11.8	5	2.1	9.8	1	1.0	2.0	51	2.1	100.0
	Region 6: Western Visayas	33	3.6	33.0	21	5.1	21.0	21	5.0	21.0	14	3.8	14.0	9	3.7	9.0	2	2.0	2.0	100	4.1	100.0
	Region 7: Central Visayas	80	8.7	43.5	31	7.5	16.8	21	5.0	11.4	28	7.6	15.2	16	6.6	8.7	8	8.2	4.3	184	7.5	100.0
	Region 8: Eastern Visayas	9	1.0	36.0	2	0.5	8.0	5	1.2	20.0	4	1.1	16.0	3	1.2	12.0	2	2.0	8.0	25	1.0	100.0
	Region 9: Zamboanga Peninsula	9	1.0	45.0	3	0.7	15.0	3	0.7	15.0	–	–	–	3	1.2	15.0	2	2.0	10.0	20	0.8	100.0
	Region 10: Northern Mindanao	21	2.3	44.7	6	1.5	12.8	8	1.9	17.0	7	1.9	14.9	3	1.2	6.4	2	2.0	4.3	47	1.9	100.0
	Region 11: Davao	32	3.5	37.6	17	4.1	20.0	14	3.3	16.5	12	3.2	14.1	6	2.5	7.1	4	4.1	4.7	85	3.4	100.0
	Region 12: SOCCSKSARGEN	7	0.8	35.0	3	0.7	15.0	7	1.7	35.0	2	0.5	10.0	1	0.4	5.0	–	–	–	20	0.8	100.0
	Region 13: Caraga	2	0.2	10.0	4	1.0	20.0	5	1.2	25.0	3	0.8	15.0	5	2.1	25.0	1	1.0	5.0	20	0.8	100.0
	BARMM (formerly ARMM)	–	–	–	–	–	–	1	0.2	100.0	–	–	–	–	–	–	–	–	–	1	0.0	100.0
	Total	922	100.0	37.4	414	100.0	16.8	419	100.0	17.0	371	100.0	15.0	244	100.0	9.9	98	100.0	4.0	2,468	100.0	100.0

– = no number; BARMM = Bangsamoro Autonomous Region in Muslim Mindanao; COVID-19 = coronavirus disease; MIMAROPA = Mindoro, Marinduque, Romblon, and Palawan (Southwestern Tagalog Region); SOCCSKSARGEN = South Cotabato, Cotabato, Sultan Kudarat, Sarangani, and General Santos.

* Share of vertical column. ** Share of horizontal line.

Source: Asian Development Bank, Philippine Enterprise Survey.

Funding after the COVID-19 Outbreak (15 March 2020)

Part 2

q2.14: Funding conditions after the COVID-19 outbreak (15 March 2020). During the Enhanced Community Quarantine period, have you:

Item		Obtained loans/overdraft/line of credit from banks for working capital		Applied for loans/overdraft/line of credit from banks for working capital		Utilized nonbank finance institutions (e.g., microfinance institutions, pawnshops) for working capital financing		Utilized digital finance platforms (e.g., peer-to-peer lending, crowdfunding) for working capital financing		Received funding support from business partner		Received funding support from the government		Borrowed from family, relatives, and friends to maintain business		Borrowed from informal moneylenders to maintain business		Used own fund/retained profit to maintain business	
		No.	%	No.	%	No.	%	No.	%	No.	%	No.	%	No.	%	No.	%	No.	%
Firm size	Micro	113	46.1	190	50.1	94	62.3	26	63.4	111	43.5	114	51.6	366	66.2	133	61.3	643	48.2
	Small	79	32.2	114	30.1	32	21.2	9	22.0	91	35.7	66	29.9	120	21.7	53	24.4	397	29.8
	Medium-sized	32	13.1	46	12.1	17	11.3	3	7.3	34	13.3	27	12.2	43	7.8	14	6.5	196	14.7
	Large	21	8.6	29	7.7	8	5.3	3	7.3	19	7.5	14	6.3	24	4.3	17	7.8	98	7.4
	Total	245	100.0	379	100.0	151	100.0	41	100.0	255	100.0	221	100.0	553	100.0	217	100.0	1,334	100.0
Industry	Agriculture, Forestry, and Fishing	1	0.4	5	1.3	1	0.7	–	–	–	–	–	–	5	0.9	3	1.4	11	0.8
	Manufacturing	35	14.3	44	11.6	18	11.9	3	7.3	31	12.2	22	10.0	59	10.7	26	12.0	131	9.8
	Electricity, Gas, Steam, and Air Conditioning Supply	1	0.4	8	2.1	2	1.3	–	–	4	1.6	3	1.4	6	1.1	2	0.9	17	1.3
	Water Supply, Sewerage, Waste Management, and Remediation Activities	–	–	–	–	–	–	–	–	–	–	–	–	–	–	–	–	4	0.3
	Construction	24	9.8	48	12.7	20	13.3	6	14.6	24	9.4	19	8.6	62	11.2	28	12.9	113	8.5
	Wholesale and Retail Trade; Repair of Motor Vehicles and Motorcycles	71	29.0	93	24.5	32	21.2	10	24.4	41	16.1	36	16.3	124	22.4	52	24.0	295	22.1
	Transportation and storage	10	4.1	8	2.1	4	2.7	2	4.9	10	3.9	8	3.6	14	2.5	6	2.8	45	3.4
	Accommodation and Food Service Activities	23	9.4	44	11.6	22	14.6	5	12.2	27	10.6	35	15.8	89	16.1	17	7.8	175	13.1
	Information and Communication	13	5.3	21	5.5	12	8.0	6	14.6	36	14.1	24	10.9	33	6.0	12	5.5	110	8.3
	Financial and Insurance Activities	11	4.5	16	4.2	6	4.0	3	7.3	16	6.3	7	3.2	14	2.5	7	3.2	63	4.7
	Real Estate Activities	8	3.3	8	2.1	1	0.7	–	–	6	2.4	4	1.8	8	1.5	2	0.9	51	3.8
	Professional, Scientific, and Technical Activities	6	2.5	9	2.4	2	1.3	2	4.9	15	5.9	8	3.6	24	4.3	6	2.8	53	4.0
	Administrative and Support Service Activities	2	0.8	5	1.3	2	1.3	1	2.4	7	2.8	6	2.7	5	0.9	4	1.8	30	2.3
	Public Administration and Defense; Compulsory Social Security	–	–	–	–	–	–	–	–	–	–	–	–	1	0.2	1	0.5	–	–

continued on next page

Funding after the COVID-19 Outbreak (15 March 2020) continued

Part 2

q2.14: Funding conditions after the COVID-19 outbreak (15 March 2020). During the Enhanced Community Quarantine period, have you:

		Obtained loans/overdraft/line of credit from banks for working capital		Applied for loans/overdraft/line of credit from banks for working capital		Utilized nonbank finance institutions (e.g., microfinance institutions, pawnshops) for working capital financing		Utilized digital finance platforms (e.g., peer-to-peer lending, crowdfunding) for working capital financing		Received funding support from business partner		Received funding support from the government		Borrowed from family, relatives, and friends to maintain business		Borrowed from informal moneylenders to maintain business		Used own fund/retained profit to maintain business	
Item		No.	%	No.	%	No.	%	No.	%	No.	%	No.	%	No.	%	No.	%	No.	%
	Education	2	0.8	4	1.1	3	2.0	1	2.4	2	0.8	2	0.9	10	1.8	5	2.3	16	1.2
	Human Health and Social Work Activities	–	–	1	0.3	–	–	–	–	1	0.4	2	0.9	1	0.2	–	–	10	0.8
	Arts, Entertainment, and Recreation	4	1.6	5	1.3	1	0.7	–	–	4	1.6	8	3.6	9	1.6	1	0.5	33	2.5
	Other Service Activities	34	13.9	60	15.8	25	16.6	2	4.9	31	12.2	37	16.7	89	16.1	45	20.7	177	13.3
	Total	245	100.0	379	100.0	151	100.0	41	100.0	255	100.0	221	100.0	553	100.0	217	100.0	1,334	100.0
Location	National Capital Region	113	46.1	162	42.7	63	41.7	19	46.3	139	54.5	134	60.6	252	45.6	88	40.6	699	52.4
	Cordillera Administrative Region	1	0.4	3	0.8	–	–	–	–	1	0.4	2	0.9	6	1.1	1	0.5	13	1.0
	Region 1: Ilocos	3	1.2	7	1.9	–	–	–	–	–	–	–	–	8	1.5	1	0.5	12	0.9
	Region 2: Cagayan Valley	4	1.6	4	1.1	2	1.3	1	2.4	–	–	4	1.8	4	0.7	1	0.5	11	0.8
	Region 3: Central Luzon	28	11.4	41	10.8	18	11.9	6	14.6	25	9.8	19	8.6	63	11.4	27	12.4	116	8.7
	Region 4A: Calabarzon	33	13.5	55	14.5	24	15.9	4	9.8	33	12.9	29	13.1	80	14.5	40	18.4	166	12.4
	MIMAROPA	2	0.8	9	2.4	3	2.0	–	–	4	1.6	3	1.4	15	2.7	10	4.6	22	1.7
	Region 5: Bicol	10	4.1	8	2.1	3	2.0	1	2.4	3	1.2	1	0.5	16	2.9	7	3.2	26	2.0
	Region 6: Western Visayas	7	2.9	18	4.8	5	3.3	3	7.3	12	4.7	7	3.2	20	3.6	7	3.2	57	4.3
	Region 7: Central Visayas	18	7.4	23	6.1	14	9.3	2	4.9	21	8.2	10	4.5	39	7.1	14	6.5	94	7.1
	Region 8: Eastern Visayas	1	0.4	3	0.8	1	0.7	–	–	2	0.8	1	0.5	4	0.7	4	1.8	16	1.2
	Region 9: Zamboanga Peninsula	1	0.4	3	0.8	2	1.3	1	2.4	1	0.4	2	0.9	4	0.7	–	–	8	0.6
	Region 10: Northern Mindanao	9	3.7	8	2.1	1	0.7	2	4.9	6	2.4	1	0.5	12	2.2	3	1.4	27	2.0
	Region 11: Davao	12	4.9	26	6.9	8	5.3	1	2.4	6	2.4	5	2.3	21	3.8	10	4.6	45	3.4
	Region 12: SOCCSKSARGEN	1	0.4	4	1.1	3	2.0	1	2.4	2	0.8	2	0.9	3	0.5	2	0.9	10	0.8
	Region 13: Caraga	2	0.8	4	1.1	4	2.7	–	–	–	–	1	0.5	6	1.1	2	0.9	12	0.9
	BARMM (formerly ARMM)	–	–	1	0.3	–	–	–	–	–	–	–	–	–	–	–	–	–	–
	Total	245	100.0	379	100.0	151	100.0	41	100.0	255	100.0	221	100.0	553	100.0	217	100.0	1,334	100.0

– = no number; BARMM = Bangsamoro Autonomous Region in Muslim Mindanao; COVID-19 = coronavirus disease; MIMAROPA = Mindoro, Marinduque, Romblon, and Palawan (Southwestern Tagalog Region); SOCCSKSARGEN = South Cotabato, Cotabato, Sultan Kudarat, Sarangani, and General Santos.

Source: Asian Development Bank, Philippine Enterprise Survey.

Sources of Funds

Part 2

q2.16: What sources of funds can you use to maintain or restart your business?

Item		Loans/overdraft/line of credit from banks		Loans from nonbank finance institutions (e.g., microfinance institutions, pawnshops) for working capital		Loans from digital finance platforms (e.g., peer-to-peer lending, crowdfunding)		Business partner(s)		Family, relatives, and friends		Loans from informal moneylenders		Own fund/retained profit	
		No.	%	No.	%	No.	%	No.	%	No.	%	No.	%	No.	%
Firm size	Micro	507	48.3	232	65.7	66	69.5	239	48.6	364	63.6	157	66.2	408	45.7
	Small	329	31.3	82	23.2	19	20.0	160	32.5	140	24.5	49	20.7	272	30.5
	Medium-sized	138	13.1	21	6.0	5	5.3	61	12.4	45	7.9	15	6.3	140	15.7
	Large	76	7.2	18	5.1	5	5.3	32	6.5	23	4.0	16	6.8	72	8.1
	Total	1,050	100.0	353	100.0	95	100.0	492	100.0	572	100.0	237	100.0	892	100.0
Industry	Agriculture, Forestry, and Fishing	11	1.1	2	0.6	1	1.1	1	0.2	6	1.1	1	0.4	8	0.9
	Manufacturing	110	10.5	34	9.6	7	7.4	51	10.4	59	10.3	23	9.7	96	10.8
	Electricity, Gas, Steam, and Air Conditioning Supply	11	1.1	1	0.3	–	–	5	1.0	8	1.4	3	1.3	10	1.1
	Water Supply, Sewerage, Waste Management, and Remediation Activities	3	0.3	–	–	–	–	1	0.2	–	–	–	–	2	0.2
	Construction	109	10.4	33	9.4	7	7.4	41	8.3	55	9.6	34	14.4	70	7.9
	Wholesale and Retail Trade; Repair of Motor Vehicles and Motorcycles	251	23.9	74	21.0	20	21.1	95	19.3	114	19.9	59	24.9	197	22.1
	Transportation and storage	45	4.3	13	3.7	3	3.2	18	3.7	13	2.3	4	1.7	24	2.7
	Accommodation and Food Service Activities	137	13.1	58	16.4	13	13.7	67	13.6	102	17.8	28	11.8	130	14.6
	Information and Communication	69	6.6	26	7.4	8	8.4	66	13.4	32	5.6	11	4.6	77	8.6
	Financial and Insurance Activities	47	4.5	12	3.4	3	3.2	25	5.1	16	2.8	4	1.7	42	4.7
	Real Estate Activities	22	2.1	4	1.1	–	–	9	1.8	10	1.8	4	1.7	38	4.3
	Professional, Scientific, and Technical Activities	39	3.7	9	2.6	6	6.3	21	4.3	19	3.3	6	2.5	31	3.5
	Administrative and Support Service Activities	24	2.3	6	1.7	2	2.1	12	2.4	10	1.8	3	1.3	19	2.1
	Public Administration and Defense; Compulsory Social Security	–	–	–	–	–	–	–	–	–	–	–	–	–	–
	Education	7	0.7	7	2.0	–	–	4	0.8	12	2.1	7	3.0	6	0.7
	Human Health and Social Work Activities	5	0.5	2	0.6	–	–	1	0.2	1	0.2	3	1.3	5	0.6
	Arts, Entertainment, and Recreation	22	2.1	7	2.0	3	3.2	9	1.8	17	3.0	4	1.7	26	2.9
	Other Service Activities	138	13.1	65	18.4	22	23.2	66	13.4	98	17.1	43	18.1	111	12.4
	Total	1,050	100.0	353	100.0	95	100.0	492	100.0	572	100.0	237	100.0	892	100.0
Location	National Capital Region	507	48.3	155	43.9	49	51.6	258	52.4	268	46.9	101	42.6	480	53.8
	Cordillera Administrative Region	7	0.7	2	0.6	1	1.1	10	2.0	8	1.4	3	1.3	8	0.9
	Region 1: Ilocos	14	1.3	5	1.4	2	2.1	3	0.6	11	1.9	6	2.5	9	1.0
	Region 2: Cagayan Valley	9	0.9	3	0.9	1	1.1	1	0.2	5	0.9	1	0.4	9	1.0
	Region 3: Central Luzon	102	9.7	40	11.3	9	9.5	43	8.7	61	10.7	27	11.4	73	8.2
	Region 4A: Calabarzon	156	14.9	46	13.0	10	10.5	63	12.8	84	14.7	36	15.2	112	12.6
	MIMAROPA	21	2.0	10	2.8	2	2.1	10	2.0	15	2.6	9	3.8	12	1.4
	Region 5: Bicol	26	2.5	6	1.7	1	1.1	9	1.8	10	1.8	4	1.7	20	2.2
	Region 6: Western Visayas	49	4.7	17	4.8	9	9.5	28	5.7	28	4.9	11	4.6	34	3.8
	Region 7: Central Visayas	65	6.2	25	7.1	6	6.3	33	6.7	30	5.2	17	7.2	64	7.2
	Region 8: Eastern Visayas	7	0.7	6	1.7	–	–	2	0.4	3	0.5	1	0.4	5	0.6
	Region 9: Zamboanga Peninsula	7	0.7	5	1.4	–	–	3	0.6	6	1.1	–	–	7	0.8
	Region 10: Northern Mindanao	22	2.1	11	3.1	3	3.2	10	2.0	15	2.6	4	1.7	15	1.7
	Region 11: Davao	41	3.9	12	3.4	–	–	17	3.5	20	3.5	10	4.2	27	3.0
	Region 12: SOCCSKSARGEN	8	0.8	2	0.6	1	1.1	2	0.4	3	0.5	4	1.7	12	1.4
	Region 13: Caraga	8	0.8	8	2.3	1	1.1	–	–	5	0.9	3	1.3	5	0.6
	BARMM (formerly ARMM)	1	0.1	–	–	–	–	–	–	–	–	–	–	–	–
	Total	1,050	100.0	353	100.0	95	100.0	492	100.0	572	100.0	237	100.0	892	100.0

– = no number; BARMM = Bangsamoro Autonomous Region in Muslim Mindanao; MIMAROPA = Mindoro, Marinduque, Romblon, and Palawan (Southwestern Tagalog Region); SOCCSKSARGEN = South Cotabato, Cotabato, Sultan Kudarat, Sarangani, and General Santos.

Source: Asian Development Bank, Philippine Enterprise Survey.

Small Amount Funding in a Short Period (1)

		Part 2								
		q2.17: If necessary, can you borrow a total of ₱50,000 from somewhere within a week?								
		Yes			No			Total		
Item		No.	%*	%**	No.	%*	%**	No.	%*	%**
Firm size	Micro	500	43.9	39.6	762	59.4	60.4	1,262	52.1	100.0
	Small	377	33.1	56.9	286	22.3	43.1	663	27.4	100.0
	Medium-sized	173	15.2	54.2	146	11.4	45.8	319	13.2	100.0
	Large	89	7.8	49.7	90	7.0	50.3	179	7.4	100.0
	Total	1,139	100.0	47.0	1,284	100.0	53.0	2,423	100.0	100.0
Industry	Agriculture, Forestry, and Fishing	6	0.5	35.3	11	0.9	64.7	17	0.7	100.0
	Manufacturing	121	10.6	48.0	131	10.2	52.0	252	10.4	100.0
	Electricity, Gas, Steam, and Air Conditioning Supply	16	1.4	57.1	12	0.9	42.9	28	1.2	100.0
	Water Supply, Sewerage, Waste Management, and Remediation Activities	3	0.3	60.0	2	0.2	40.0	5	0.2	100.0
	Construction	102	9.0	47.9	111	8.6	52.1	213	8.8	100.0
	Wholesale and Retail Trade; Repair of Motor Vehicles and Motorcycles	272	23.9	52.3	248	19.3	47.7	520	21.5	100.0
	Transportation and storage	37	3.3	45.1	45	3.5	54.9	82	3.4	100.0
	Accommodation and Food Service Activities	148	13.0	42.3	202	15.7	57.7	350	14.4	100.0
	Information and Communication	99	8.7	53.8	85	6.6	46.2	184	7.6	100.0
	Financial and Insurance Activities	47	4.1	44.8	58	4.5	55.2	105	4.3	100.0
	Real Estate Activities	39	3.4	55.7	31	2.4	44.3	70	2.9	100.0
	Professional, Scientific, and Technical Activities	50	4.4	52.1	46	3.6	47.9	96	4.0	100.0
	Administrative and Support Service Activities	21	1.8	40.4	31	2.4	59.6	52	2.2	100.0
	Public Administration and Defense; Compulsory Social Security	–	–	–	1	0.1	100.0	1	0.0	100.0
	Education	8	0.7	25.8	23	1.8	74.2	31	1.3	100.0
	Human Health and Social Work Activities	6	0.5	40.0	9	0.7	60.0	15	0.6	100.0
	Arts, Entertainment, and Recreation	17	1.5	30.4	39	3.0	69.6	56	2.3	100.0
	Other Service Activities	147	12.9	42.5	199	15.5	57.5	346	14.3	100.0
	Total	1,139	100.0	47.0	1,284	100.0	53.0	2,423	100.0	100.0
Location	National Capital Region	631	55.4	52.4	573	44.6	47.6	1,204	49.7	100.0
	Cordillera Administrative Region	12	1.1	52.2	11	0.9	47.8	23	1.0	100.0
	Region 1: Ilocos	7	0.6	26.9	19	1.5	73.1	26	1.1	100.0
	Region 2: Cagayan Valley	7	0.6	30.4	16	1.3	69.6	23	1.0	100.0
	Region 3: Central Luzon	95	8.3	42.6	128	10.0	57.4	223	9.2	100.0
	Region 4A: Calabarzon	139	12.2	41.1	199	15.5	58.9	338	14.0	100.0
	MIMAROPA	15	1.3	32.6	31	2.4	67.4	46	1.9	100.0
	Region 5: Bicol	20	1.8	40.0	30	2.3	60.0	50	2.1	100.0
	Region 6: Western Visayas	35	3.1	35.7	63	4.9	64.3	98	4.0	100.0
	Region 7: Central Visayas	82	7.2	45.6	98	7.6	54.4	180	7.4	100.0
	Region 8: Eastern Visayas	11	1.0	47.8	12	0.9	52.2	23	1.0	100.0
	Region 9: Zamboanga Peninsula	7	0.6	36.8	12	0.9	63.2	19	0.8	100.0
	Region 10: Northern Mindanao	25	2.2	54.3	21	1.6	45.7	46	1.9	100.0
	Region 11: Davao	42	3.7	50.6	41	3.2	49.4	83	3.4	100.0
	Region 12: SOCCSKSARGEN	4	0.4	20.0	16	1.3	80.0	20	0.8	100.0
	Region 13: Caraga	7	0.6	35.0	13	1.0	65.0	20	0.8	100.0
	BARMM (formerly ARMM)	–	–	–	1	0.1	100.0	1	0.0	100.0
	Total	1,139	100.0	47.0	1,284	100.0	53.0	2,423	100.0	100.0

– = no number; BARMM = Bangsamoro Autonomous Region in Muslim Mindanao; MIMAROPA = Mindoro, Marinduque, Romblon, and Palawan (Southwestern Tagalog Region); SOCCSKSARGEN = South Cotabato, Cotabato, Sultan Kudarat, Sarangani, and General Santos.

* Share of vertical column. ** Share of horizontal line.

Source: Asian Development Bank, Philippine Enterprise Survey.

Small Amount Funding in a Short Period (2)

Part 2

q2.18: Is it more difficult to borrow ₱50,000 now than last year (2019)?

Item	Category	More difficult No.	%*	%**	Same as last year (2019) No.	%*	%**	Easier now No.	%*	%**	Don't know No.	%*	%**	Total No.	%*	%**
Firm size	Micro	804	57.8	63.6	98	38.3	7.8	17	48.6	1.3	345	46.4	27.3	1,264	52.1	100.0
	Small	357	25.7	53.8	77	30.1	11.6	12	34.3	1.8	218	29.3	32.8	664	27.4	100.0
	Medium-sized	141	10.1	44.3	59	23.1	18.6	4	11.4	1.3	114	15.3	35.8	318	13.1	100.0
	Large	88	6.3	49.2	22	8.6	12.3	2	5.7	1.1	67	9.0	37.4	179	7.4	100.0
	Total	1,390	100.0	57.3	256	100.0	10.6	35	100.0	1.4	744	100.0	30.7	2,425	100.0	100.0
Industry	Agriculture, Forestry, and Fishing	14	1.0	77.8	1	0.4	5.6	–	–	–	3	0.4	16.7	18	0.7	100.0
	Manufacturing	137	9.9	54.6	28	10.9	11.2	1	2.9	0.4	85	11.4	33.9	251	10.4	100.0
	Electricity, Gas, Steam, and Air Conditioning Supply	14	1.0	50.0	3	1.2	10.7	–	–	–	11	1.5	39.3	28	1.2	100.0
	Water Supply, Sewerage, Waste Management, and Remediation Activities	3	0.2	60.0	2	0.8	40.0	–	–	–	–	–	–	5	0.2	100.0
	Construction	128	9.2	60.4	16	6.3	7.5	6	17.1	2.8	62	8.3	29.2	212	8.7	100.0
	Wholesale and Retail Trade; Repair of Motor Vehicles and Motorcycles	280	20.1	53.6	64	25.0	12.3	7	20.0	1.3	171	23.0	32.8	522	21.5	100.0
	Transportation and storage	53	3.8	64.6	10	3.9	12.2	1	2.9	1.2	18	2.4	22.0	82	3.4	100.0
	Accommodation and Food Service Activities	224	16.1	63.8	28	10.9	8.0	3	8.6	0.9	96	12.9	27.4	351	14.5	100.0
	Information and Communication	96	6.9	52.2	27	10.6	14.7	4	11.4	2.2	57	7.7	31.0	184	7.6	100.0
	Financial and Insurance Activities	58	4.2	56.9	12	4.7	11.8	1	2.9	1.0	31	4.2	30.4	102	4.2	100.0
	Real Estate Activities	20	1.4	28.6	14	5.5	20.0	3	8.6	4.3	33	4.4	47.1	70	2.9	100.0
	Professional, Scientific, and Technical Activities	59	4.2	61.5	9	3.5	9.4	1	2.9	1.0	27	3.6	28.1	96	4.0	100.0
	Administrative and Support Service Activities	31	2.2	60.8	2	0.8	3.9	2	5.7	3.9	16	2.2	31.4	51	2.1	100.0
	Public Administration and Defense; Compulsory Social Security	–	–	–	–	–	–	–	–	–	1	0.1	100.0	1	0.0	100.0
	Education	22	1.6	71.0	2	0.8	6.5	–	–	–	7	0.9	22.6	31	1.3	100.0
	Human Health and Social Work Activities	9	0.7	60.0	–	–	–	–	–	–	6	0.8	40.0	15	0.6	100.0
	Arts, Entertainment, and Recreation	30	2.2	53.6	4	1.6	7.1	2	5.7	3.6	20	2.7	35.7	56	2.3	100.0
	Other Service Activities	212	15.3	60.6	34	13.3	9.7	4	11.4	1.1	100	13.4	28.6	350	14.4	100.0
	Total	1,390	100.0	57.3	256	100.0	10.6	35	100.0	1.4	744	100.0	30.7	2,425	100.0	100.0
Location	National Capital Region	655	47.1	54.3	135	52.7	11.2	20	57.1	1.7	397	53.4	32.9	1,207	49.8	100.0
	Cordillera Administrative Region	17	1.2	73.9	–	–	–	–	–	–	6	0.8	26.1	23	1.0	100.0
	Region 1: Ilocos	19	1.4	73.1	3	1.2	11.5	–	–	–	4	0.5	15.4	26	1.1	100.0
	Region 2: Cagayan Valley	13	0.9	56.5	2	0.8	8.7	–	–	–	8	1.1	34.8	23	1.0	100.0
	Region 3: Central Luzon	131	9.4	58.5	31	12.1	13.8	2	5.7	0.9	60	8.1	26.8	224	9.2	100.0
	Region 4A: Calabarzon	199	14.3	58.9	31	12.1	9.2	7	20.0	2.1	101	13.6	29.9	338	13.9	100.0
	MIMAROPA	33	2.4	71.7	3	1.2	6.5	–	–	–	10	1.3	21.7	46	1.9	100.0
	Region 5: Bicol	34	2.5	68.0	8	3.1	16.0	–	–	–	8	1.1	16.0	50	2.1	100.0
	Region 6: Western Visayas	64	4.6	66.0	3	1.2	3.1	–	–	–	30	4.0	30.9	97	4.0	100.0
	Region 7: Central Visayas	96	6.9	53.9	16	6.3	9.0	3	8.6	1.7	63	8.5	35.4	178	7.3	100.0
	Region 8: Eastern Visayas	13	0.9	54.2	6	2.3	25.0	–	–	–	5	0.7	20.8	24	1.0	100.0
	Region 9: Zamboanga Peninsula	11	0.8	57.9	1	0.4	5.3	–	–	–	7	0.9	36.8	19	0.8	100.0
	Region 10: Northern Mindanao	24	1.7	51.1	6	2.3	12.8	2	5.7	4.3	15	2.0	31.9	47	1.9	100.0
	Region 11: Davao	54	3.9	65.1	8	3.1	9.6	1	2.9	1.2	20	2.7	24.1	83	3.4	100.0
	Region 12: SOCCSKSARGEN	13	0.9	65.0	3	1.2	15.0	–	–	–	4	0.5	24.0	20	0.8	100.0
	Region 13: Caraga	14	1.0	73.7	–	–	–	–	–	–	5	0.7	26.3	19	0.8	100.0
	BARMM (formerly ARMM)	–	–	–	–	–	–	–	–	–	1	0.1	100.0	1	0.0	100.0
	Total	1,390	100.0	57.3	256	100.0	10.6	35	100.0	1.4	744	100.0	30.7	2,425	100.0	100.0

– = no number; BARMM = Bangsamoro Autonomous Region in Muslim Mindanao; MIMAROPA = Mindoro, Marinduque, Romblon, and Palawan (Southwestern Tagalog Region); SOCCSKSARGEN = South Cotabato, Cotabato, Sultan Kudarat, Sarangani, and General Santos.

* Share of vertical column. ** Share of horizontal line.

Source: Asian Development Bank, Philippine Enterprise Survey.

Employees Who Reside in the Same Municipality

Part 2

Item		q2.19: Among employees, how many reside in the same municipality?												Total		
		less than 25%			25%–50%			51%–75%			76%–100%					
		No.	%*	%**	No.	%*	%**	No.	%*	%**	No.	%*	%**	No.	%*	%**
Firm size	Micro	397	52.5	31.2	244	44.9	19.2	217	46.2	17.1	413	61.4	32.5	1,271	52.1	100.0
	Small	208	27.5	31.1	164	30.2	24.6	150	31.9	22.5	146	21.7	21.9	668	27.4	100.0
	Medium-sized	96	12.7	29.9	89	16.4	27.7	65	13.8	20.2	71	10.6	22.1	321	13.1	100.0
	Large	55	7.3	30.2	46	8.5	25.3	38	8.1	20.9	43	6.4	23.6	182	7.5	100.0
	Total	756	100.0	31.0	543	100.0	22.2	470	100.0	19.2	673	100.0	27.6	2,442	100.0	100.0
Industry	Agriculture, Forestry, and Fishing	2	0.3	11.1	5	0.9	27.8	2	0.4	11.1	9	1.3	50.0	18	0.7	100.0
	Manufacturing	47	6.2	18.6	59	10.9	23.3	77	16.4	30.4	70	10.4	27.7	253	10.4	100.0
	Electricity, Gas, Steam, and Air Conditioning Supply	7	0.9	25.0	5	0.9	17.9	6	1.3	21.4	10	1.5	35.7	28	1.2	100.0
	Water Supply, Sewerage, Waste Management, and Remediation Activities	3	0.4	60.0	–	–	–	1	0.2	20.0	1	0.2	20.0	5	0.2	100.0
	Construction	71	9.4	33.5	52	9.6	24.5	46	9.8	21.7	43	6.4	20.3	212	8.7	100.0
	Wholesale and Retail Trade; Repair of Motor Vehicles and Motorcycles	175	23.2	33.5	106	19.5	20.3	99	21.1	18.9	143	21.3	27.3	523	21.4	100.0
	Transportation and storage	26	3.4	31.7	21	3.9	25.6	20	4.3	24.4	15	2.2	18.3	82	3.4	100.0
	Accommodation and Food Service Activities	92	12.2	26.0	75	13.8	21.2	62	13.2	17.5	125	18.6	35.3	354	14.5	100.0
	Information and Communication	71	9.4	38.4	45	8.3	24.3	28	6.0	15.1	41	6.1	22.2	185	7.6	100.0
	Financial and Insurance Activities	34	4.5	32.4	23	4.2	21.9	20	4.3	19.0	28	4.2	26.7	105	4.3	100.0
	Real Estate Activities	19	2.5	26.4	20	3.7	27.8	13	2.8	18.1	20	3.0	27.8	72	3.0	100.0
	Professional, Scientific, and Technical Activities	45	6.0	46.9	25	4.6	26.0	9	1.9	9.4	17	2.5	17.7	96	3.9	100.0
	Administrative and Support Service Activities	22	2.9	41.5	11	2.0	20.8	11	2.3	20.8	9	1.3	17.0	53	2.2	100.0
	Public Administration and Defense; Compulsory Social Security	–	–	–	1	0.2	100.0	–	–	–	–	–	–	1	0.0	100.0
	Education	–	–	–	6	1.1	19.4	4	0.9	12.9	21	3.1	67.7	31	1.3	100.0
	Human Health and Social Work Activities	4	0.5	26.7	4	0.7	26.7	4	0.9	26.7	3	0.5	20.0	15	0.6	100.0
	Arts, Entertainment, and Recreation	23	3.0	40.4	7	1.3	12.3	8	1.7	14.0	19	2.8	33.3	57	2.3	100.0
	Other Service Activities	115	15.2	32.7	78	14.4	22.2	60	12.8	17.0	99	14.7	28.1	352	14.4	100.0
	Total	756	100.0	31.0	543	100.0	22.2	470	100.0	19.2	673	100.0	27.6	2,442	100.0	100.0
Location	National Capital Region	500	66.1	41.2	286	52.7	23.6	206	43.8	17.0	221	32.8	18.2	1,213	49.7	100.0
	Cordillera Administrative Region	3	0.4	13.0	3	0.6	13.0	4	0.9	17.4	13	1.9	56.5	23	0.9	100.0
	Region 1: Ilocos	7	0.9	26.9	6	1.1	23.1	6	1.3	23.1	7	1.0	26.9	26	1.1	100.0
	Region 2: Cagayan Valley	6	0.8	26.1	8	1.5	34.8	4	0.9	17.4	5	0.7	21.7	23	0.9	100.0
	Region 3: Central Luzon	47	6.2	20.9	52	9.6	23.1	52	11.1	23.1	74	11.0	32.9	225	9.2	100.0
	Region 4A: Calabarzon	80	10.6	23.5	64	11.8	18.8	77	16.4	22.6	120	17.8	35.2	341	14.0	100.0
	MIMAROPA	5	0.7	11.1	6	1.1	13.3	9	1.9	20.0	25	3.7	55.6	45	1.8	100.0
	Region 5: Bicol	10	1.3	19.6	7	1.3	13.7	11	2.3	21.6	23	3.4	45.1	51	2.1	100.0
	Region 6: Western Visayas	26	3.4	26.3	24	4.4	24.2	18	3.8	18.2	31	4.6	31.3	99	4.1	100.0
	Region 7: Central Visayas	46	6.1	25.4	50	9.2	27.6	38	8.1	21.0	47	7.0	26.0	181	7.4	100.0
	Region 8: Eastern Visayas	1	0.1	4.0	6	1.1	24.0	6	1.3	24.0	12	1.8	48.0	25	1.0	100.0
	Region 9: Zamboanga Peninsula	1	0.1	5.0	2	0.4	10.0	4	0.9	20.0	13	1.9	65.0	20	0.8	100.0
	Region 10: Northern Mindanao	6	0.8	13.0	7	1.3	15.2	11	2.3	23.9	22	3.3	47.8	46	1.9	100.0
	Region 11: Davao	12	1.6	14.5	16	3.0	19.3	16	3.4	19.3	39	5.8	47.0	83	3.4	100.0
	Region 12: SOCCSKSARGEN	4	0.5	20.0	2	0.4	10.0	3	0.6	15.0	11	1.6	55.0	20	0.8	100.0
	Region 13: Caraga	2	0.3	10.0	4	0.7	20.0	5	1.1	25.0	9	1.3	45.0	20	0.8	100.0
	BARMM (formerly ARMM)	–	–	–	–	–	–	–	–	–	1	0.2	100.0	1	0.0	100.0
	Total	756	100.0	31.0	543	100.0	22.2	470	100.0	19.2	673	100.0	27.6	2,442	100.0	100.0

– = no number; BARMM = Bangsamoro Autonomous Region in Muslim Mindanao; MIMAROPA = Mindoro, Marinduque, Romblon, and Palawan (Southwestern Tagalog Region); SOCCSKSARGEN = South Cotabato, Cotabato, Sultan Kudarat, Sarangani, and General Santos.

* Share of vertical column. ** Share of horizontal line.

Source: Asian Development Bank, Philippine Enterprise Survey.

Expected Volume of Order from Clients after the ECQ

Part 2

q2.20: After the Enhanced Community Quarantine (ECQ), what is your expected volume of order from client?

Item		Increase No.	%*	%**	Decrease No.	%*	%**	Remain the same No.	%*	%**	Total No.	%*	%**
Firm size	Micro	231	50.7	18.2	782	53.6	61.6	256	48.5	20.2	1,269	51.9	100.0
	Small	124	27.2	18.5	393	26.9	58.7	152	28.8	22.7	669	27.4	100.0
	Medium-sized	62	13.6	19.3	183	12.5	56.8	77	14.6	23.9	322	13.2	100.0
	Large	39	8.6	21.3	101	6.9	55.2	43	8.1	23.5	183	7.5	100.0
	Total	456	100.0	18.7	1,459	100.0	59.7	528	100.0	21.6	2,443	100.0	100.0
Industry	Agriculture, Forestry, and Fishing	1	0.2	5.6	11	0.8	61.1	6	1.1	33.3	18	0.7	100.0
	Manufacturing	46	10.1	18.2	157	10.8	62.1	50	9.5	19.8	253	10.4	100.0
	Electricity, Gas, Steam, and Air Conditioning Supply	8	1.8	28.6	8	0.6	28.6	12	2.3	42.9	28	1.2	100.0
	Water Supply, Sewerage, Waste Management, and Remediation Activities	2	0.4	40.0	1	0.1	20.0	2	0.4	40.0	5	0.2	100.0
	Construction	47	10.3	22.1	109	7.5	51.2	57	10.8	26.8	213	8.7	100.0
	Wholesale and Retail Trade; Repair of Motor Vehicles and Motorcycles	108	23.7	20.6	325	22.3	61.9	92	17.4	17.5	525	21.5	100.0
	Transportation and storage	20	4.4	24.4	40	2.7	48.8	22	4.2	26.8	82	3.4	100.0
	Accommodation and Food Service Activities	32	7.0	9.1	277	19.0	78.5	44	8.3	12.5	353	14.5	100.0
	Information and Communication	42	9.2	22.8	90	6.2	48.9	52	9.9	28.3	184	7.5	100.0
	Financial and Insurance Activities	45	9.9	43.3	38	2.6	36.5	21	4.0	20.2	104	4.3	100.0
	Real Estate Activities	9	2.0	12.5	37	2.5	51.4	26	4.9	36.1	72	3.0	100.0
	Professional, Scientific, and Technical Activities	12	2.6	12.4	61	4.2	62.9	24	4.6	24.7	97	4.0	100.0
	Administrative and Support Service Activities	11	2.4	20.8	30	2.1	56.6	12	2.3	22.6	53	2.2	100.0
	Public Administration and Defense; Compulsory Social Security	1	0.2	100.0	–	–	–	–	–	–	1	0.0	100.0
	Education	2	0.4	6.5	20	1.4	64.5	9	1.7	29.0	31	1.3	100.0
	Human Health and Social Work Activities	2	0.4	13.3	9	0.6	60.0	4	0.8	26.7	15	0.6	100.0
	Arts, Entertainment, and Recreation	6	1.3	10.5	44	3.0	77.2	7	1.3	12.3	57	2.3	100.0
	Other Service Activities	62	13.6	17.6	202	13.9	57.4	88	16.7	25.0	352	14.4	100.0
	Total	456	100.0	18.7	1,459	100.0	59.7	528	100.0	21.6	2,443	100.0	100.0
Location	National Capital Region	200	43.9	16.5	750	51.4	61.7	265	50.2	21.8	1,215	49.7	100.0
	Cordillera Administrative Region	6	1.3	26.1	14	1.0	60.9	3	0.6	13.0	23	0.9	100.0
	Region 1: Ilocos	7	1.5	26.9	13	0.9	50.0	6	1.1	23.1	26	1.1	100.0
	Region 2: Cagayan Valley	6	1.3	26.1	10	0.7	43.5	7	1.3	30.4	23	0.9	100.0
	Region 3: Central Luzon	42	9.2	18.6	129	8.8	57.1	55	10.4	24.3	226	9.3	100.0
	Region 4A: Calabarzon	77	16.9	22.6	181	12.4	53.1	83	15.7	24.3	341	14.0	100.0
	MIMAROPA	3	0.7	6.5	34	2.3	73.9	9	1.7	19.6	46	1.9	100.0
	Region 5: Bicol	6	1.3	12.0	34	2.3	68.0	10	1.9	20.0	50	2.1	100.0
	Region 6: Western Visayas	25	5.5	25.3	59	4.0	59.6	15	2.8	15.2	99	4.1	100.0
	Region 7: Central Visayas	37	8.1	20.4	108	7.4	59.7	36	6.8	19.9	181	7.4	100.0
	Region 8: Eastern Visayas	8	1.8	32.0	12	0.8	48.0	5	1.0	20.0	25	1.0	100.0
	Region 9: Zamboanga Peninsula	5	1.1	27.8	8	0.6	44.4	5	1.0	27.8	18	0.7	100.0
	Region 10: Northern Mindanao	11	2.4	23.4	24	1.6	51.1	12	2.3	25.5	47	1.9	100.0
	Region 11: Davao	14	3.1	16.9	59	4.0	71.1	10	1.9	12.0	83	3.4	100.0
	Region 12: SOCCSKSARGEN	5	1.1	25.0	9	0.6	45.0	6	1.1	30.0	20	0.8	100.0
	Region 13: Caraga	3	0.7	15.8	15	1.0	78.9	1	0.2	5.3	19	0.8	100.0
	BARMM (formerly ARMM)	1	0.2	100.0	–	–	–	–	–	–	1	0.0	100.0
	Total	456	100.0	18.7	1,459	100.0	59.7	528	100.0	21.6	2,443	100.0	100.0

– = no number; BARMM = Bangsamoro Autonomous Region in Muslim Mindanao; COVID-19 = coronavirus disease; MIMAROPA = Mindoro, Marinduque, Romblon, and Palawan (Southwestern Tagalog Region); SOCCSKSARGEN = South Cotabato, Cotabato, Sultan Kudarat, Sarangani, and General Santos.

* Share of vertical column. ** Share of horizontal line.

Source: Asian Development Bank, Philippine Enterprise Survey.

Part 3: Policy Interventions
Policy Measures Required during the COVID-19 Crisis

Part 3

q3.1: What policy measures are most needed to support your business during the COVID-19 crisis?

Item	No support required No.	%	Payroll subsidy for workers No.	%	Low-interest loan/ subsidized loan No.	%	Credit guarantee No.	%	Government purchase of goods and services from my business No.	%	Deferment of payment to government (e.g, tax payment, withholding tax, VAT, SSS, PhilHealth) No.	%	Payment deferment to debtors (e.g, banks, microfinance institutions) No.	%	Payment deferment of utility bills (e.g, electricity, gas, water supply) No.	%	Utility subsidies No.	%	Tax discounts or tax credits No.	%
Firm size																				
Micro	18	41.9	746	52.5	473	52.9	126	52.5	88	53.7	690	53.8	188	45.3	385	57.0	201	56.8	426	48.6
Small	4	9.3	407	28.6	247	27.6	72	30.0	39	23.8	349	27.2	137	33.0	170	25.2	86	24.3	254	29.0
Medium-sized	12	27.9	178	12.5	109	12.2	24	10.0	26	15.9	169	13.2	59	14.2	76	11.2	44	12.4	135	15.4
Large	9	20.9	90	6.3	65	7.3	18	7.5	11	6.7	75	5.9	31	7.5	45	6.7	23	6.5	62	7.1
Total	43	100.0	1,421	100.0	894	100.0	240	100.0	164	100.0	1,283	100.0	415	100.0	676	100.0	354	100.0	877	100.0
Sector																				
Agriculture, Forestry, and Fishing	1	2.3	14	1.0	9	1.0	1	0.4	5	3.1	4	0.3	1	0.2	4	0.6	1	0.3	7	0.8
Manufacturing	5	11.6	152	10.7	83	9.3	22	9.2	13	7.9	143	11.2	54	13.0	78	11.5	32	9.0	90	10.3
Electricity, Gas, Steam, and Air Conditioning Supply	–	–	17	1.2	8	0.9	1	0.4	2	1.2	14	1.1	4	1.0	8	1.2	2	0.6	17	1.9
Water Supply, Sewerage, Waste Management, and Remediation Activities	–	–	2	0.1	2	0.2	–	–	1	0.6	3	0.2	1	0.2	1	0.2	1	0.3	2	0.2
Construction	3	7.0	139	9.8	89	10.0	23	9.6	20	12.2	120	9.4	35	8.4	42	6.2	20	5.7	82	9.4
Wholesale and Retail Trade; Repair of Motor Vehicles and Motorcycles	8	18.6	264	18.6	218	24.4	63	26.3	52	31.7	274	21.4	114	27.5	133	19.7	54	15.3	201	22.9
Transportation and storage	1	2.3	41	2.9	31	3.5	8	3.3	1	0.6	40	3.1	22	5.3	19	2.8	16	4.5	27	3.1
Accommodation and Food Service Activities	4	9.3	192	13.5	120	13.4	31	12.9	20	12.2	187	14.6	62	14.9	132	19.5	59	16.7	126	14.4
Information and Communication	1	2.3	112	7.9	57	6.4	13	5.4	12	7.3	97	7.6	27	6.5	48	7.1	32	9.0	76	8.7
Financial and Insurance Activities	3	7.0	62	4.4	48	5.4	15	6.3	3	1.8	43	3.4	12	2.9	23	3.4	11	3.1	40	4.6
Real Estate Activities	4	9.3	38	2.7	17	1.9	3	1.3	2	1.2	38	3.0	13	3.1	23	3.4	17	4.8	29	3.3
Professional, Scientific, and Technical Activities	2	4.7	67	4.7	33	3.7	10	4.2	7	4.3	46	3.6	13	3.1	16	2.4	15	4.2	40	4.6
Administrative and Support Service Activities	1	2.3	35	2.5	16	1.8	4	1.7	1	0.6	24	1.9	4	1.0	13	1.9	9	2.5	17	1.9
Public Administration and Defense; Compulsory Social Security	–	–	–	–	–	–	–	–	1	0.6	1	0.1	–	–	–	–	–	–	–	–

continued on next page

Policy Measures Required during the COVID-19 Crisis continued

Part 3

q3.1: What policy measures are most needed to support your business during the COVID-19 crisis?

Item		No support required		Payroll subsidy for workers		Low-interest loan/ subsidized loan		Credit guarantee		Government purchase of goods and services from my business		Deferment of payment to government (e.g., tax payment, withholding tax, VAT, SSS, PhilHealth)		Payment deferment to debtors (e.g., banks, microfinance institutions)		Payment deferment of utility bills (e.g., electricity, gas, water supply)		Utility subsidies		Tax discounts or tax credits	
		No.	%	No.	%	No.	%	No.	%	No.	%	No.	%	No.	%	No.	%	No.	%	No.	%
	Education	–	–	19	1.3	11	1.2	2	0.8	–	–	14	1.1	9	2.2	14	2.1	7	2.0	6	0.7
	Human Health and Social Work Activities	–	–	7	0.5	2	0.2	2	0.8	–	–	8	0.6	1	0.2	6	0.9	4	1.1	8	0.9
	Arts, Entertainment, and Recreation	3	7.0	37	2.6	17	1.9	3	1.3	6	3.7	30	2.3	4	1.0	14	2.1	13	3.7	19	2.2
	Other Service Activities	7	16.3	223	15.7	133	14.9	39	16.3	18	11.0	197	15.4	39	9.4	102	15.1	61	17.2	90	10.3
	Total	43	100.0	1,421	100.0	894	100.0	240	100.0	164	100.0	1,283	100.0	415	100.0	676	100.0	354	100.0	877	100.0
Location	National Capital Region	15	34.9	722	50.8	412	46.1	118	49.2	78	47.6	667	52.0	196	47.2	318	47.0	206	58.2	459	52.3
	Cordillera Administrative Region	–	–	13	0.9	7	0.8	1	0.4	1	0.6	10	0.8	4	1.0	8	1.2	6	1.7	8	0.9
	Region 1: Ilocos	1	2.3	13	0.9	9	1.0	2	0.8	2	1.2	13	1.0	6	1.5	4	0.6	1	0.3	10	1.1
	Region 2: Cagayan Valley	–	–	11	0.8	10	1.1	3	1.3	2	1.2	11	0.9	2	0.5	5	0.7	2	0.6	8	0.9
	Region 3: Central Luzon	7	16.3	124	8.7	83	9.3	21	8.8	17	10.4	113	8.8	49	11.8	74	11.0	24	6.8	77	8.8
	Region 4A: Calabarzon	9	20.9	179	12.6	142	15.9	32	13.3	18	11.0	168	13.1	59	14.2	97	14.4	41	11.6	115	13.1
	MIMAROPA	1	2.3	21	1.5	20	2.2	8	3.3	5	3.1	24	1.9	7	1.7	23	3.4	4	1.1	14	1.6
	Region 5: Bicol	1	2.3	27	1.9	29	3.2	4	1.7	3	1.8	31	2.4	8	1.9	11	1.6	7	2.0	22	2.5
	Region 6: Western Visayas	1	2.3	64	4.5	33	3.7	7	2.9	7	4.3	50	3.9	23	5.5	27	4.0	13	3.7	34	3.9
	Region 7: Central Visayas	2	4.7	115	8.1	56	6.3	15	6.3	14	8.5	101	7.9	22	5.3	57	8.4	26	7.3	65	7.4
	Region 8: Eastern Visayas	1	2.3	17	1.2	9	1.0	2	0.8	2	1.2	10	0.8	8	1.9	7	1.0	3	0.9	3	0.3
	Region 9: Zamboanga Peninsula	–	–	12	0.8	7	0.8	4	1.7	–	–	6	0.5	3	0.7	3	0.4	1	0.3	6	0.7
	Region 10: Northern Mindanao	2	4.7	30	2.1	19	2.1	6	2.5	5	3.1	23	1.8	4	1.0	15	2.2	5	1.4	13	1.5
	Region 11: Davao	1	2.3	50	3.5	40	4.5	11	4.6	6	3.7	39	3.0	13	3.1	17	2.5	11	3.1	35	4.0
	Region 12: SOCCSKSARGEN	2	4.7	12	0.8	7	0.8	4	1.7	3	1.8	5	0.4	4	1.0	3	0.4	2	0.6	3	0.3
	Region 13: Caraga	–	–	11	0.8	11	1.2	2	0.8	1	0.6	12	0.9	6	1.5	7	1.0	2	0.6	4	0.5
	BARMM (formerly ARMM)	–	–	–	–	–	–	–	–	–	–	–	–	1	0.2	–	–	–	–	1	0.1
	Total	43	100.0	1,421	100.0	894	100.0	240	100.0	164	100.0	1,283	100.0	415	100.0	676	100.0	354	100.0	877	100.0

– = no number; BARMM = Bangsamoro Autonomous Region in Muslim Mindanao; COVID-19 = coronavirus disease; MIMAROPA = Mindoro, Marinduque, Romblon, and Palawan (Southwestern Tagalog Region); PhilHealth = Philippine Health Insurance Corporation; SOCCSKSARGEN = South Cotabato, Cotabato, Sultan Kudarat, Sarangani, and General Santos; SSS = Social Security System; VAT = value-added tax.

Source: Asian Development Bank, Philippine Enterprise Survey.

Policy Measures Required after the COVID-19 Crisis

Part 3

q3.2: What policy measures are most needed to support your business to be adopted after the COVID-19 crisis is resolved?

Item		Provide financial assistance on teleworking arrangement		Tax incentives for adopting digital technologies (e.g, e-payments, e-commerce)		Provide support in upgrading skills of workers to keep them competitive under the "new normal"		Facilitate access to new financing models (e.g, crowdfunding, peer-to-peer (P2P) lending)		Improve public ICT infrastructure and regulation to increase internet speed and lower internet cost		Review BIR, SEC, and COA regulations to be compatible with digital payments and transactions		Streamline government transaction processes and shift to digital platforms		Streamline labor regulations for remote working arrangements	
		No.	%	No.	%	No.	%	No.	%	No.	%	No.	%	No.	%	No.	%
Firm size	Micro	314	58.0	417	54.4	443	49.6	272	55.6	266	48.5	536	50.9	351	46.6	208	47.4
	Small	122	22.6	198	25.8	255	28.6	128	26.2	156	28.4	301	28.6	241	32.0	122	27.8
	Medium-sized	64	11.8	100	13.0	123	13.8	56	11.5	79	14.4	135	12.8	120	15.9	70	16.0
	Large	41	7.6	52	6.8	72	8.1	33	6.8	48	8.7	82	7.8	42	5.6	39	8.9
	Total	541	100.0	767	100.0	893	100.0	489	100.0	549	100.0	1,054	100.0	754	100.0	439	100.0
Sector	Agriculture, Forestry, and Fishing	3	0.6	6	0.8	7	0.8	5	1.0	1	0.2	7	0.7	10	1.3	4	0.9
	Manufacturing	45	8.3	71	9.3	113	12.7	54	11.0	49	8.9	110	10.4	80	10.6	40	9.1
	Electricity, Gas, Steam, and Air Conditioning Supply	4	0.7	8	1.0	14	1.6	2	0.4	6	1.1	17	1.6	14	1.9	4	0.9
	Water Supply; Sewerage, Waste Management, and Remediation Activities	1	0.2	1	0.1	1	0.1	1	0.2	2	0.4	2	0.2	1	0.1	–	–
	Construction	40	7.4	65	8.5	102	11.4	59	12.1	28	5.1	87	8.3	58	7.7	53	12.1
	Wholesale and Retail Trade; Repair of Motor Vehicles and Motorcycles	109	20.2	182	23.7	186	20.8	106	21.7	119	21.7	240	22.8	165	21.9	74	16.9
	Transportation and storage	16	3.0	22	2.9	30	3.4	17	3.5	15	2.7	34	3.2	30	4.0	16	3.6
	Accommodation and Food Service Activities	74	13.7	135	17.6	124	13.9	72	14.7	63	11.5	152	14.4	90	11.9	47	10.7
	Information and Communication	62	11.5	68	8.9	40	4.5	36	7.4	75	13.7	68	6.5	73	9.7	56	12.8
	Financial and Insurance Activities	20	3.7	31	4.0	43	4.8	30	6.1	20	3.6	50	4.7	30	4.0	14	3.2
	Real Estate Activities	13	2.4	22	2.9	20	2.2	6	1.2	21	3.8	31	2.9	32	4.2	12	2.7
	Professional, Scientific, and Technical Activities	30	5.6	35	4.6	25	2.8	12	2.5	36	6.6	44	4.2	28	3.7	21	4.8
	Administrative and Support Service Activities	13	2.4	13	1.7	19	2.1	2	0.4	17	3.1	21	2.0	12	1.6	8	1.8
	Public Administration and Defense; Compulsory Social Security	–	–	–	–	1	0.1	–	–	1	0.2	–	–	–	–	–	–

continued on next page

Policy Measures Required after the COVID-19 Crisis continued

Part 3

q3.2. What policy measures are most needed to support your business to be adopted after the COVID-19 crisis is resolved?

Item		Provide financial assistance on teleworking arrangement.		Tax incentives for adopting digital technologies (e.g, e-payments, e-commerce).		Provide support in upgrading skills of workers to keep them competitive under the "new normal".		Facilitate access to new financing models (e.g., crowdfunding, peer-to-peer (P2P) lending).		Improve public ICT infrastructure and regulation to increase internet speed and lower internet cost.		Review BIR, SEC, and COA regulations to be compatible with digital payments and transactions.		Streamline government transaction processes and shift to digital platforms.		Streamline labor regulations for remote working arrangements.	
		No.	%	No.	%	No.	%	No.	%	No.	%	No.	%	No.	%	No.	%
	Education	8	1.5	7	0.9	15	1.7	10	2.0	15	2.7	14	1.3	6	0.8	4	0.9
	Human Health and Social Work Activities	3	0.6	2	0.3	6	0.7	2	0.4	3	0.6	8	0.8	2	0.3	3	0.7
	Arts, Entertainment, and Recreation	13	2.4	12	1.6	17	1.9	6	1.2	12	2.2	26	2.5	23	3.1	16	3.6
	Other Service Activities	87	16.1	87	11.3	130	14.6	69	14.1	66	12.0	143	13.6	100	13.3	67	15.3
	Total	541	100.0	767	100.0	893	100.0	489	100.0	549	100.0	1,054	100.0	754	100.0	439	100.0
Location	National Capital Region	246	45.5	387	50.5	392	43.9	226	46.2	305	55.6	551	52.3	415	55.0	241	54.9
	Cordillera Administrative Region	–	–	11	1.4	12	1.3	5	1.0	4	0.7	11	1.0	12	1.6	2	0.5
	Region 1: Ilocos	3	0.6	6	0.8	9	1.0	5	1.0	5	0.9	10	1.0	7	0.9	4	0.9
	Region 2: Cagayan Valley	3	0.6	2	0.3	8	0.9	5	1.0	4	0.7	9	0.9	9	1.2	5	1.1
	Region 3: Central Luzon	50	9.2	73	9.5	91	10.2	45	9.2	41	7.5	97	9.2	69	9.2	37	8.4
	Region 4A: Calabarzon	84	15.5	106	13.8	147	16.5	63	12.9	66	12.0	136	12.9	84	11.1	56	12.8
	MIMAROPA	17	3.1	15	2.0	16	1.8	11	2.3	11	2.0	21	2.0	13	1.7	9	2.1
	Region 5: Bicol	11	2.0	14	1.8	17	1.9	14	2.9	13	2.4	28	2.7	16	2.1	8	1.8
	Region 6: Western Visayas	28	5.2	29	3.8	46	5.2	21	4.3	15	2.7	50	4.7	21	2.8	17	3.9
	Region 7: Central Visayas	38	7.0	58	7.6	69	7.7	37	7.6	51	9.3	68	6.5	62	8.2	25	5.7
	Region 8: Eastern Visayas	5	0.9	6	0.8	11	1.2	4	0.8	7	1.3	9	0.9	8	1.1	7	1.6
	Region 9: Zamboanga Peninsula	2	0.4	5	0.7	5	0.6	6	1.2	1	0.2	5	0.5	4	0.5	3	0.7
	Region 10: Northern Mindanao	14	2.6	13	1.7	28	3.1	12	2.5	9	1.6	14	1.3	16	2.1	8	1.8
	Region 11: Davao	30	5.6	31	4.0	24	2.7	21	4.3	15	2.7	37	3.5	13	1.7	10	2.3
	Region 12: SOCCSKSARGEN	4	0.7	4	0.5	10	1.1	7	1.4	–	–	2	0.2	2	0.3	4	0.9
	Region 13: Caraga	6	1.1	7	0.9	8	0.9	7	1.4	2	0.4	5	0.5	3	0.4	3	0.7
	BARMM (formerly ARMM)	–	–	–	–	–	–	–	–	–	–	1	0.1	–	–	–	–
	Total	541	100.0	767	100.0	893	100.0	489	100.0	549	100.0	1,054	100.0	754	100.0	439	100.0

– = no number; BARMM = Bangsamoro Autonomous Region in Muslim Mindanao; BIR = Bureau of Internal Revenue; COA = Commission on Audit; COVID-19 = coronavirus disease; ICT = information and communication technology; MIMAROPA = Mindoro, Marinduque, Romblon, and Palawan (Southwestern Tagalog Region); SEC = Securities and Exchange Commission; SOCCSKSARGEN = South Cotabato, Cotabato, Sultan Kudarat, Sarangani, and General Santos.

Source: Asian Development Bank, Philippine Enterprise Survey.

Availability of the Department of Labor and Employment's COVID-19 Adjustment Measures Program

Part 3

q3.3: Has your company availed of the Department of Labor and Employment's COVID-19 Adjustment Measures Program to provide financial assistance to employees unable to work due to quarantine measures?

Item		Yes			No			Total		
		No.	%*	%**	No.	%*	%**	No.	%*	%**
Firm size	Micro	365	44.8	28.4	922	55.4	71.6	1,287	51.9	100.0
	Small	259	31.8	38.3	417	25.1	61.7	676	27.3	100.0
	Medium-sized	126	15.5	38.2	204	12.3	61.8	330	13.3	100.0
	Large	65	8.0	34.9	121	7.3	65.1	186	7.5	100.0
	Total	815	100.0	32.9	1,664	100.0	67.1	2,479	100.0	100.0
Sector	Agriculture, Forestry, and Fishing	6	0.7	33.3	12	0.7	66.7	18	0.7	100.0
	Manufacturing	92	11.3	35.2	169	10.2	64.8	261	10.5	100.0
	Electricity, Gas, Steam, and Air Conditioning Supply	6	0.7	20.7	23	1.4	79.3	29	1.2	100.0
	Water Supply, Sewerage, Waste Management, and Remediation Activities	1	0.1	20.0	4	0.2	80.0	5	0.2	100.0
	Construction	64	7.9	29.9	150	9.0	70.1	214	8.6	100.0
	Wholesale and Retail Trade; Repair of Motor Vehicles and Motorcycles	185	22.7	34.7	348	20.9	65.3	533	21.5	100.0
	Transportation and storage	26	3.2	31.7	56	3.4	68.3	82	3.3	100.0
	Accommodation and Food Service Activities	126	15.5	35.4	230	13.8	64.6	356	14.4	100.0
	Information and Communication	60	7.4	31.7	129	7.8	68.3	189	7.6	100.0
	Financial and Insurance Activities	34	4.2	31.2	75	4.5	68.8	109	4.4	100.0
	Real Estate Activities	17	2.1	22.7	58	3.5	77.3	75	3.0	100.0
	Professional, Scientific, and Technical Activities	31	3.8	32.0	66	4.0	68.0	97	3.9	100.0
	Administrative and Support Service Activities	14	1.7	26.4	39	2.3	73.6	53	2.1	100.0
	Public Administration and Defense; Compulsory Social Security	–	–	–	1	0.1	100.0	1	0.0	100.0
	Education	10	1.2	32.3	21	1.3	67.7	31	1.3	100.0
	Human Health and Social Work Activities	6	0.7	40.0	9	0.5	60.0	15	0.6	100.0
	Arts, Entertainment, and Recreation	24	2.9	42.9	32	1.9	57.1	56	2.3	100.0
	Other Service Activities	113	13.9	31.8	242	14.5	68.2	355	14.3	100.0
	Total	815	100.0	32.9	1,664	100.0	67.1	2,479	100.0	100.0
Location	National Capital Region	428	52.5	34.8	802	48.2	65.2	1,230	49.6	100.0
	Cordillera Administrative Region	17	2.1	73.9	6	0.4	26.1	23	0.9	100.0
	Region 1: Ilocos	8	1.0	30.8	18	1.1	69.2	26	1.1	100.0
	Region 2: Cagayan Valley	11	1.4	47.8	12	0.7	52.2	23	0.9	100.0
	Region 3: Central Luzon	85	10.4	37.0	145	8.7	63.0	230	9.3	100.0
	Region 4A: Calabarzon	99	12.2	28.5	248	14.9	71.5	347	14.0	100.0
	MIMAROPA	23	2.8	50.0	23	1.4	50.0	46	1.9	100.0
	Region 5: Bicol	16	2.0	31.4	35	2.1	68.6	51	2.1	100.0
	Region 6: Western Visayas	10	1.2	10.0	90	5.4	90.0	100	4.0	100.0
	Region 7: Central Visayas	51	6.3	27.6	134	8.1	72.4	185	7.5	100.0
	Region 8: Eastern Visayas	8	1.0	32.0	17	1.0	68.0	25	1.0	100.0
	Region 9: Zamboanga Peninsula	7	0.9	35.0	13	0.8	65.0	20	0.8	100.0
	Region 10: Northern Mindanao	13	1.6	27.1	35	2.1	72.9	48	1.9	100.0
	Region 11: Davao	29	3.6	34.1	56	3.4	65.9	85	3.4	100.0
	Region 12: SOCCSKSARGEN	7	0.9	36.8	12	0.7	63.2	19	0.8	100.0
	Region 13: Caraga	3	0.4	15.0	17	1.0	85.0	20	0.8	100.0
	BARMM (formerly ARMM)	–	–	–	1	0.1	100.0	1	0.0	100.0
	Total	815	100.0	32.9	1,664	100.0	67.1	2,479	100.0	100.0

– = no number; BARMM = Bangsamoro Autonomous Region in Muslim Mindanao; COVID-19 = coronavirus disease; MIMAROPA = Mindoro, Marinduque, Romblon, and Palawan (Southwestern Tagalog Region); SOCCSKSARGEN = South Cotabato, Cotabato, Sultan Kudarat, Sarangani, and General Santos.

* Share of vertical column. ** Share of horizontal line.

Source: Asian Development Bank, Philippine Enterprise Survey.

Part 4: Social Contact Indices
Actions to Be Taken after Business Reopening

Part 4

q4.3: Which of the following activities will be performed by your firm after reopening?

Item		Separate staff by smaller groups and restrict interaction between groups.			For contact tracing purpose, keep record of contacted personnel for all staff.			Canteen rationing to ensure social distancing during lunch.			Routine temperature checks for all staff.			Provide all staff enough face masks for business days.			Total		
		No.	%*	%**	No.	%*	%**	No.	%*	%**	No.	%*	%**	No.	%*	%**	No.	%*	%**
Firm size	Micro	199	47.5	15.5	87	57.2	6.8	5	29.4	0.4	123	38.6	9.5	874	55.5	67.9	1,288	51.9	100.0
	Small	120	28.6	17.8	38	25.0	5.6	5	29.4	0.7	117	36.7	17.3	396	25.2	58.6	676	27.3	100.0
	Medium-sized	67	16.0	20.2	17	11.2	5.1	3	17.7	0.9	47	14.7	14.2	197	12.5	59.5	331	13.3	100.0
	Large	33	7.9	17.7	10	6.6	5.4	4	23.5	2.2	32	10.0	17.2	107	6.8	57.5	186	7.5	100.0
	Total	419	100.0	16.9	152	100.0	6.1	17	100.0	0.7	319	100.0	12.9	1,574	100.0	63.4	2,481	100.0	100.0
Industry	Agriculture, Forestry, and Fishing	4	1.0	22.2	3	2.0	16.7	–	–	–	3	0.9	16.7	8	0.5	44.4	18	0.7	100.0
	Manufacturing	34	8.1	13.0	18	11.8	6.9	5	29.4	1.9	46	14.4	17.6	158	10.0	60.5	261	10.5	100.0
	Electricity, Gas, Steam, and Air Conditioning Supply	5	1.2	17.2	3	2.0	10.3	–	–	–	4	1.3	13.8	17	1.1	58.6	29	1.2	100.0
	Water Supply, Sewerage, Waste Management, and Remediation Activities	–	–	–	–	–	–	–	–	–	–	–	–	5	0.3	100.0	5	0.2	100.0
	Construction	53	12.7	24.8	12	7.9	5.6	1	5.9	0.5	24	7.5	11.2	124	7.9	57.9	214	8.6	100.0
	Wholesale and Retail Trade; Repair of Motor Vehicles and Motorcycles	77	18.4	14.4	26	17.1	4.9	2	11.8	0.4	59	18.5	11.0	370	23.5	69.3	534	21.5	100.0
	Transportation and storage	13	3.1	15.9	2	1.3	2.4	–	–	–	16	5.0	19.5	51	3.2	62.2	82	3.3	100.0
	Accommodation and Food Service Activities	51	12.2	14.3	26	17.1	7.3	4	23.5	1.1	44	13.8	12.4	231	14.7	64.9	356	14.4	100.0
	Information and Communication	61	14.6	32.3	8	5.3	4.2	–	–	–	28	8.8	14.8	92	5.8	48.7	189	7.6	100.0
	Financial and Insurance Activities	17	4.1	15.6	9	5.9	8.3	1	5.9	0.9	9	2.8	8.3	73	4.6	67.0	109	4.4	100.0
	Real Estate Activities	9	2.2	12.0	3	2.0	4.0	–	–	–	13	4.1	17.3	50	3.2	66.7	75	3.0	100.0
	Professional, Scientific, and Technical Activities	18	4.3	18.6	5	3.3	5.2	–	–	–	19	6.0	19.6	55	3.5	56.7	97	3.9	100.0
	Administrative and Support Service Activities	9	2.2	17.0	3	2.0	5.7	–	–	–	6	1.9	11.3	35	2.2	66.0	53	2.1	100.0
	Public Administration and Defense; Compulsory Social Security	–	–	–	–	–	–	–	–	–	–	–	–	1	0.1	100.0	1	0.0	100.0

continued on next page

Actions to Be Taken after Business Reopening continued

Part 4

q4.3: Which of the following activities will be performed by your firm after reopening?

Item		Separate staff by smaller groups and restrict interaction between groups.			For contact tracing purpose, keep record of contacted personnel for all staff.			Canteen rationing to ensure social distancing during lunch.			Routine temperature checks for all staff.			Provide all staff enough face masks for business days.			Total		
		No.	%*	%**	No.	%*	%**	No.	%*	%**	No.	%*	%**	No.	%*	%**	No.	%*	%**
	Education	5	1.2	16.1	2	1.3	6.5	–	–	–	5	1.6	16.1	19	1.2	61.3	31	1.3	100.0
	Human Health and Social Work Activities	2	0.5	13.3	–	–	–	–	–	–	2	0.6	13.3	11	0.7	73.3	15	0.6	100.0
	Arts, Entertainment, and Recreation	11	2.6	19.3	5	3.3	8.8	1	5.9	1.8	8	2.5	14.0	32	2.0	56.1	57	2.3	100.0
	Other Service Activities	50	11.9	14.1	27	17.8	7.6	3	17.7	0.8	33	10.3	9.3	242	15.4	68.2	355	14.3	100.0
	Total	419	100.0	16.9	152	100.0	6.1	17	100.0	0.7	319	100.0	12.9	1,574	100.0	63.4	2,481	100.0	100.0
Location	National Capital Region	219	52.3	17.8	65	42.8	5.3	10	58.8	0.8	165	51.7	13.4	772	49.1	62.7	1,231	49.6	100.0
	Cordillera Administrative Region	2	0.5	8.7	3	2.0	13.0	–	–	–	4	1.3	17.4	14	0.9	60.9	23	0.9	100.0
	Region 1: Ilocos	2	0.5	7.7	3	2.0	11.5	–	–	–	3	0.9	11.5	18	1.1	69.2	26	1.1	100.0
	Region 2: Cagayan Valley	4	1.0	17.4	1	0.7	4.3	–	–	–	2	0.6	8.7	16	1.0	69.6	23	0.9	100.0
	Region 3: Central Luzon	41	9.8	17.8	11	7.2	4.8	1	5.9	0.4	33	10.3	14.3	144	9.2	62.6	230	9.3	100.0
	Region 4A: Calabarzon	45	10.7	13.0	20	13.2	5.8	1	5.9	0.3	43	13.5	12.4	238	15.1	68.6	347	14.0	100.0
	MIMAROPA	13	3.1	28.3	4	2.6	8.7	1	5.9	2.2	6	1.9	13.0	22	1.4	47.8	46	1.9	100.0
	Region 5: Bicol	12	2.9	23.5	3	2.0	5.9	–	–	–	6	1.9	11.8	30	1.9	58.8	51	2.1	100.0
	Region 6: Western Visayas	9	2.2	9.0	8	5.3	8.0	–	–	–	13	4.1	13.0	70	4.5	70.0	100	4.0	100.0
	Region 7: Central Visayas	35	8.4	18.9	15	9.9	8.1	4	23.5	2.2	25	7.8	13.5	106	6.7	57.3	185	7.5	100.0
	Region 8: Eastern Visayas	4	1.0	16.0	4	2.6	16.0	–	–	–	1	0.3	4.0	16	1.0	64.0	25	1.0	100.0
	Region 9: Zamboanga Peninsula	2	0.5	10.0	3	2.0	15.0	–	–	–	1	0.3	5.0	14	0.9	70.0	20	0.8	100.0
	Region 10: Northern Mindanao	12	2.9	25.0	3	2.0	6.3	–	–	–	6	1.9	12.5	27	1.7	56.3	48	1.9	100.0
	Region 11: Davao	10	2.4	11.8	6	4.0	7.1	–	–	–	8	2.5	9.4	61	3.9	71.8	85	3.4	100.0
	Region 12: SOCCSKSARGEN	7	1.7	35.0	2	1.3	10.0	–	–	–	1	0.3	5.0	10	0.6	50.0	20	0.8	100.0
	Region 13: Caraga	2	0.5	10.0	1	0.7	5.0	–	–	–	2	0.6	10.0	15	1.0	75.0	20	0.8	100.0
	BARMM (formerly ARMM)	–	–	–	–	–	–	–	–	–	–	–	–	1	0.1	100.0	1	0.0	100.0
	Total	419	100.0	16.9	152	100.0	6.1	17	100.0	0.7	319	100.0	12.9	1,574	100.0	63.4	2,481	100.0	100.0

– = no number; BARMM = Bangsamoro Autonomous Region in Muslim Mindanao; MIMAROPA = Mindoro, Marinduque, Romblon, and Palawan (Southwestern Tagalog Region); SOCCSKSARGEN = South Cotabato, Cotabato, Sultan Kudarat, Sarangani, and General Santos.

* Share of vertical column. ** Share of horizontal line.

Source: Asian Development Bank, Philippine Enterprise Survey.

ANNEX 2: SURVEY QUESTIONNAIRE

Asian Development Bank

Enterprise Survey for the COVID-19 Impact in the Philippines

Dear Head/Owner of the company,

Thank you for your valuable participation in this survey.

The Asian Development Bank (ADB) is a multilateral development bank owned by 68 members, and its main mission is to reduce poverty in the Asia and Pacific region.

ADB is conducting a rapid survey on companies in the Philippines to assess the impact of the coronavirus disease (COVID-19) on your business and explore possible assistance to firms devastated by COVID-19.

To this end, we would very much appreciate your cooperation in answering following questions. It will take around 30 minutes to complete this survey.

In accordance with the Data Privacy Act of 2012, by participating in this survey, you consent to the collection, use, storage, and all other forms of processing of your information in relation to the purpose of the survey. Information you provided is strictly confidential and utilized only for aggregate analysis without individual identity.

Company Information

Company Name:

Name of head of the company:

☐ Mr. ☐ Ms.

Email of person responsible for answering the questions:

Address (names of municipality and province):

Part 1: Company Profile

1.1 What best describes your company?

-- *Please select one* --
☐ Corporation or a partnership
☐ Cooperative or foundation
☐ Sole proprietorship
☐ Others, please specify: _____

1.2 Is the company registered with the following government agency?

-- *Please select all that apply* --
☐ DTI – Department of Trade and Industry
☐ SEC – Securities and Exchange Commission
☐ PSE – Philippine Stock Exchange
☐ SSS – Social Security System
☐ BIR – Bureau of Internal Revenue
☐ CDA – Cooperative Development Authority
☐ LGU – Local Government Unit (City/Municipal Office)
☐ None of the above
☐ Others, please specify: _____

1.3 What is your primary business sector?

-- *Please select one* --
☐ Agriculture, forestry and fisheries
☐ Manufacturing – Food and beverages
☐ Manufacturing – Electronics
☐ Manufacturing – Garments
☐ Manufacturing – Other manufacturing activities
☐ Power and energy (e.g., electricity, gas, petrol stations)
☐ Construction

☐ Wholesale and retail trade

☐ Repair of motor vehicles and motorcycles

☐ Transportation and storage

☐ Tourism and accommodation services

☐ Food service activities

☐ Information and communication technology – Business process outsourcing (BPO)

☐ Information and communication technology – Others

☐ Finance and insurance activities

☐ Real estate activities

☐ Arts, entertainment, and recreation

☐ Others, please specify: _____.

1.4 What type of product or service represents your company's largest share of annual sales?

_____.

(name of product or service with the largest share of annual sales)

1.5 Your company location:

--Please select the Region--

☐ National Capital Region

☐ Cordillera Administrative Region

☐ Region 1: Ilocos

☐ Region 2: Cagayan Valley

☐ Region 3: Central Luzon

☐ Region 4A: Calabarzon

☐ MIMAROPA

☐ Region 5: Bicol

☐ Region 6: Western Visayas

☐ Region 7: Central Visayas

☐ Region 8: Eastern Visayas

☐ Region 9: Zamboanga Peninsula

☐ Region 10: Northern Mindanao

- ☐ Region 11: Davao
- ☐ Region 12: SOCCSKSARGEN
- ☐ Region 13: Caraga
- ☐ BARMM (formerly ARMM)

1.6   Period of your operations since establishment (as of the end of 2019):

-- Please select one --

☐ 0–5 years   ☐ 6–10 years   ☐ 11–15 years   ☐ 16–30 years   ☐ 31 years and above

1.7   How many full-time and part-time paid workers did your company have (as of the end of 2019)?

1.7.a. Number of full-time regular workers	_____.
1.7.b. Number of part-time or contractual workers	_____.

1.8   Percentage (%) of female employees to total employees (as of the end of 2019):

-- Please select one --

☐ 0%–10%   ☐ 11%–30%   ☐ 31%–50%   ☐ 51%–80%   ☐ 81% and above

1.9   Monthly wage per full-time regular worker (as of the end of 2019):

<=₱9,000	[number] _____.
₱9,001 – ₱20,000	[number] _____.
₱20,001 – ₱26,000	[number] _____.
>₱26,000	[number] _____.

1.10   Total assets (including fixed assets such as buildings and equipment, and financial assets such as bank savings, but excluding land, as of the end of 2019):

-- Please select one --
- ☐ Not more than ₱3,000,000
- ☐ ₱3,000,001 – ₱15,000,000
- ☐ ₱5,000,001 – ₱100,000,000
- ☐ Over ₱100,000,000

1.11 Annual total revenue (as of the end of 2019):

Please indicate amount **in pesos:** .

1.12 Are you engaged in online selling or e-commerce?

-- Select --

☐ Yes   ☐ No

1.13 Do you export your products or services?

--Select--

☐ Yes *(proceed to **question 1.13.1 to 1.13.2**)*

☐ No *(proceed to **question 1.14**)*

1.13.1 What is the share of exports to your total sales as of the end of 2019?

-- Please select one --

☐ 0%

☐ 1%–20%

☐ 21%–50%

☐ 51%–70%

☐ 71%–90%

☐ More than 90%

1.13.2 To which countries did you **export** your goods and services last year (2019)?

-- Please select all that apply --

☐ People's Republic of China   ☐ Japan   ☐ Republic of Korea   ☐ Other Asian countries

☐ United States   ☐ Europe   ☐ Latin America   ☐ Middle East and North Africa

☐ Other regions   ☐ Don't know

1.14 Do you import for your business?

> *--Select--*
>
> ☐ Yes *(proceed to **question 1.14.1 to 1.14.6**)*
>
> ☐ No *(proceed to **part 2**)*

1.14.1 What is the share of imports to your total inputs?

> *-- Please select one --*
>
> ☐ 0%
>
> ☐ 1%–20%
>
> ☐ 21%–50%
>
> ☐ 51%–70%
>
> ☐ 71%–90%
>
> ☐ More than 90%

1.14.2 From which countries did you **import** goods/materials last year (2019)?

> *-- Please select all that apply --*
>
> ☐ People's Republic of China   ☐ Japan   ☐ Republic of Korea   ☐ Other Asian countries
>
> ☐ United States   ☐ Europe   ☐ Latin America   ☐ Middle East and North Africa
>
> ☐ Other regions   ☐ Don't know

1.14.3 What has happened to **the cost of supplies** from abroad after the COVID-19 outbreak (15 March 2020)?

> *-- Please select one --*
>
> ☐ Rather, cost decreased   ☐ No change   ☐ 1%–5% increase   ☐ 6%–10% increase
>
> ☐ More than 10% increase

1.14.4 **Buyers** of your products and services are principally in which sectors?

> *-- Please select all that apply --*
>
> ☐ Individual
>
> ☐ Agriculture, forestry and fisheries

☐ Manufacturing – Food and beverages

☐ Manufacturing – Electronics

☐ Manufacturing – Garments

☐ Manufacturing – Other manufacturing activities

☐ Power and energy (e.g., electricity, gas, petrol stations)

☐ Construction

☐ Wholesale and retail trade

☐ Repair of motor vehicles and motorcycles

☐ Transportation and storage

☐ Tourism and accommodation services

☐ Food service activities

☐ Information and communication technology – Business process outsourcing (BPO)

☐ Information and communication technology – Others

☐ Finance and insurance activities

☐ Real estate activities

☐ Arts, entertainment, and recreation

☐ Others, please specify: _____.

1.14.5 **From what sectors** do you buy most of your business's inputs?

-- Please select all that apply --

☐ Agriculture, forestry and fisheries

☐ Manufacturing – Food and beverages

☐ Manufacturing – Electronics

☐ Manufacturing – Garments

☐ Manufacturing – Other manufacturing activities

☐ Power and energy (e.g., electricity, gas, petrol stations)

☐ Construction

☐ Wholesale and retail trade

☐ Repair of motor vehicles and motorcycles

☐ Transportation and storage

☐ Tourism and accommodation services

☐ Food service activities

☐ Information and communication technology – Business process outsourcing (BPO)

☐ Information and communication technology – Others

☐ Finance and insurance activities

☐ Real estate activities

☐ Arts, entertainment, and recreation

☐ Others, please specify: _____.

1.14.6 Where is the location of your domestic input/raw material supplier?

☐ Within the same municipality

☐ In a different municipality/region, easily substitutable

☐ In a different municipality/region, not easily substitutable

☐ Not applicable, only use import inputs

Part 2: Impact of COVID-19 on Your Business

Business conditions

2.1   What is the status of your business after the Enhanced Community Quarantine (15 March 2020)?

-- Please select one --

☐ Open

☐ Open, but limited operations *(proceed to **question 2.1.1**)*

☐ Temporarily closed

☐ Permanently closed (will not reopen)

2.1.1   If you have faced limited operations, what is the status?

-- Please select one --

☐ Less than 25% operational

☐ 25%–50% operational

☐ 51%–75% operational

☐ More than 75% operational

2.2   What is the expected timeframe on your business recovery from the end of the Enhanced Community Quarantine*?

-- Please select one --

☐ Within 2 weeks

☐ 1 month

☐ 1 to 3 months

☐ More than 3 months

☐ Unable to judge

---

* Business recovery means one of the following conditions: return to profitability, return to previous production level, and return to previous workforce level.

2.3   What is the status of your sales (value) in April 2020 as compared to March 2020?

-- Please select one --

☐ Increased *(proceed to **question 2.3.1**)*

☐ Decreased *(proceed to **question 2.3.2**)*

☐ Remain the same *(proceed to **question 2.4**)*

2.3.1   The sales value **increased** by:

% in April 2020 from March 2020

2.3.2   The sales value **decreased** by:

% in April 2020 from March 2020

Employment

2.4   As of the end of April 2020, how many **full-time regular workers** were/have been*:

-- Please select one --

☐ Hired *(proceed to **question 2.4.1**)*

☐ Laid off *(proceed to **question 2.4.2**)*

☐ Granted leave of absence (e.g. sick leave, vacation leave, etc.) *(proceed to **question 2.4.3**)*

☐ Had their salary, wages, or benefits reduced *(proceed to **question 2.4.4**)*

☐ Had their working hours reduced (*proceed to* **question 2.4.5**)

☐ No change

* Use absolute values (number of workers), more than one condition may apply to the same worker (e.g., salary and hours reduced).

2.4.1 How many full-time regular workers did your company **hire** in April 2020 as compared to March 2020?

Number:_____.

2.4.2 How many full-time regular workers did your company **lay off** in April 2020 as compared to March 2020?

Number:_____.

2.4.3 How many full-time regular workers did your company **grant for existing leave days** in April 2020 as compared to March 2020?

Number:_____.

2.4.4 How many full-time regular workers did your company **reduce their salary/wages/benefits** in April 2020 as compared to March 2020?

Number:_____.

2.4.5 How many full-time regular workers did your company **reduce working hours** in April 2020 as compared to March 2020?

Number:_____.

2.5 As of the end of April 2020, how many **part-time or contractual workers** were/have been*:

-- *Please select one* --

☐ Hired (*proceed to* **question 2.5.1**)

☐ Laid off (*proceed to* **question 2.5.2**)

☐ Granted leave of absence (e.g. sick leave, vacation leave, etc.) (*proceed to* **question 2.5.3**)

☐ Had their salary, wages, or benefits reduced (*proceed to* **question 2.5.4**)

☐ Had their working hours reduced (*proceed to* **question 2.5.5**)

☐ No change

* use absolute values (number of workers), more than one condition may apply to the same worker (e.g., salary and hours reduced).

2.5.1   How many part-time or contractual workers did your company **hire** in April 2020 as compared to March 2020?

Number:_____.

2.5.2   How many part-time or contractual workers did your company **lay off** in April 2020 as compared to March 2020?

Number:_____.

2.5.3   How many part-time or contractual workers did your company **grant for existing leave days** in April 2020 as compared to March 2020?

Number:_____.

2.5.4   How many part-time or contractual workers did your company **reduce their salary/wages/benefits** in April 2020 as compared to March 2020?

Number:_____.

2.5.5   How many part-time or contractual workers did your company **reduce working hours** in April 2020 as compared to March 2020?

Number:_____.

2.6 Changes in **total wage payments** to all employees after the COVID-19 outbreak (15 March 2020):

-- *Please select one* --

☐ Temporarily no payment ☐ More than 50% decrease ☐ 31%–50% decrease   ☐ 11%–30% decrease

☐ 1%–10% decrease   ☐ No change   ☐ Less than 10% increase ☐ 10%–30% increase

☐ 31%–50% increase   ☐ More than 50% increase

2.7a What do you think will be **the employment level** of your business on 15 June 2020 as compared to 15 March 2020 (when the Enhanced Community Quarantine started)?

[   ] % of total number of workers on 15 June 2020 against 15 March 2020

2.7b What do you think will be **the employment level** of your business on 15 June 2020 as compared to 15 March 2020 if the economy recovers QUICKER than expected (COVID-19 settled down before end May 2020)?

| | % of total number of workers on 15 June 2020 against 15 March 2020

2.7c   What do you think will be **the employment level** of your business on 15 June 2020 as compared to 15 March 2020 if the economy recovers SLOWER than expected (COVID-19 continues to spread beyond end May 2020)?

| | % of total number of workers on 15 June 2020 against 15 March 2020

Operations

2.8 What percentage of your workers can **work from home** without major disruption in your operations?

> -- *Please select one* --
>
> ☐ Work from home not possible for any workers
>
> ☐ More than 50%   ☐ 26%-50%   ☐ 6%-25%   ☐ 1%-5%

2.9 What **assistance** has your company provided to employees during the Enhanced Community Quarantine?

> -- *Please select all that apply* --
>
> ☐ Shuttle service to and from home or designated pick-up points
>
> ☐ Accommodation near the workplace
>
> ☐ Additional leave credits
>
> ☐ Internet/data allowance
>
> ☐ Personal protective equipment (PPE; e.g., face masks)
>
> ☐ Vitamins and hygiene products (e.g., alcohol-based)
>
> ☐ Others, please specify: _____

2.10 Have you experienced or are you expecting to experience any **bottlenecks in your supply chain?**

> -- *Please select one* --
>
> ☐ Yes, minor bottlenecks (i.e., less than half of your capacity impacted) (*proceed to* **question 2.10.1**)
>
> ☐ Yes, severe bottlenecks (i.e., more than half of your capacity impacted) (*proceed to* **question 2.10.1**)
>
> ☐ No (*proceed to* **question 2.11**)

2.10.1 What are **the main reasons** for bottlenecks in supply chain?

-- Please select up to 3 --

☐ Delay in importing goods / raw materials because of international suppliers' problems

☐ Delay in importing goods / raw materials because of slow customs clearance

☐ Local suppliers or distributors have ceased or have reduced operations

☐ Delayed logistics because of checkpoints or border shutdown

☐ Delayed logistics because limited availability of trucks/drivers

☐ Prices of goods / raw materials have become too expensive

☐ Others, please specify: _____

2.11   How have your **cost of supplies/raw materials** changed since imposition of the Enhanced Community Quarantine in April 2020 against March 2020?

-- Please select one --

☐ Increased *(proceed to **question 2.11.1**)*

☐ Decreased *(proceed to **question 2.11.2**)*

☐ No change *(proceed to **question 2.12**)*

2.11.1 The cost of supplies/raw materials **increased** by:

% between end March and end April 2020

2.11.2 The cost of supplies/raw materials **decreased** by:

% between end March and end April 2020

2.12 **Financial condition** after the COVID-19 outbreak (15 March 2020):

-- Please select one --

☐ Enough savings, liquid assets, and other contingency budget to maintain business for more than 6 months

☐ Cash/funds covering operation costs to be run out in 3-6 months

☐ Cash/funds covering operation costs to be run out in 1-3 months

☐ Already no cash and savings

☐ Others, please specify: _____.

2.13 What are **the most significant financial problems** for your company during the COVID-19 outbreak?

-- Please select one --

☐ Staff wages and social security charges

☐ Rent

☐ Repayment of loans

☐ Payments of invoices

☐ Other expenses

☐ No specific problem

2.14 **Funding conditions** after the COVID-19 outbreak (15 March 2020). During the Enhanced Community Quarantine period, have you:

-- Please select all that apply --

☐ Obtained loans/overdraft/line of credit from banks for working capital

☐ Applied for loans/overdraft/line of credit from banks for working capital

☐ Utilized nonbank finance institutions (e.g., microfinance institutions, pawnshops) for working capital financing

☐ Utilized digital finance platforms (e.g., peer-to-peer lending, crowdfunding) for working capital financing

☐ Received funding support from business partner

☐ Received funding support from the government

☐ Borrowed from family, relatives, and friends to maintain business

☐ Borrowed from informal moneylenders to maintain business

☐ Used own fund/retained profit to maintain business

☐ Others, please specify: _____.

2.15 How much **funding** would you need to raise to maintain or restart your business in the next 3 months?

Amount **in pesos:**_____.

2.16   What **sources of funds** can you use to maintain or restart your business?

> *-- Please select all that apply --*
>
> ☐ Loans/overdraft/line of credit from banks
>
> ☐ Loans from nonbank finance institutions (e.g., microfinance institutions, pawnshops) for working capital financing
>
> ☐ Loans from digital finance platforms (e.g., peer-to-peer lending, crowdfunding)
>
> ☐ Business partner(s)
>
> ☐ Family, relatives, and friends
>
> ☐ Loans from informal moneylenders
>
> ☐ Own fund/retained profit
>
> ☐ Others, please specify: _____.

2.17   If necessary, can you borrow a total of ₱50,000 from somewhere within a week?

> *-- Select--*
>
> ☐ Yes   ☐ No

2.18   Is it more difficult to borrow ₱50,000 now than last year (2019)?

> *-- Select--*
>
> ☐ More difficult
>
> ☐ Same as last year (2019)
>
> ☐ Easier now
>
> ☐ Don't know

2.19 Among employees, how many reside in the same municipality?

> ☐ Less than 25%
>
> ☐ 25%–50%
>
> ☐ 51%–75%
>
> ☐ 76%–100%

2.20 After the Enhanced Community Quarantine, what is your expected volume of order from client?

☐ Increase *(proceed to **question 2.20.1**)*

☐ Decrease *(proceed to **question 2.20.2**)*

☐ Remain the same *(proceed to **Part 3**)*

2.20.1   Please indicate approximate % increase: %

2.20.2   Please indicate approximate % decrease: %

Part 3: Policy Interventions

Please click the appropriate box below:

3.1 What **policy measures** are most needed to support your business **during** the COVID-19 crisis?

-- *Please select up to 3* --

☐ No support required

☐ Payroll subsidy for workers

☐ Low-interest loan/subsidized loan

☐ Credit guarantee

☐ Government purchase of goods and services from my business

☐ Deferment of payment to government (e.g., tax payment, withholding tax, VAT, SSS, PhilHealth)

☐ Payment deferment to debtors (e.g., banks, microfinance institutions)

☐ Payment deferment of utility bills (e.g., electricity, gas, water supply)

☐ Utility subsidies

☐ Tax discounts or tax credits

☐ Others, please specify: _____.

3.2 What **policy measures** are most needed to support your business to be adopted **after** the COVID-19 crisis is resolved? (Select up to 3)

> *-- Please select up to 3 --*
>
> ☐ Provide financial assistance on teleworking arrangement.
>
> ☐ Tax incentives for adopting digital technologies (e.g., e-payments, e-commerce).
>
> ☐ Provide support in upgrading skills of workers to keep them competitive under the "new normal".
>
> ☐ Facilitate access to new financing models (e.g., crowdfunding, peer-to-peer (P2P) lending).
>
> ☐ Improve public ICT infrastructure and regulation to increase internet speed and lower internet cost.
>
> ☐ Review BIR (Bureau of Internal Revenue), SEC (Securities and Exchange Commission), and COA (Commission on Audit) regulations to be compatible with digital payments and transactions.
>
> ☐ Streamline government transaction processes and shift to digital platforms.
>
> ☐ Streamline labor regulations for remote working arrangements.
>
> ☐ Others, please specify: _____.

3.3 Has your company availed of the **Department of Labor and Employment's COVID-19 Adjustment Measures Program** to provide financial assistance to employees unable to work due to quarantine measures?

> *-- Select--*
>
> ☐ Yes   ☐ No

Part 4: Social Contact Indices

4.1 Existing social contacts of employees:

4.1a What is the major type of role within your company?

> *-- Please select all that apply --*
>
> ☐ Cashier
>
> ☐ Accountant
>
> ☐ Machinist
>
> ☐ Waiter
>
> ☐ Others, please specify: _____.

4.1b Number of employees normally performing the role in the company.	(number)

4.1c What share of the employees spend more than 30 minutes commuting each way by public transport from home (%)?	(percentage)

4.1d What share of the employees spend more than 1 hour commuting each way by public transport from home (%)?	(percentage)

4.1e Typical physical proximity of your workers to each other during work (meter).	(meter)

4.1f Number of other employees that the role contacts within 2 meters distance in a typical workday.	(number)

4.1g Average time that the role spends in contact within 2 meters distance of each of these employees (minutes) in a typical workday.	(minutes)

4.1h Number of people outside the company that the role contacts within 2 meters distance in a typical workday.	(number)

4.1i Average time that the role spends in contact within 2 meters distance of each of these people (minutes) in a typical workday.	(minutes)

4.2. Potential to reduce social contacts and introduce social distancing:

4.2a What is the major type of role within your company?

-- *Please select all that apply* --

☐ Cashier

☐ Accountant

☐ Machinist

☐ Waiter

☐ Others, please specify: _____.

4.2b Minimum number of employees needed to perform the role for the company to function.	(number)

4.2c What share of these workers could be physically spaced at 2 meters distance or more during routine work (%)?	(percentage)

4.2d Minimum number of other employees that the role must contact within 2 meters distance in a typical workday.	(number)

4.3. Which of the following activities will be performed by your firm after reopening?

☐ Separate staff by smaller groups and restrict interaction between groups.

☐ For contact tracing purpose, keep record of contacted personnel for all staff.

☐ Canteen rationing to ensure social distancing during lunch.

☐ Routine temperature checks for all staff.

☐ Provide all staff enough face masks for business days.

Reference: How did you learn about this survey?

-- Please select one --

☐ Industry association

☐ Other private organization

☐ Government agency

☐ Social media (Facebook, Twitter, etc.)

☐ Friends and family

☐ Others, please specify:

-- End of Survey. Thank you very much for your cooperation. –